AMAZING
TALES FROM THE
BOSTON RED SOX
DUGOUT

AMAZING
TALES FROM THE
BOSTON RED SOX
DUGOUT

A COLLECTION OF THE GREATEST
RED SOX STORIES EVER TOLD

JIM PRIME AND BILL NOWLIN

SPORTS
PUBLISHING

Sports Publishing books may be purchased in bulk at special discounts for sales promotion, corporate gifts, fund-raising, or educational purposes. Special editions can also be created to specifications. For details, contact the Special Sales Department, Sports Publishing, 307 West 36th Street, 11th Floor, New York, NY 10018 or sportspubbooks@skyhorsepublishing.com.

Sports Publishing® is a registered trademark of Skyhorse Publishing, Inc.®, a Delaware corporation.

Visit our website at www.sportspubbooks.com.

10 9 8 7 6 5 4 3 2 1

Library of Congress Cataloging-in-Publication Data is available on file.

Jacket design by Tom Lau
Jacket photograph: AP Images

Photographs on pages 5, 164, 168, 227, 233, and 246 are from AP Images

ISBN: 978-1-68358-063-8
Ebook ISBN: 978-1-68358-064-5

Printed in the United States of America

To all my Red Sox heroes, from Ted Williams to Carl Yastrzemski; from Tony C to Freddie Lynn; from Luis Tiant to Mookie Betts; and all those in between.
And to my own impressive starting nine: Glenna, Jeff, Jung, Catherine, Dave, Fin, Sam, Margaret, and Ray —JP

To the chroniclers of Red Sox lore from years gone by – among others, to Harold Kaese and George Sullivan and Ed Walton and Ellery Clark and Al Hirshberg and Ed Linn, and the more recent writers like Glenn Stout and Dick Johnson and Dan Shaughnessy. All wrote books which preceded us and inspired us. —BN

ACKNOWLEDGMENTS

The Boston Red Sox inspire people to talk, often with great eloquence and always with great passion. People from all walks of life enjoy sharing their stories about this colorful team. Some of the people who helped, encouraged and/or inspired me in the writing of *Amazing Tales from the Boston Red Sox Dugout* are: Dr. Philip Belitsky, Dave Canton, Dabney Coleman, Peter Cornu, Maureen Cronin, Bobby Doerr, Keith Foulke, Nomar Garciaparra, Victor Garciaparra, Dick Gernert, Paul Gleason, Bob Jackson, Gabe Kapler, Bill Lee, Larry Lucchino, Dave McCarty, Mickey McDermott, Doug Mirabelli, Bill Mueller, Mel Parnell, Glenna Prime, Catherine Prime, Ben Robicheau, Curt Schilling, Sam Snead, Dr. Charles Steinberg, Virgil Trucks, Mickey Vernon, Bill Wilder, Karen Wilder and Ted Williams. I thank them all. A special thank-you to my son Jeffrey, whose intimate knowledge of computers was instrumental in the writing of this book. Thanks, Jeff!

—JHP

Bill Nowlin would like to extend his thanks to: Walter Cherniak, Jr., Bill Consolo, Maureen Cronin, Kate Gordon, Mike Ipavec, Ted Lepcio, Pedro Martinez, Slade Mead, Steve Mastroyin, Lou Merloni, Eddie Pellagrini, Paul Penta, Johnny Pesky, Kevin Shea, Bob Stanley, John Valentin, Charlie Wagner, Gary Williams, Brian Wilson, Janet Zauchin, and Tony, a waiter at Valbella's in Greenwich, Connecticut.

CONTENTS

Introduction xiii

Harry Agganis 1
Dale Alexander 1
Larry Andersen 3
Luis Aparicio... 3
Elden Auker... 4
The Killer B's... 5
Jim Bagby 5
Daniel Bard 6
Jack Baker... 6
Matt Batts... 7
Don Baylor 7
Rod Beck 9
Mark Bellhorn 10
Andrew Benintendi 11
Dennis "The Menace" Bennett 13
Moe Berg 15
Mookie Betts 17
Clarence "Climax" Blethen 22
Xander Bogaerts... 22
Wade Boggs 25
Dennis "Oil Can" Boyd 27
Jackie Bradley Jr... 29
Darren Bragg 30
Bill Buckner 30
Don Buddin 33
Rick Burleson 33
Jose Canseco 34
Bernie Carbo 34
Bill Carrigan/Joe Kerrigan.. 36
Roger Clemens 39
Reggie Cleveland 43
Eddie Collins... 44

Tony Conigliaro 44
Gene Conley 48
Marty Cordova 49
Joe Cronin 49
Bill Crowley 53
Ray Culp 54
Tom Daly 54
Brian Daubach 54
Dom DiMaggio 56
Bill Dinneen 58
Bobby Doerr 58
Patsy Donovan 59
Lib Dooley 59
Patsy Dougherty 61
Walt Dropo 61
Dennis Eckersley 64
Howard Ehmke 67
Dwight Evans 68
Carl Everett 70
Sherm Feller 72
The Ferrell Brothers—Wes and Rick 73
Rick Ferrell 73
Wes Ferrell 75
Dave "Boo" Ferriss 76
Carlton Fisk 77
Fats Fothergill 80
Jimmie Foxx 80
Rich Garces 84
Nomar Garciaparra 84
Rich Gedman 90
Gary Geiger 91
Dick Gernert 91
Don Gile... 92
Billy Goodman 92
Mike Greenwell 93
Lefty Grove 94
Creighton Gubanich 95
Devern Hansack 96

Carroll Hardy 96
Tommy Harper 97
Ken Harrelson 98
Bucky Harris 98
Scott Hatteberg 98
Dave (Hendu) Henderson : From Goat to Gloat...................... 99
Jim Henry 99
John Henry 100
Mike Herrera 101
Butch Hobson 102
Brock Holt 102
Harry Hooper 103
Ralph Houk 106
Tex Hughson 106
Bruce Hurst 106
Pete Jablonowski 107
Jackie Jensen 107
Smead Jolley 110
John Kennedy 111
Kevin Kennedy 111
Marty Keough 112
Henry Killilea 112
Wendell Kim 113
Ellis Kinder 113
Jack Kramer 115
Roger LaFrancois 116
Bill Lee 117
The World According to Chairman Lee 125
Sang-Hoon Lee 127
Dutch Leonard 128
Jon Lester 129
Ted Lewis 129
Grady Little 130
Dick Littlefield 130
Jim Lonborg 130
Derek Lowe 132
Larry Lucchino 132
Sparky Lyle 133

Fred Lynn 133
Steve Lyons 135
Sam Malone 136
Frank Malzone..139
Pedro Martinez...139
Carl Mays 145
Mickey McDermott 147
Sam Mele 153
Oscar Melillo 154
Lou Merloni 154
Doug Mirabelli..156
Dave Morehead 156
Ed Morris 157
Daniel Nava..157
Bobo Newsom 158
Trot Nixon 158
Russ Nixon 160
Hideo Nomo 161
Buck O'Brien 161
Troy O'Leary 162
Gene Oliver 162
Johnny Orlando...162
David Ortiz 163
Mel Parnell 167
Dustin Pedroia..168
Eddie Pellagrini 169
Johnny Pesky 169
Rico Petrocelli 175
Jimmy Piersall 175
Eddie Popowski 180
Dick Radatz 181
Manny Ramirez 182
Jim Rice 184
Dave Roberts 187
Si Rosenthal...188
Red Ruffing 189
Pete Runnels 189
Babe Ruth 190

Gene "Half-Pint" Rye 194
Ray Scarborough..194
Curt Schilling..195
George Scott 197
Eddie Shore 199
Reggie Smith 199
Tris Speaker 201
Tracy Stallard 202
Bob Stanley 202
Dave Stapleton 203
Vern Stephens 204
Jerry Stephenson 205
Dick Stuart... 205
Jim Tabor 210
Birdie Tebbetts 211
George Thomas 213
Luis Tiant 213
Bob Tillman 221
John Valentin...221
Jason Varitek 226
Mo Vaughn.. 228
Mickey Vernon 229
"Broadway" Charlie Wagner 230
Tim Wakefield.. 232
Murray Wall 234
Wally "The Green Monster" 234
John Wasdin 238
Earl Webb 238
Billy Werber 239
Tom Werner 241
Sammy White 241
Del Wilber 243
Dick Williams 243
Ted Williams 243
Ted's Philadelphia Story... 272
Jimy Williams 274
Jim Willoughby 276
Rick Wise 277

Smoky Joe Wood 277
Tris and Smoky 280
John Wyatt 280
Carl Yastrzemski 280
Tom Yawkey 292
Bill Lee on Tom Yawkey 296
Rudy York 296
Cy Young 298
Matt Young 301
Norm Zauchin 302
Don Zimmer 302
Bill Zuber/Bob Zupcic... 305
Sox Populi... 305
Popeye's Chicken 307
Just the Facts.. 307
Jokes 308
Stealing Home 312
Epilogue..314
Bibliography.. 322

INTRODUCTION

It isn't much of an exaggeration to say that the history of the Boston Red Sox is the history of baseball. Born in 1901, the Boston franchise was a founding member of the American League. The first modern World Series was played in 1903 between the Boston Americans, as they were then known, and the Pittsburg Pirates, with the Boston nine emerging victorious. Rechristened the Red Sox by 1908, they won again in 1912, 1915, and 1916. In 1918, as the First World War was ending, a young Boston pitcher named Babe Ruth led the American League with 11 homers (and compiled a 13-7 record on the pitching mound), Ted Williams was born, and the Sox won their fifth World Series. Then, just when it was beginning to look as if the 20th century belonged to the Boston Red Sox, Ruth was sold to the New York Yankees (who became the "hated New York Yankees"). Eight decades later, the annual New England cry of "Wait 'til next year!" had been replaced with "Maybe next millennium!"

When the first *Tales from the Red Sox Dugout* was published, we were still waiting.

Despite the extended championship drought, it could nevertheless be argued that the Bosox showcased the greatest practitioners of the two basic facets of the game: hitting and pitching. They boasted Ted Williams, whose name will forever be synonymous with the science of hitting, and Cy Young, the man permanently identified with excellence in the art of pitching. Of course Babe Ruth, the personification of baseball around the world, perfected both skills at Fenway before that carpet-bagging New Yorker named Harry Frazee sold him to the Yankees for cold, hard cash (and even gave the Yankees a mortgage on Fenway Park). Frazee failed to realize that the real drama and melodrama was to be found with his Red Sox. The rise of Ruth as a bona fide Boston star and that eventual sale to the Yankees sums up the Red Sox saga—blessed and cursed in equal measure. Blessed with wonderful heroes and unforgettable heroics; cursed with bad luck and squandered opportunities.

All this made the Red Sox more than just an American institution; it made them a beloved team. You can't say that about many multimillion dollar corporations. You certainly can't say it about the Yankees: maybe the Mets...sometimes; the Cubs and the old Brooklyn Dodgers, certainly; but never the Yanks. Teams don't become beloved strictly by winning, nor do they achieve this status by being just plain bad. Elements of both are necessary. There must be a core of greatness—tempered with comedic relief and at least one tragic flaw. The Red Sox have had stars, heroes and anti-heroes in abundance. Like Sisyphus, the Sox keep pushing the rock up the mountain—only to have it roll right down again. They have shown periodic flashes of brilliance—only to fall just short, often in dramatic style. For every Ted Williams hitting a home run in his last at-bat, there is a Bill Buckner with the ball going through his legs. For every Carlton Fisk game-winning home run, there is the specter of Bucky Dent's devastating 1978 playoff homer. For every 1967 Impossible Dream, there is the very real nightmare of the 1986 "One Strike Away" World Series. And then along came 2004. And 2007. Did success make the Red Sox less eccentric? Less interesting? Not on your life. More on that later, but let's also keep in mind 2011. Sox fans have been reminded what humility (and humiliation) is all about.

The Red Sox image is a curious mix of vulnerability, humanity, and humor. America loves underdogs, and for decades the Sox were the perpetual underdog. As such, they were more convincing in the role of "America's Team" than the media-hyped and image-conscious Atlanta Braves or Yankees.

This book is meant to capture the many sides of the Boston Red Sox: the humor, the brilliance, the humanity, and the countless eccentricities that make them what they are. Anyone who has followed the Red Sox even casually has a favorite story about this team.

My own favorite anecdote about the Red Sox? In the early '80s, I wrote a number of articles on Ted Williams and in 1995 co-authored a book with Williams, entitled *Ted Williams' Hit List*, a ranking of the greatest hitters in baseball history. As a result of all this, Ted's name became a household word in our home. In 1983, I visited Fenway Park to see a game between the Red Sox and Kansas City Royals. By the third inning, my three- year-old daughter Catherine had dozed off in the hot August sun just as Carl Yastrzemski launched a long homer into the bleachers. Abruptly awakened by the cheers, Catherine joined in the spirit if not the substance of the celebration. "Hooray for Ted Williams!" she said. Although those words had probably not been uttered at Fenway much since September 28, 1960, they sounded not at all out of place. Fans around us seemed to understand and smiled approvingly, as if those unspoken words had been rattling through Fenway Park for decades and needed only a naïve child to give voice to them. The Red Sox are like that—a great, unfinished novel with lots of intriguing characters. To get the full impact of what happens in any one chapter, you should have a working knowledge of previous chapters. The effect is cumulative. The Red Sox are connected to the past yet timeless, and what happened in 1939 or 1960 still means something today.

Red Sox fans know that for good or for bad they are cheering for an American original; the most fascinating franchise in professional sports. I hope the stories in this book help to capture some of their magic for you.

—Jim Prime

Harry Agganis

Harry Agganis' promising career was cut short when he died at the age of 25 in 1955. The man known as the Golden Greek appeared in an official capacity at both Braves Field and Fenway Park on the same day in 1954. He began the day by hitting a game-winning homer for the Bosox and ended it by receiving his Boston University degree in ceremonies at Braves Field. The former pigskin star at B.U. was one of the few to go from horsehide to sheepskin all in one day in two major league ballparks in two different leagues. We are not sure if there is a record for this sort of thing, but if there is, we're sure Harry holds it.

*   *   *   *

Billy Consolo was Agganis' teammate with the Red Sox. He has fond memories of the former football All-American, who could have been a pro on the gridiron as well as the diamond. "Man, I tell you, if you're talking about a man's man, it was Harry Agganis. When I was rooming with him in '53, the Cleveland Browns called him up saying, 'Otto Graham has retired and you're our number-one draft choice. You don't want to play baseball.' I heard all those conversations, man. He could have been a professional football player, quarterback for the Cleveland Browns."

Dale Alexander

Alexander is a forgotten Red Sox player, but in 1932, despite totaling only 392 at-bats, he led the league with a .372 average. Author Ed Walton documented how the Tennessee farmer's career came to an unexpected halt. Doc Woods, a former trainer for the Yankees, was hired and decided that a leg injury Alexander had suffered should be treated by heat therapy. He placed Alexander under a heat lamp and went out to check on how the game was going. It must have been a good one, because he forgot to go back in to check on Alexander, who was out for a

Luis Aparicio

couple of weeks after being cooked to a "well-done" degree. Talk about your red-hot hitters!

Larry Andersen

In Red Sox lore, he will forever be known as the player whom Lou Gorman obtained for Jeff Bagwell. Larry Andersen was in his 13th year of baseball at the time, an excellent reliever. Gorman acquired him at a crucial point in the 1990 pennant race, and Andersen threw 22 innings, with 25 strikeouts compared to just three walks. His ERA was 1.23. He was extremely effective in helping the Sox to win the division by just two games over the Blue Jays. Meanwhile, native son Bagwell, born in Boston, became a star with Houston the very next year—and after 15 years with the Astros sports a lifetime .297 average with 449 homers and 1,529 RBI. Gorman has long been ridiculed but when the trade was made, it reflected good baseball sense.

*   *   *   *

Andersen was, in Floyd Conner's choice words, "the Steven Wright of baseball. He pondered such matters as why slim chance and fat chance meant the same thing, and how do you know when invisible ink is dry?" The reliever was puzzled by something he saw most every day: "Why does everybody stand up and sing 'Take Me Out to the Ball Game' when they're already there?"

Luis Aparicio

It was 1971, and Red Sox shortstop Luis Aparicio was mired in the worst slump of his long and distinguished major-league career. He had been held hitless for 11 games and 44 at-bats. On June 1, he singled, a small oasis in a desert of batting futility, but then went hitless for two more games and was now l-for-55. On June

4, he received a note from President Richard Nixon, who wrote: "In my own career, I have experienced long periods when I couldn't seem to get a hit, regardless of how hard I tried, but in the end, I was able to hit a home run." Inspired by the President's support, the 37-year-old Aparicio went out that day and earned a standing ovation for knocking in two runs. His slump was over. As for Nixon, his next slump would prove to be his last.

* * * *

On the final day of the 1971 season, Luis was preparing to head back to Venezuela. Something of a fashion plate, he wore his Oleg Cassini jacket, his Oleg Cassini pants and his Oleg Cassini shoes to the ballpark. He had already sent the rest of his luggage to the airport, and all he had was his ticket, his uniform and the elegant clothes on his back. Carl Yastrzemski, a brutal practical joker who wasn't playing that day, went to the clubhouse in the late innings of the game and cut his pants at the knees, cut the lapels off his jacket, cut his tie in half and nailed his shoes to the hardwood floor. Luis was forced to make his way back home in borrowed Bermuda shorts.

Elden Auker

Ted Williams once told Elden Auker, "You're about the only friend I have who doesn't want something from me. You've never even asked for my autograph." Auker replied, "You never ask me for my autograph so why should I ask for yours?"

* * * *

Before John Valentin (1992-2001), the only Red Sox players to wear a number 13 jersey were Bob Fothergill (1933), Elder Auker (1939), Reid Nichols (1985) and Billy Joe Robidoux (1990.) After five seasons with the Red Sox, Nichols was traded the year he donned the number. 1990 proved to be Robidoux's last year in the majors.

The Killer B's

They are known as the Killer B's, a swarm of young Red Sox stars that includes Mookie Betts, Xavier Bogaerts, Jackie Bradley Jr., and Andrew Benintendi. Also part of the hive is Brock Holt who achieved honorary membership because of his first name and the fact that he can sting opposing pitchers with the best of them.

The Killer B's swarm. Andrew Benintendi, Jackie Bradley Jr., and Mookie Betts perform a victory dance

Jim Bagby

Red Sox reliever Jim Bagby was once warming up in the bullpen while consuming a hotdog. Cronin called the kid in the bullpen and said, "Tell Bagby to get in here." Bagby hands the hotdog to the kid. "What am I going to do with the hotdog, it'll get cold?" the kid says. Bagby said, "Well, who am I going to pitch to?" The kid said "DiMaggio, Henrich and Keller." Bagby said "Hold the f—ing hotdog, I'll be right back!"

Daniel Bard

Daniel Bard was part of the first swarm of "B's" for the Red Sox—the trio of pitchers with Michael Bowden and Clay Buchholz who it was thought would ensure a home-grown Red Sox rotation for years to come.

Buchholz threw a no-hitter in his second start, and has had success with the Red Sox, including a remarkable 12-1 (1.74) season in 2013 sandwiched around injury.

Bard, a first-round draft pick who had a 100-mph fastball, was effective working out of the Red Sox bullpen, particularly with his 1.93 ERA in 2010. But he wanted to be a starter and manager Bobby Valentine gave him the opportunity in 2012. He just couldn't seem to harness it, and saw his ERA climb to 6.22 that year. He was gone from the majors with only two appearances in 2013, and couldn't manage a comeback in the low minors or Puerto Rican Winter League ball. There was even the time in 2014, pitching in Single-A in the Rangers system that he recorded two outs (and that's all) while walking nine and hitting seven batters. Raw talent for sure, but something had gone awry.

Jack Baker

Late in the 1977 season, Jack Baker stepped to the plate for the Red Sox, and his first major league hit was a home run into the screen at Fenway. Was this a new "Home Run" Baker in the making? Not quite. This Baker lacked the Ruthian recipe. In 22 other at-bats at the tail end of 1977 and in three more in 1978, he only managed two other hits. The career .115 hitter moved on to another career—perhaps as a butcher, or candlestick maker.

Matt Batts

B lessed with one of the most fitting—and Suessian—
names in baseball history, Batts once incurred the wrath
of legendary Boston manager Joe McCarthy. In August
of 1948, the Red Sox were locked in a pennant race with the
Cleveland Indians. Indians sparkplug Lou Boudreau stole home
against Red Sox pitcher Mickey McDermott and catcher Batts.
McCarthy stormed out of the Red Sox dugout to dispute the call at
home plate and ended his tirade by kicking Batts in the posterior.
Or as Dr. Suess might put it: Manager Mac attacks Matt Batts'
slats.

Don Baylor

D on Baylor was a stylish hitter, an intelligent ballplayer,
a born leader with fire in his belly—and a winner.
He came to the Red Sox late in his career, bringing
that winning tradition with him. The best designated hitter in
baseball at the time, he became the first player to reach the World
Series in three consecutive seasons for three different teams—the
1986 Red Sox, the 1987 Minnesota Twins and the 1988 Oakland
Athletics. Baylor was fearless. He'd stand close to the plate and
defy pitchers to throw at him, yelling as a reliever strode to
the mound: "You're the guy I've been waiting for since batting
practice!" Often they obliged, making Baylor number one on the
all-time hit-by-pitch list. Baylor was hit by a season-record 35
pitches in 1986 and took one for the team a total of 267 times in
his career. Ouch!

*   *   *   *

When Baylor came to the Red Sox in 1986 from the New York
Yankees, Yankee owner George Steinbrenner predicted that the
aging, 36-year-old slugger's bat would be "dead by August."
August came, and Baylor hit seven home runs and drove in 14

Rod Beck

runs. Steinbrenner later apologized, claiming he had been mis-
quoted. Actually it was his Yankees that were on life support.

✳   ✳   ✳   ✳

Baylor was perhaps best known for the Kangaroo Courts he
established. The idea was to have some fun while at the same
time keeping players loose and boosting morale. Baylor was
the judge, and fines could be imposed for almost any on-field
"infraction." Some players, of course, were repeat offenders.
Steve "Psycho" Lyons was fined for fraternizing with opposing
players, socializing with fans, being on the field without his cap
and so on. When Lyons was traded from the Red Sox, Baylor
lamented: "There goes half our Kangaroo Court fund."

Rod Beck

It may have been the longest trip in from the bullpen in the
history of baseball. He had never been to Boston, let alone
Fenway Park, but when reliever Rod Beck came over to the
Red Sox in a trade with the National League's Chicago Cubs in
the middle of the '99 stretch drive, the long-haired, mustachioed
right-hander was immediately pressed into action. Arriving at
Fenway after a six-hour flight from California followed by a
stressful 40-minute cab ride from the airport, the Sox's brand
new closer had scarcely located the bullpen when he was called
in against the Kansas City Royals in the ninth inning. "The Red
Sox fans gave him a great ovation," said Nomar Garciaparra. "I
mean, he was with the Cubs—in the other league—but they still
knew how good he is, and they give him a great reception. It
just shows how knowledgeable Boston fans are." First baseman
Mike Stanley literally had to introduce himself to Beck during
the meeting at the mound: "How you doing, Rod? Welcome to
the Red Sox. I'm Mike Stanley, and I'll be your first baseman
today." Catcher Jason Varitek extended his hand in greeting. "Hi,
I'm Jason Varitek," he said. "What do ya got?" Despite his long
trip, Beck's first outing was successful. He threw eleven pitches

and recorded his first save for the Red Sox. "I'd never met him either," recalls Garciaparra, "but I figured I'd introduce myself after the game." In his initial eight appearances in a Sox uniform he was almost untouchable, allowing just four hits in his first 10 pressure-packed innings of work.

*   *   *   *

Rod Beck wishes no one—especially his dental hygienist—had noticed. But the TV cameras caught it all one summer night in an inter-league game with the Expos in Montreal during the 2001 season. Beck, celebrating after a key strikeout, accidentally spit out his gum. Not missing a beat, Beck bent down, picked it up, and popped it back in his mouth. "Now it looks even more like I'm the dirt bag everybody thinks I am," Beck said. "It landed on the turf, not on the mound," he insisted. "It fell on a clean spot." But he admitted that had it landed in the dirt he still would have chewed it. "That had never happened before," he explained. "I considered that my lucky gum."

Mark Bellhorn

One of the very few Red Sox players born in Boston, Mark Bellhorn sometimes seem to just stand at the plate without swinging the bat. He led the A.L. with 117 strikeouts in 2004, but he was third in the league with 88 bases on balls. And he hit 17 homers during the regular season, with 93 runs scored and 88 driven in. But it was the postseason where he made a big mark. After hardly hitting at all for the first seven games, he hit a three-run homer against the Yankees in Game Six (the initial call of a double was overturned) and a two-run homer in Game Seven, then snapped a 9-9 tie in the eighth inning of Game One of the World Series with yet another home run. The Yankees may have thought they were getting something big when they picked him up later in 2005, but he only hit .118 for them.

Andrew Benintendi

I t may be heresy. It may be premature. These words you are reading may someday be looked at with scorn and ridicule. But Andrew Benintendi has a Ted Williams swing. That's not to say that he will be the next Ted Williams. There were many qualities that made Ted the greatest hitter in baseball history and The Swing was only one of them. Ted had a passion for hitting, a willingness to learn from others, intelligence, power, and an intimate knowledge of the strike zone. But Benintendi has the swing. A swing that renders even cynical, battle-hardened baseball men rhapsodic in their enthusiasm.

✶　　✶　　✶　　✶

Andrew Benintendi ascended to the majors so quickly that it's a wonder he didn't suffer from the bends. Benintendi went directly from Double-A Portland to the Boston Red Sox, comparable to skipping your senior year at college and being awarded your degree anyway. In 2015, as a member of the University of Arkansas Razorbacks, he had won the Golden Spikes Award, as the best amateur player in the country. Other future Red Sox players to win the prestigious award include Jason Varitek, David Price, and J.D. Drew. Benintendi was the seventh outfielder to capture the honor; the first was Terry Francona in 1980.

✶　　✶　　✶　　✶

Benintendi's major league debut came on August 2, 2016, when he was sent to the plate to pinch hit. The next day he got his first big league start and collected two hits. In 34 games, he batted .295 with 31 hits, 2 homers, and 14 RBIs.

*   *   *   *

It didn't take long for Andrew Benintendi to win over the populace of Red Sox Nation. On August 9, 2016, sports columnist, author, and passionate Red Sox fan Bill Simmons tweeted the following: "Benintendi rapidly climbing the ladder of most important people in my life . . . I think he just passed 10 cousins, 4 uncles, and 3 aunts."

*   *   *   *

Although the Red Sox were swept by Cleveland in the 2016 ALDS, Benintendi batted .333 in the series. Batting out of the ninth spot in the lineup, the 22-year old outfielder hit a home run in Game One, making him the youngest Red Sox player to go deep in a postseason contest.

*   *   *   *

The garage of Andrew Benintendi's uncle Brian has become a repository for assorted family memorabilia, both athletic and academic. Naturally many of the recent additions have to do with Andrew's rapid advancement to the major leagues. Brian and Andrew's dad Chris also use the place to watch ballgames on the internet. It is known as the Garage Mahal.

*   *   *   *

Benintendi's hair has garnered a lot of attention since he joined the Red Sox. His flowing black locks started innocently enough, but as they grew and he moved from Double-A to the majors, baseball superstition took over and Andrew was loath to shear them. His coif became so large that he was in the market for a larger hat. And then his mom came to Boston for a visit and he suddenly decided to get a haircut. The power of superstition takes a backseat to mom power.

*   *   *   *

Dennis "The Menace" Bennett

Pitcher Dennis Bennett used to carry five guns with him on road trips. One evening, he got into a heated argument with roommate Lee "Mad Dog" Thomas over who should get up to turn out the light in their room. Players in the next room overheard the angry shouts and then were startled by a loud gunshot. Expecting the worst, the players rushed to the scene of the mayhem, passing a rapidly retreating Thomas in the hallway. When they reached Bennett's room, they discovered that he had solved the dispute by shooting out the light with his pistol.

*   *   *   *

Lacking sufficient money for a plane ticket to a teammate's wedding, Bennett enlisted the help of a stewardess friend and stowed away on a cross-country flight. Giving new meaning to the term "relief pitcher," Bennett remained in one of the plane's toilets, protected by a sign that read "Out of Service."

Moe Berg

Moe Berg

Red Sox catcher Moe Berg was a spy. No, not just another one of those guys who gets to second base and tries to steal the catcher's signs in order to relay them to the batter—although had he *reached* second more often, he doubtless would have become quite adept at that too. Berg was a real spy for the U.S. during World War II.

In 1934, Berg visited Japan as part of an All-Star barnstorming tour. With a puny .251 average, Berg's credentials for such a trip paled beside those of teammates such as Ruth and Gehrig. Why then was he chosen? While there he reportedly took a large number of photographs which years later were used by U.S. intelligence to plan air attacks on Tokyo.

* * * *

It was once said of Berg: "He could speak a dozen languages and couldn't hit in any of them." During a 15-year career, he compiled a modest .243 batting average, with just six home runs.

* * * *

Prior to departure for the series of games in Japan, Babe Ruth asked Berg: "You're such a brilliant linguist; do you speak Japanese?" The catcher replied that he did not. After two weeks on the high seas, the ship carrying the baseball stars arrived in Japan. As they were disembarking, Berg engaged a welcoming committee in animated conversation—in apparently fluent Japanese. Ruth was astounded. "I thought you didn't speak Japanese," he said. "That was two weeks ago," Berg replied.

* * * *

On one 1937 trip between Washington and Philadelphia, the Red Sox had four players fluent in four languages on the team. Mel

Almada was born in Mexico, Fabian Gaffke was German, Gene Desautels was French and Dom Dallessandro was Italian. Moe Berg was able to talk with each reasonably fluently. Impressive, but would he have been able to communicate with Jimy Williams in Jimywocky?

✳   ✳   ✳   ✳

Moe Berg was a Phi Beta Kappa Ivy Leaguer (Princeton), a Rhodes Scholar and an attorney. Apparently Berg could write in Japanese, too. Once he startled some visitors from Japan by autographing their ball in Japanese. When Joe Garagiola described catcher's equipment as "the tools of ignorance," he was obviously not talking about Moe.

✳   ✳   ✳   ✳

In the *Big Book of Jewish Baseball*, the author claims that catcher and part-time spy (or is it the other way around?) Moe Berg actually met with Albert Einstein in 1945. Now that would be a conversation worth recording. Berg reportedly impressed Einstein with detailed knowledge of his recent writings on atomic warfare. And then it was Berg's turn to be impressed when Einstein described an article that Berg had penned on the subject of catching. Little wonder! The physics of splitting the atom are one thing, but the physics of the knuckleball remain beyond the realm of human knowledge. The two men had something else in common; neither could hit worth a darn.

✳   ✳   ✳   ✳

Berg was a back-up catcher and rarely started a game. Instead, he spent long periods of time warming up pitchers in the Red Sox dugout. So when manager Joe Cronin once brought him in to catch the final innings of a game, Berg broke up the dugout by loudly inquiring of Cronin, "Joe, I can't remember. Do the batters still get three strikes in this league?"

*   *   *   *

Berg graduated *magna cum laude* from Columbia University Law School and pursued the study of philosophy at the Sorbonne in Paris but in some quarters that just doesn't measure up with being able to deliver a whack on the head, a tweak of the nose or a poke in the eye. When a publisher approached Berg with an offer to pen his autobiography, it looked like Berg's fascinating life story would finally be told. Unfortunately, the editor mistakenly believed he was negotiating with Moe Howard of the Three Stooges, and when it was discovered that Berg was only a major league ballplayer and international spy, the offer was promptly rescinded.

Mookie Betts

Aside from an Elvis style sneer when he looks out at the pitcher, he does not have the look of a star and at 5'9", 180 pounds he is far from intimidating.

In 2016, he committed only one error all season and was awarded a Gold Glove as the best right fielder in the league. He topped the major leagues in defensive runs with 32. The home opener against the Washington Nationals was the Mookie Betts Show. In the outfield he committed grand larceny, robbing Bryce Harper of a sure homer. The robbery continued on the base paths as he swiped two bases. He topped off the crime wave by stealing the hearts of the Fenway faithful, blasting a home run over the Green Monster.

*   *   *   *

Betts's break-out year was 2016, as he was selected to his first AL All Star team. He also reached the coveted 200-hit plateau with

214, second best in the junior circuit. The right fielder was at or near the top in an assortment of offensive categories, leading the league in at-bats (672) and total bases (359). He finished second in runs scored (122), beat out 42 doubles, hit 31 homers and contributed 113 RBIs. His batting average was .318 (2nd). Once on the base paths he continued to be a threat, stealing 26 bases and rattling opposing pitchers.

*   *   *   *

As a child, Mookie was so small that even his extra small pair of baseball pants were in constant danger of falling down. His mother, Diana Benedict, solved the problem by buying him suspenders. He chose the ones with Teenage Mutant Ninja Turtles on them and his mom bought him a matching Ninja Turtle glove.

*   *   *   *

For such a clean cut ballplayer, Mookie spends a lot of time hanging out in alleys. Bowling alleys that is. He is so good that he someday hopes to join the PBA tour. He has bowled four perfect games and participated in the 2015 PBA World Series of Bowling in Reno, Nevada. Baseball experts see a World Series of another kind in his future.

*   *   *   *

Mookie has a guardian angel. At the age of 12 he was returning from a bowling trip with three teammates. His stepfather was driving and his mother was in the front seat as the boys snoozed in the back. Suddenly the car struck a utility pole and careened across the busy interstate, finally coming to rest upside-down next to the median.

Ignoring her broken shoulder, his mother tried frantically to open the door. She could see the other three kids scramble through a window but Mookie, who hadn't been wearing a seatbelt, was nowhere in sight. A few desperate moments later, he was spotted lying face down and stunned in the middle of rush hour traffic. For his mother, the next sequence of events seemed to play out in slow motion.

Seemingly out of nowhere, a driver got out of his car and carried Mookie to safety, away from the oncoming traffic. The man then stopped the two-way traffic until emergency vehicles arrived. "To this day I don't know who saved him," Diana Benedict told Sports Illustrated's Tom Verducci in 2015. "He was God's little angel." As for Mookie, he escaped with a broken jaw and an assortment of scrapes and bruises.

✳   ✳   ✳   ✳

It couldn't have been scripted any better. Betts' first major league hit came against the Red Sox archrivals, the New York Yankees, at Yankee Stadium. His mother, father and fiancée were at the game. To put a cherry on top of a perfect day, Yankee shortstop and future Hall of famer Derek Jeter realized the significance of the hit, retrieved the ball and rolled it to the dugout for the budding superstar.

✳   ✳   ✳   ✳

Mookie's favorite TV show is SpongeBob SquarePants, and he confesses to binge watching it during the offseason. Aside from SpongeBob himself, his favorite character is Squidward.

✳   ✳   ✳   ✳

Despite his young age, Mookie is already a pioneer. Betts was still a student at Overton High School in Nashville in 2011 when Red Sox scout Danny Watkins came calling. Watkins asked the young ballplayer to play a series of computer games. These games were not your usual shoot 'em ups however. They were actually a battery of state-of-the art baseball tests designed to measure the previously unmeasurable. It is relatively easy for an experienced scout to assess a player's swing. Such things as bat speed, technique and mechanics are all tangible, or at least quantifiable elements in a hitter's skill set. But what about pitch recognition and decision making?

Mookie was a guinea pig in a concept known as neuroscouting, a tool developed to rate a player's baseball mind, how fast and intuitive his baseball IQ is in real time. It tests how well a players sees a pitch and how well he reads the pitch. Former Red Sox general manager Theo Epstein was one of the first to embrace the technology. Mookie was told to tap the space bar when he saw a certain spin on the ball.

Incredibly, neuroscouting also attempts to assess the character of the player being tested. To that end, certain errors are built into the program. If a player is frustrated or makes excuses based on the irregularities, he is likely to be a complainer in the majors; if he ignores it continues to perform, he is more likely to handle the ups and downs of major league play. Not surprisingly, Betts scored incredibly high in all aspects of the test, "ridiculously high," according to one source.

Little wonder that Theo Epstein saw enough potential to draft Betts in 2011, his last season as Red Sox GM before moving over to the Chicago Cubs.

*   *   *   *

Betts is among the most opportunistic of players, especially on the base paths. He once pulled off the rare double-steal-by-one-person-on-a-single-pitch trick. It happened on Opening Day at Fenway on April 13, 2015, in a game against the Washington Nationals. On first with David Ortiz at the plate, he took off for second and just beat the throw from the catcher. As he popped out of his slide he glanced toward third and saw that no one was covering the base. He took off, leaving the helpless shortstop holding the ball. By the time third baseman Ryan Zimmerman received the throw ran back to his base, Betts slid in just beyond the tag. The Nats challenged both safe calls—at second and third—but after a lengthy pause, Betts was declared safe at both bases. He later scored on a David Ortiz hit.

✶   ✶   ✶   ✶

Mookie is a key member of the outfield dance troupe that performs "win dance repeat" after every Sox win. His contributions include "The Carlton," "Jump On It," and the "Macarena."

✶   ✶   ✶   ✶

Humble, team-oriented, talented, Mookie is the poster boy for the sport. Jerry West's silhouetted image is the symbol for the NBA. Betts already has a head start to be his baseball counterpart. His full name is Marcus Lynn Betts, as in MLB. His best Red Sox pal Jackie Bradley Jr. still addresses him by that name.

✶   ✶   ✶   ✶

Betts was once asked about his biggest fear. His answer? "Rust. I hate rust, it messes me up. It makes my skin crawl," he told Katie Nolan of Garbage Time. "I have to get away from it. It's been this way pretty much my entire life. I don't know why I don't like it, if I see rust it just really messes me up." This might have been a legitimate concern for atrocious fielding former Red Sox first baseman Dick Stuart, aka "The Man With The Iron Glove" but not for the sure-handed Red Sox right fielder. It's just a matter of time before he is the proud owner of multiple Gold Gloves. And gold doesn't rust.

✶   ✶   ✶   ✶

Mookie's mom was his first Little League coach. Mookie's uncle is Terry Shumpert, a former major leaguer with several teams. The nickname Mookie was inspired by his parents watching Mookie Blaylock, then a guard for the NBA's Atlanta Hawks.

Clarence "Climax" Blethen

Some major league ballplayers exit the game having left a mark on posterity; still others depart with a mark on their own posterior. Red Sox pitcher Blethen was one of those players who left little mark on the game, but the game made a distinct mark on him. He was once bitten on the butt by his own teeth! He wore dentures and placed them in his back pocket when he played. Maybe he didn't trust his 1923 teammates enough to leave them in the clubhouse. One day, on a slide into second base, the teeth snapped shut on part of his anatomy.

Xander Bogaerts

David Ortiz has called Xander Bogaerts "the best shortstop in the game, by far" and few would argue that he's at least in the top echelon at that position. At the plate, his bat is lightning quick. He once hit a home run on a pitch that was so far inside, he actually apologized after the game. "I had no business swinging at it," he told reporters.

* * * *

Xander Bogaerts, nicknamed X-Man, is a native of Aruba and can speak four languages: English, Dutch, Papiamento, and Spanish. Unlike former Red Sox catcher Moe Berg of whom it was said, "He could speak a dozen languages and couldn't hit in any of them," Bogaerts can hit fluently in all of them.

✷　✷　✷　✷

As a 21-year old with only two month in the big leagues, Bogaerts helped lead the Red Sox to a World Series championship in 2013, prompting a hero's welcome back home in Aruba. The red carpet was rolled out, a stretch limo provided. Even the Prime Minister turned out for the occasion. But for Bogaerts, the highlight was being awarded the first star on the Aruba Walk of Fame at the local mall. "That's our Hollywood Boulevard," he explained. "I guess that means I've really made it."

✷　✷　✷　✷

Bogaerts wears uniform number 2 in honor of his hero, Derek Jeter.

✷　✷　✷　✷

Even before Bogaerts joined the Red Sox, writer Michael Schur saw promotional opportunities for the young prospect: "I'm excited for when Bogaerts gets to the majors, has a great first week, and Baskin-Robbins releases 'Xander Bogaerts Frozen Yogaerts.'

✷　✷　✷　✷

Xander's twin brother Jair Bogaerts was also Red Sox property for a short while but he will always be part of a great Sox trivia question. He was dealt to the Chicago Cubs in 2012 as part of the deal that allowed Red Sox GM and executive vice-president Theo Epstein to take over as president of baseball operations in the windy city. Jair now works for the Beverly Hills Sports Council as a player agent.

Wade Boggs

*　　*　　*　　*

Bogaerts was discovered by Red Sox scout Mike Lord during a 2009 recruiting trip to Aruba. Lord had watched several young players work out, including Xander's brother Jair. He casually asked if there was anyone else he should see. Jair mentioned his 16-year old twin who was sick in bed with chicken pox. His mother, Sandra Brown, was finally convinced to let him leave his sick bed to try out and the rest is history.

The Bogaerts twins were first instructed in the fine art of hitting by their uncle Glenroy. Instead of baseballs, he threw them almonds from the tree in the backyard. The trunk of a discarded Christmas tree was used as a bat.

Wade Boggs

Ballplayers are a superstitious lot; none more so than former Red Sox third baseman and Hall of Fame inductee Wade Boggs. Boggs was known for drawing Hebrew letters in the batter's box for luck. He also had a fixation with the numbers 7 and 17. He took his wind sprints at 7:17 each evening (this was before the days of the 7:05 start) and in 1984 asked the Red Sox for the precise sum of $717,000. Boggs' major quirk was a daily diet of chicken, prepared one of fifty different ways. His wife Debbie was so inspired that she even went so far as to author a cookbook entitled *Fowl Tips*.

*　　*　　*　　*

During the 1985 season, Boggs batted .368 and showed his great patience as a hitter. He popped up just three times in 653 at-bats, and two of those were foul. During that same season, he compiled 240 hits, and 124 of those came with two strikes on him—something that would make Ted "a walk is as good as a hit" Williams smile. Boggs swung at and missed a grand total of one first pitch all season long. In 1987, he hit a robust .390 with the count at 0 and 2.

*   *   *   *

Boggs' days with the Red Sox were not without controversy. In 1989, a very public scandal involving Margo Adams tarnished his image and threatened to scuttle his marriage, and for a while he was forced to endure brutal heckling both at home and on the road. His season batting average fell from .366 the previous year to a slightly more earthly .330, and for the first time in recent memory he failed to capture the batting title. Boggs endured however, and when he retired at the end of the 1999 campaign with a .328 average and 3010 hits, he was a sure bet for a spot in baseball's Hall of Fame. Defying those who dismiss him as a doubles hitter, his 3000th hit was a 372-foot home run.

*   *   *   *

Ted Williams redux? Well, not quite maybe, but not bad. On the final day of the 1985 season, Boggs admits he was counting numbers, shooting for 240 hits which would represent the highest total since 1930. With 11 games left, he still needed 19 hits.

The last day, he still needed three, and John McNamara asked him how many at-bats he wanted. "I'll go 3-for-3 and come out of the game," replied Boggs. First two times up, he got a double and then a single. Next at-bat, he made an out. McNamara informed Boggs that with that 2-for-3 he was in a dead tie with Rod Carew for the batting title, and asked if Wade wanted to share the title or go for hit #240, possibly risking the loss of both goals. Boggs said, "Just give me another at-bat," and got his hit.

*   *   *   *

Boggs started the season going 3-for-4 and closed it the same way. On the season, he hit 187 singles, seven more than the previous A.L. record. He hit safely in 135 games, tying the major league mark set in 1930.

*   *   *   *

Boggs averaged .338 during his 11 years as a Red Sox, getting over 200 hits in seven straight seasons. Too often in the press for one escapade or another, Boggs "left the Red Sox for the Yankees becoming perhaps the only sports star ever to move to the Big Apple in search of anonymity." —Friend & Zminda.

*   *   *   *

"According to *The Sporting News*, over the last four years, Wade Boggs hit .800 with women in scoring position." —David Letterman.

Dennis "Oil Can" Boyd

"I sometimes act like I'm from another planet."
                                        —Dennis "Oil Can" Boyd

Oil Can Boyd courted controversy during his fiery tenure with the Red Sox. General Manager Lou Gorman describes why, after the disastrous sixth-game loss to the Mets, Oil Can didn't pitch in Game seven of the 1986 World Series.

"Then it all fell apart. The wild pitch. The error. Then the loss. We were devastated. The next day, we were rained out and I met with [manager] John McNamara about what we were going to do in the seventh game. Oil Can Boyd was fresh, rested, and wanted to pitch the game. But Mac decided to go with Bruce Hurst. Hurst had won two games already in that series, though he was going to go without his normal rest. If he got in trouble early, we were going to bring in Boyd, and then finish up with [Calvin] Schiraldi. We had the lead going into the sixth inning, but then Bruce started to get into trouble. We were going to go to Boyd, but we couldn't find him." Will McDonough, (Boston Globe 4/8/2000)

✳   ✳   ✳   ✳

The Can recalled meeting The Kid: "The first thing Ted Williams ever said to me, he saw me throw in minor league camp, the first time he ever seen me, he was standing behind the backstop, and I'll never forget the day, he called time and said, 'Holy Cow, if it ain't Satchel in reincarnation.' And from that point on, he has been so good to me, he used to say he wanted to represent me, he talked me into the big leagues. He pulled for me every day, with other coaches, he said 'I don't care who you're lookin' at down here, that's the man you should have your eye on.' He was always telling people who were in charge of things to keep their eye on me, and sayin' 'I want to represent him, I want to be his agent!'"

✳   ✳   ✳   ✳

In Bruce Shalin's book *Oddballs*, Oil Can compares himself to Satchel Paige: "Satchel had to pitch five innings every day. He warmed up over a matchbox. I know those kinds of things were true because I came up with the same kind of makeup as a ballplayer, knowing that the things that they said may seem kind of farfetched, but they were true. I warmed up as a Little Leaguer, I used to be able to throw a curveball and drop it into a bucket on home plate. That's how I learned to make my curveball go down. I had a perfect curveball."

✳   ✳   ✳   ✳

Dennis Boyd hailed from Meridian, Mississippi, the home of legendary Satchel Paige and—because he is black, wiry, countrified, loves to talk and has a colorful nickname—many people thought of him as the reincarnation of Satch. In some parts of the south, beer is known as "oil," and since Boyd loved beer as a teenager, he was given the name Oil Can. The son of an ex-Negro League star, the Can even kept a picture of Paige in his locker. Boyd did not share Satch's laid-back philosophy, however. He had a temper. When he was left off the 1985 All-Star team by manager Sparky Anderson, he was upset. When he was left off by Dick Howser in 1986, he went ballistic, throwing a tantrum in the Red Sox dressing room and verbally abusing several teammates. He was suspended for three days without pay.

Jackie Bradley Jr.

Jackie Bradley Jr. is the son of Jackie Bradley and Alfreda Hagans. The elder Bradley was christened with the name in tribute to soul singer Jackie Wilson. He has been a driver for the Greater Richmond Transit Company in Virginia for 25 years. Junior's mother is a former Virginia state trooper. Although the couple divorced when he was only 3, they made sure that their son's transfer was smooth. "On the weekend, when it was time for me to get him, she'd bring him and put him on the bus with me till I got off (work)," says Jackie Sr.

*   *   *   *

Pay attention the next time Bradley Jr. catches the final out of an inning. He immediately channels Tom Brady by throwing a lead pass to his close friend and wide receiver Mookie Betts as he runs his route to the dugout.

Red Sox manager John Farrell does not exhibit quite as much confidence in Bradley Jr. that Bill Belichick does in Tom Brady. "I'm always fearful some fan is going to get it in their nachos and their beer," he once admitted.

*   *   *   *

For most major league ballplayers, life on the road can be tedious. For Jackie Bradley Jr., each road trip is an opportunity to expand his horizons and soak up the cultural and culinary delights of the area. When the Red Sox visit Seattle for instance, he takes in the

Space Needle and Pike's Place Market. But his two favorite cities are Baltimore and Toronto. Baltimore is the nearest park to his home state of Virginia and gives him a chance to reconnect with family and friends. |As for Toronto, he says he likes the infrastructure of the city and the people.

Darren Bragg

Trying desperately to beat the throw from shortstop, Darren Bragg slid headfirst into first base on a close play at Fenway. The only problem was that he started his slide too soon and ended up several feet short of his goal. The next day, during batting practice, his Red Sox teammates decided to help him out. "We put another base 10 feet in front of the actual bag," said Nomar Garciaparra. "Right where he ended up. We said, this is Darren Bragg's first base. He plays by different rules. We told him if first base were right here, you would have been safe."

Bill Buckner

Game Six of the 1986 World Series was hardly a laugh riot for Red Sox fans. It was as if Wile E. Coyote had finally caught the tasty but elusive Roadrunner, only to have the annoying little creature escape once again from the boiling pot. Beep! Beep! The '86 Red Sox came within one pitch of a World Series championship and let it slip through their hands—or more accurately, through Bill Buckner's legs. (Bleep! Bleep!) The humor that the game does present is of the darkest possible variety. Before the game, Sox manager John McNamara was asked who would start at first base, Buckner or Don Baylor. His reply: "Probably Buckner. He was hobbling at one hundred percent today." Buckner later let a ground ball go through his legs, resulting in the most devastating loss in Sox history. He later moved to Idaho to escape his infamy.

Bill Buckner (Brace Photography)

*   *   *   *

He won the National League batting championship in 1980 with a .324 average. He accumulated 2,715 career base hits. He led the National League in doubles not once but twice. He drove in 110 runs for the Red Sox in 1985 and another 102 runs in '86. He was a team leader for the Red Sox, perhaps the most respected man on the team. Nevertheless, the man known as Billy Bucks is best remembered for a ball that eluded his grasp and led to the most disappointing loss in Red Sox franchise history. The ball that went through his legs untouched in Game Six is now the object of a rather dark sort of fame. It was purchased at auction by actor Charlie Sheen and now presumably is a conversation piece in some Beverly Hills home. The price of the infamous spheroid: $93,000 and a million broken New England hearts.

*   *   *   *

Buckner excelled in bases-loaded situations. With the bases full in the 1985 season, Buckner batted .389 (7-18). He did not strike out a single time, hit into no double-plays and drove in 21 runs.

*   *   *   *

Buckner's infamous misplay of the grounder in the '86 World Series has inspired jokes such as:

Q: "What do Michael Jackson and Bill Buckner have in common?"
A: "They both wear one glove for no apparent reason."

Buckner actually had an excellent lifetime .992 fielding average.

Don Buddin

Don Buddin had a reputation as an erratic fielder. In 1956, '58 and '59, the clean-cut Red Sox shortstop led the American League in double plays. Unfortunately, in two of those years he also topped the league in errors. Former Boston writer and radio personality Clif Keane once incurred Buddin's wrath by suggesting in print that he should have "E-6" as his license plate.

Rick Burleson

Announcer Joe Garagiola once described shortstop "Rooster" Burleson as follows: "He's even-tempered. He comes to the ballpark mad, and he stays that way."

*   *   *   *

According to teammate Bill Lee, Rick Burleson, known to Red Sox teammates and fans as "Rooster", "was mad all the time." During a 1977 game against the hated Yankees, Burleson even managed to take his anger out on an inanimate object. When the Yankee scoreboard encouraged cheers for Reggie Jackson, Burleson turned and yelled epithets at the blinking lights.

*   *   *   *

In his May 4, 1974 debut, a nervous bantam Burleson committed three errors.

*   *   *   *

Bill Lee remembers Rick Burleson as a typical middle-infielder in temperament. "He reminded me of Billy Martin a lot. He was a hothead. We were in an elevator once in Minnesota and some drunk made a derogatory comment about him and Rooster started pounding on him. And finally I said, 'Leave him alone, let him fall down.' He was tough. He was pugnacious like all those middle infielders. Eddie Stanley, Don Zimmer, Billy Martin, Leo Durocher. They're all the same. They're all pains in the ass."

Jose Canseco

While with the Red Sox, Jose Canseco expressed some rather interesting views on fuel economy: "The faster you drive, the less time you spend with your foot on the gas."

Bernie Carbo

"Bernie was baseball's Forrest Gump." —Bill Lee

Bernie Carbo was an unorthodox ballplayer who traveled with a stuffed gorilla named Mighty Joe Young who he occasionally ordered for in restaurants. Bernie Carbo's chief claim to fame was the clutch home run that he hit in Game Six of the 1975 World Series, a contest that many consider the greatest ever played. With two strikes, and the Red Sox down 6-3 in the bottom of the eighth, Carbo hit a three-run homer off ace Cincinnati reliever Rawly Eastwick to tie the game. The unlikely home run set the stage for Carlton Fisk's dramatic game-winning homer in the bottom of the 12th inning.

★   ★   ★   ★

In 1977, Carbo slugged a bases-loaded homer against Seattle Mariners' left-hander Mike Kekich. After the game, reporters gathered around his locker to ask him about the grand slam. "Grand slam?" said a startled Carbo, who had failed to notice that the bases were loaded while he was at-bat. Another reporter asked when he had last homered off a southpaw pitcher. Carbo laughed. "Now I know you're pulling my leg, because he was a right-handed pitcher," he said confidently. "(Red Sox manager Don) Zimmer would never let me hit against a left-hander with the bases loaded."

*　　*　　*　　*

When Carbo was sold to Cleveland in 1978, his best friend Bill Lee went on an unofficial strike. He confronted his manager Don Zimmer. "I thought you said that Bernie was like a son to you?" said Lee. "Well, I've got news for you; you don't trade your son to Cleveland."

*　　*　　*　　*

During the 1975 Red Sox run for the pennant, Laurie Cabot—a witch from Salem—attempted to energize Bernie Carbo's slumping bat by putting a spell on it.

*　　*　　*　　*

In the summer of '75, Carbo crashed into the bullpen at Fenway Park in a successful effort to prevent a home run by the Yankee batter. The jarring contact with the wall caused him to lose the plug of tobacco he had been chewing, and Carbo held up the game for a full ten minutes while he looked for his missing "chaw" on the dirt of the warning track. When he finally found it, he put it back in his mouth and the game continued.

*　　*　　*　　*

Bill Lee, unofficial leader of the subversive group known as the Buffalo Heads, was a good friend of Carbo. "All of the Buffalo Heads, except Bernie Carbo, were pitchers," he recalls. "Jenkins, Willoughby, Wise, and myself—Bernie just wanted to be in there, he didn't want to be left behind. There are a million Buffalo Head stories in the naked jungle. A lot of mean tricks were played on Bernie. He was very intuitive, not well educated, flew by the seat of his pants. I considered him like a negative barometer. If anything was going to go wrong, he'd give me foresight into it."

Bill Carrigan/Joe Kerrigan

Bill "Rough" Carrigan really lived up to his nickname. Carrigan single-handedly put an end to Ty Cobb's infamous practice of sliding into home with sharpened spikes raised. He tagged The Georgia Peach hard in the face with the ball in his hand. Cobb was out, and also knocked out, and carried out of Fenway on a stretcher. Carrigan was a good receiver and actually caught three no-hitters for the Sox.

* * * *

A few years later, Carrigan was manager when young Babe Ruth joined the Sox. In his first 3 1/2 years, the Red Sox won two championships. Ruth called him "the greatest manager I ever played for"—despite the fact that Rough had once slugged the slugger.

* * * *

The only manager to win back-to-back World Series tides who is not in the Hall of Fame is Bill Carrigan. His Red Sox won the 1915 and 1916 championships.

* * * *

The naming of Joe Kerrigan as Sox skipper in August 2001 restored a name steeped in Red Sox club history. During the 1913 season, on July 14, William F. "Rough" Carrigan assumed the managerial reins at Fenway, and ran the club for the 1914, 1915 and 1916 seasons—winning the World Series in both '15 and '16. Though just 33 at the time, his wife was pregnant, and he left the game to start a family in his home state of Maine. Years later, he was lured back by new owner Bob Quinn and managed the Sox for three less-than-stellar seasons 1927-9 (well, to be blunt, Boston finished dead last all three years.)

*   *   *   *

As it turns out, Joe Kerrigan's tenure was brief (17-26, .395 winning percentage working with a team decimated by injuries and discord.) That .395 was still better than any of the last three years of Carrigan's second coming. Kerrigan (maybe the best pitching coach the Red Sox ever had and the man Dennis Eckersley called Stats Masterson) was relieved of his duties during spring training 2002, only the fourth manager in major league history to lose his position during the preseason. Except for the bizarre 1907 Sox season, which saw four managers at the helm, Kerrigan's was the shortest tenure of any manager. In 1907, Chick Stahl committed suicide on March 27 (apparently more related to his playing the field than the team's play on the field), George Huff quit after eight games, and then first baseman Bob Unglaub managed for 29. Cy Young managed on an interim basis for six games. Finally, a true man of the flannel—Deacon McGuire—finished out the season. McGuire batted .750 that year in four well-chosen plate appearances.

Managers with even worse statistical records than Kerrigan's include Del Baker, Shano Collins, Lee Fohl, Marty McManus, Heinie Wagner, and Rudy York—as well as Huff and Unglaub.

Roger Clemens

Roger Clemens

Rocket Roger Clemens has had some memorable days on the mound for the Red Sox, but none greater than the day in May of 1986 when he set a new major-league record by striking out 20 Seattle Mariners. At that point, the record for a nine-inning game was 19, shared by Steve Carlton, Nolan Ryan and Tom Seaver. In the contest, Clemens threw 138 pitches—97 of them strikes. Of the 97 strikes only 29 were sullied by contact with wood, and 19 of those were foul balls. In baseball's version of "float like a butterfly and sting like a bee," he painted the corners like an artist and threw inside like a hired assassin. What makes Clemens' achievement even more amazing was the fact that just eight months earlier he had undergone shoulder surgery. As the strikeout totals continued to build, the Fenway faithful reacted enthusiastically when first baseman Mike Easler dropped a foul ball, allowing Clemens to notch yet another K. Clemens went on to earn American League MVP honors and capture the Cy Young award.

✳   ✳   ✳   ✳

The names of Clemens' kids all begin with K—the baseball symbol for strikeout. For the record, they are Koby, Kory, Kacy and Kody. Klever!

✳   ✳   ✳   ✳

And he's thinking of wearing a New York cap into the Hall of Fame? During the 1986 World Series with the Mets, one of the problems the Red Sox players had to endure was the treatment they suffered from the security forces at Shea Stadium. Roger Clemens, in his book *Rocket Man,* recalls, "I have nothing against the fans, who except for a few nuts were fine. It was the security—the police and the way the place was handled. The security guards were screaming at our wives. ... There was the fan who threw the golf ball out of the upper deck that just missed Rice's head. When we were coming in from the bullpen after we'd lost the final game, there were all sorts of security guards screaming obscenities at us and calling us all kinds of names." On the way to the bus, someone threw a can that hit traveling secretary Jack Rogers on the head and knocked him unconscious. As he lay there bleeding, Clemens says two New York cops stood around snickering.

* * * *

When the Red Sox clinched the 1986 pennant, Texan Roger Clemens celebrated like a true cowboy. "One of the Boston policemen was on a horse named Timothy, and Rice yelled, 'There's your horse, Tex, get on it.' I looked up at the policeman, asked if I could get up there, and he said sure. When I got up and started riding around, the fans went crazy. ... I can imagine what the Red Sox and the fans would have thought if I had fallen off. I've been riding all my life, so they shouldn't have worried, but since I was in back of the policeman and far back on Timothy, I put too much pressure on his bladder, he started bucking, and I did nearly get thrown off. I got off—in a hurry."

* * * *

When Roger's first child Koby was born, Roger carried around a baseball card that indicated that Koby is a switch hitter and then the following: career highlights "In the year 2005, he stars at the University of Texas in baseball, beats Arizona State for the national title, and catches winning touchdown pass to beat Oklahoma 21-14 in Cotton Bowl."

Roger also says: "I'm the kind of guy who likes to eat cereal in the morning while I'm watching TV in my undershorts." Which inspired *Baseball Cards* columnist Irwin Cohen to quip: "To paraphrase Groucho Marx, how the TV got in his undershorts we'll never know."

* * * *

In a memorable game in Oakland, Roger Clemens wore eyeblack and Ninja Turtle shoelaces and told umpire Terry Cooney, "I know where you live!" Just another one of those flaky northpaws that Bill Lee is always talking about.

*   *   *   *

Roger Clemens won his sixth Cy Young Award in 2001. Red Sox fans are still trying to figure out how a guy who was once a hero in Boston could manage to rack up seasons like his last four with the Red Sox:

1993	11-14	4.46 ERA
1994	9-7	2.85 ERA
1995	10-5	4.18 ERA
1996	10-13	3.63 ERA total of 40-39

And then go on to win three Cy Youngs in the next five years.

*   *   *   *

Is Roger Clemens really the anti-Christ? It's been said that Clemens— this six-time Cy Young winner—doesn't really have any fans. He's burnt too many bridges in both Boston and Toronto, and never really earned a true fan base in New York. He may wear a Yankees cap into Cooperstown, but will anyone really care?

*   *   *   *

He began as a true hero in Boston, but (in Will McDonough's words) "put it on cruise control his last four years in Boston, allowing himself to balloon like the poster child for the Pillsbury Doughboy, letting his fastball drop to the high 80s, making sure he didn't get hurt." He said if he ever left the Red Sox, it would be to move closer to his home outside

Dallas. He went to Toronto and immediately won two Cy Youngs there. He'd arranged and then invoked some clause in his contract—it was never fully explained—which resulted in the Blue Jays trading him to the Yankees.

*   *   *   *

There's one entire website devoted to anti-Roger material. Hating Roger has become an acceptable popular pastime in Boston. When the Yankees last visited Fenway in the 2001 season, sports talk radio station WEEI printed up thousands of cardboard posters as a giveaway promotion prior to the game. The posters read: WE HATE ROGER.

*   *   *   *

A few Clemens quotes of note from the website:

"I wish he were still playing. I'd probably crack his head open to show him how valuable I was."—Roger on Hank Aaron, after baseball's home run king suggested that pitchers should not be eligible for the MVP award.

"I thought it was the ball."—Roger, who apparently wanted to throw the baseball at Mike Piazza, on throwing a splintered bat at the Mets catcher.

"I could never come back and pitch against the Red Sox, so it would have to be in the other league."—Roger, as quoted by Will McDonough of the *Boston Globe*.

"I've thrown the ball well in postseason play."—Roger, after being beaten by Pedro Martinez in the 1999 ALCS, comparing his 1-2 record in nine postseason starts with Boston versus Pedro's 3-0 career during the playoffs.

"I think undercover [Red Sox fans] are going to be rooting for me, too."—Roger, before being booed and taunted mercilessly by Red Sox nation at Fenway Park during Game Three of the 1999 ALCS.

"I would only leave Boston to go back to Houston to be closer to my family."—Roger, as quoted by Will McDonough

"I have all the nice things in life because of the fact that [Red Sox owner] Mr. Harrington took care of me. I don't need a lot of money."—Roger, also as quoted by McDonough

"You just don't leave the Sox to go to the Yanks, That's like a black man joining the KKK," wrote an anonymous poster. "Roger Clemens represents everything that's wrong with sports today," editorialized the webmaster.

But is he really the anti-Christ? Bill Simmons of ESPN.COM said his bosses at ESPN gave him the following assignment: "Please explain to the world why Boston fans believe that Roger Clemens might be the anti-Christ." One suspects that Bill needed little prompting. "With pleasure," he wrote and then launched into a 3,325-word diatribe.

Reggie Cleveland

Red Sox pitcher Reggie Cleveland rolled his car over in a Storrow Drive tunnel, reportedly while reaching into the back seat for a doughnut. That inspired this immortal line from Dennis Eckersley reported by Gordon Edes: "We need driver's ed, not a pitching coach."

*   *   *   *

Cleveland was one of the rare Red Sox to hail from Swift Current, Saskatchewan, Canada. "He dressed like Herb Tarlek from WKRP," says teammate Bill Lee. "He's probably a used car salesman somewhere. His weight used to fluctuate 15 pounds between starts."

Eddie Collins

W hile still a player, future Hall of Famer Eddie Collins—who went on to become Red Sox GM and was instrumental in signing a young prospect named Ted Williams—always placed his chewing gum on the button on top of his cap for good luck. It must have worked; Collins was one of the first major leaguers to accumulate over 3,000 career hits. Like many ballplayers of his day, Collins had other quirks. He used to bury his bats in shallow graves to keep them lively. In the midst of the 'dead ball era,' it kind of makes sense . . . no, wait a minute, we take that back. It makes no sense at all.

Tony Conigliaro

"He was baseball's JFK." —Dick Johnson

I t was the kind of debut that every kid dreams about. Just two years out of St. Mary's High School in Lynn, Massachusetts, 19-year-old rookie right fielder Tony Conigliaro stepped into the batter's box and homered off Chicago's Joel Horlen on the first pitch thrown to him at Fenway Park. One writer suggested that it was the fastest start by anyone in town "since Paul Revere beat the British out of the gate." It was 1964, and the home opener was a special game to benefit the planned John F. Kennedy Memorial Library. Conigliaro was performing before a celebrity-filled crowd that included Bobby and Teddy Kennedy, the governor of Massachusetts, Boston's mayor, boxers Jack Dempsey and Gene Tunney, Cardinal Cushing, the Harvard University band and an impressive array of film stars, including Carol Channing. Despite missing more than 50 games due to injury, Conigliaro, with a swing ideally suited to Fenway, poked 24 home runs over the Green Monster while hitting at a .290 clip. In his sophomore year, he became baseball's youngest home run king, leading the American League with 32 at the age of 20. He added 28 more in 1966, but both the production and the injury were harbingers of things to come.

Tony Conigliaro (Brace Photography)

*   *   *   *

There have been two great tragedies in Red Sox history, both involving local Boston boys with matinee-idol good looks and seemingly limitless futures. The first involved the Golden Greek, Harry Agganis, who died tragically in 1953 at the age of 23. The second of the Greco-Roman tragedies came more than a decade later on August 18, 1967, a steamy night in the midst of one of the hottest and most memorable pennant races in American League history. Hometown hero Tony Conigliaro was hit in the head by a fastball thrown by California Angels pitcher Jack Hamilton. The blow almost killed him and he was never the same again. He had 20 home runs at the time of his beaning.

*   *   *   *

Red Sox manager Darrell Johnson once spied Conigliaro coming out of a nightclub after curfew. Tony C insisted that he had only ducked into the establishment to get directions to Midnight Mass.

*   *   *   *

Before "vanity plates" were commonplace, the governor of Massachusetts issued a set of personalized plates to Conigliaro in recognition of the great rookie season the hometown boy had put together. The plates bore only the letters "T. C." Unfortunately, some over-zealous fans decided that the plates would make a nice souvenir and stole them, bumpers and all.

*   *   *   *

New England fans loved Tony C. Following his beaning, his eyesight took a long time to come back and never did return completely. After striking out four times in one game, he complained about fans wearing white shirts in the bleacher triangle. He said the glare off the shirts made it difficult to see the ball and created a dangerous situation for hitters, and proposed that fans sitting in that area be given green or blue vests to wear during the game. The Red Sox responded, posting a sign which read: "Dear Patron, please do not sit in green seat section unless you are wearing dark-colored clothing. Conig thanks you. Management thanks you." Fans entering the seats in this area were given cards stating: "You are now an official member of Conig's Corner. The Red Sox and Tony C appreciate your cooperation in helping to provide a good hitting background."

*   *   *   *

Before becoming the Red Sox manager and leading them to the 1967 "Impossible Dream" pennant, Dick Williams was Tony C's teammate. Management requested that he room with the handsome young star in order to provide some positive influence from a major league veteran. There was only one small flaw in the strategy. "Never saw him," claimed Williams in his book *No More Mr. Nice Guy*. "Not late at night, not first thing in the morning, never. I was providing veteran influence to a suitcase."

*   *   *   *

Like crooner Mickey McDermott before him, Tony C became a New England singing idol as well as a baseball idol. It began with him singing old rock & roll songs with teammates Rico Petrocelli and Mike Ryan but quickly grew more serious as record companies tried to cash in on his huge popularity in the Boston area. His first big chartbuster was the aptly named "Playing the Field", with "Why Don't They Understand?" on the flip side. His Red Sox teammates went out of their way to keep the young heartthrob humble. When the record was first released Conigliaro rushed to the ballpark before the players arrived and left a copy in each of his teammates' lockers. He then went onto the field to work out. When he returned expecting congratulations and gratitude, he was greeted instead with stony silence. "What happened to the records?" he asked. One of the players motioned toward the trash barrel, overflowing with Tony C's records. Conigliaro immediately saw what was going on and laughed harder than anyone.

Gene Conley

Following a game at Yankee Stadium in July 1962, losing pitcher Gene Conley and teammate Pumpsie Green, the first black man to play for the Red Sox, were traveling back to the hotel in the team bus. When the bus became trapped in a New York traffic jam, Conley and Green jumped ship and disappeared into the crowd. They checked into a hotel and proceeded to get inebriated. At least one of the two defectors then seems to have undergone a profound religious experience. Green's pilgrimage was back to the Red Sox, but Conley headed for the airport with every intention of flying to Israel "to get nearer to God." A ticket agent pointed out that he had no passport, and he sheepishly returned to the Boston fold. Both were fined by owner Tom Yawkey, and Green was later banished to the then-lowly New York Mets.

* * * *

Someone once spotted Gene Conley alone and crying in a church. The concerned observer asked him if he had lost a loved one. "Yes," he sobbed. "My fastball."

* * * *

In addition to being something of a flake, Red Sox pitcher Gene Conley was an all-around athlete and no stranger to the thrill of victory. Before coming to the Red Sox, he was a member of the 1957

World Series champion Milwaukee Braves. He also performed with the NBA champion Boston Celtics of 1959, 1960 and 1961.

Marty Cordova

During the 2000 season, a short-staffed Boston newspaper was forced to send a non-baseball person to Fenway Park to interview former Red Sox player Marty Cordova. Cordova had been released by the Red Sox during spring training a few months earlier and this was his first time he'd visited Boston since his release.

On entering the visitors' dressing room, the apprehensive newsman approached the man he believed to be Cordova and tentatively began asking him questions. To his surprise and delight the ballplayer responded vigorously to his inquiries. He was obviously a man who wanted to vent his feelings to the public following a terrible injustice. Warming to his task, the reporter asked Cordova to expand on his feelings about being released—whereupon the ballplayer launched into a passionate, vitriolic diatribe on the entire Red Sox organization from top to bottom. He condemned the team and everyone associated with it, past and present. He concluded by stating that the Boston Red Sox were the most despised franchise in sport and that he would exact revenge upon them if it took him the rest of his natural life. The reporter was flushed with success. He thanked the ballplayer profusely for his frankness and headed for the door, thoughts of Pulitzers no doubt dancing in his head. Just as he was about to exit the room, the irate ballplayer hailed him once again. "I have one more thing I want to add," he said. "What's that?" asked the eager reporter, tape recorder poised to capture more venomous rhetoric. "I'm John Frascatore," he said. "That's Cordova over there."

Joe Cronin

In a 1935 game against Cleveland at Fenway Park, Red Sox shortstop Joe Cronin (later to become Red Sox manager and eventually American League president) came to bat with none out, the bases loaded and the Red Sox down by a 5-3 count. Cronin drove a vicious line drive down the third base line that handcuffed Indians third baseman Odell "Bad News" Hale. The ball struck him in the forehead and ricocheted to shortstop William Knickerbocker for the first out. Knickerbocker relayed it to second baseman Billy Werber to get the runner, and Werber threw it to first baseman Hal Trosky to complete the triple play. Three outs—possibly four if you include Hale, who was nearly out cold.

*   *   *   *

"Curt Gowdy once told me that Yawkey fired my dad at least twice a week," says Joe Cronin's daughter Maureen. "Ten times more than Steinbrenner fired Billy Martin, because Yawkey was a big drinker and he'd have a few and say 'You're fired!' I mean it was kind of a joke, but I felt badly for my poor dad."

*   *   *   *

On August 25, 1937, the Red Sox faced Cleveland ace Bob Feller. Rapid Robert proceeded to strike out 16 Red Sox hitters en route to a four-hit, 8-1 victory. After being called out on strikes for his second strikeout of the day, Red Sox player-manager Joe Cronin turned to umpire Lou Kolls and asked reasonably, "If I can't see it, how did you see it?"

*   *   *   *

When Cronin became General Manager of the Boston Red Sox, he soon had old friends from the west coast calling to ask favors. Frank Keneally, a fan of the San Francisco Seals and an old school friend of Cronin's, called to urge Cronin to send a few expendable Red Sox players west to help out his team. Faced with lineup problems of his own, Cronin had to refuse the request. A few weeks later Keneally was reading the San Francisco newspapers and noticed that the Red Sox were mired in the depths of the American League standings while the Seals were near the top of their league. He rushed to send a telegram to Cronin: "Dear Joe—maybe we can help you."

✳   ✳   ✳   ✳

As a player Cronin was good enough to be named Allstar short-stop seven times by *The Sporting News* and capture an American league MVP award in 1930; as a player-manager he led teams to two pennants. He then became general manager of the Red Sox before becoming president of the American League.

He was one of the most successful pinch hitters in major league history. On a record five different occasions in 1943, Cronin, at the ripe old baseball age of 37, called his own number to pinch hit and responded with a home run each time. In total, the player-manager went to the plate 49 times in the pinch-hitting role and produced seven bases-on-balls, nine singles, four doubles, and five homers. In short, the man who earned the nickname "Mr. Clutch" set the standard for pinch hitters of his or any era. Former sports editor Bob Broeg of the *St. Louis Post-Dispatch,* in his book *Superstars of Baseball* summed it up nicely:

"Cronin in a pinch was Capt. Blood, a swashbuckler. In the era of the playing managers, a period of considerable color, charm and drama, Joe would put himself on the spot with a flair and courage that would make lesser men gulp." For his part, Cronin was much more modest about his pinchhitting accomplishments. "I pulled rank and waited until the wind blew out," he claimed.

✳   ✳   ✳   ✳

Brawls between the Red Sox and Yankees are as predictable as Harry Potter sequels, and almost as entertaining. On May 30, 1938, the Red Sox were playing a doubleheader with the Yankees in front of a capacity crowd of 83,533 at Yankee Stadium in the Bronx. In the first game Red Sox pitcher Archie McKain threw a purpose pitch a bit too close to Yankees batter Jake Powell. Powell charged the mound with his mind on mayhem, but his progress was blocked by shortstop-manager Joe Cronin. As the benches

Joe Cronin (Brace Photography)

emptied and fists flew, Cronin protected his pitcher from several wayward punches. "We couldn't afford to have our pitcher ejected for fighting," he explained later. Cronin and Powell were tossed from the game by umpire Cal Hubbard, and order was eventually restored. However, as the ejected manager headed for the showers he was physically assaulted by several Yankee players in the tunnel leading to the Red Sox locker room.

When umpire Hubbard glanced at the Yankees dugout and saw it was vacant he rushed to the scene and attempted a rescue. "Three or four of them were going to town on poor dad," recounts Cronin's daughter Maureen. "They were beating him up and Cal Hubbard appeared. Cal was huge, he used to play against Bronko Nagurski, so he knew how to handle the rough stuff." Hubbard, it should be noted, is the only person to be inducted into the baseball, college football and pro football halls of fame. The former Green Bay Packer stood an imposing 6-foot-4 and tipped the scales at 255 pounds. "This big hand came down and grabbed dad by the collar and pulled him out of this melee. Years later, when dad was made president of the American League, he made Cal Hubbard his chief of umpires."

Bill Crowley

Bill Crowley first joined the Red Sox as one of Curt Gowdy's broadcast partners in 1958. He went on to become the longtime Director of Public Relations for the Boston ballclub. It was his job to let both reporters and the general public know about the latest developments within the franchise and thereby build interest in the Red Sox. In 1972, when superstar pitcher Vida Blue was in a contract dispute with Charlie Finley and the Oakland Athletics, it was rumored that Blue was about to be dealt to the Red Sox. A reporter finally asked Crowley if he'd heard the rumor about Blue coming to Boston. "Hear it?" replied Crowley with a twinkle in his eye. "I started it."

Ray Culp

Red Sox pitcher Ray Culp was once hit in the head by a line drive off the bat of Detroit Tigers strongman Willie Horton. The ball bounced high into the air toward center field, where Reggie Smith made a diving catch for the second out of the inning. Culp hung in there and retired the next batter to end the game. When questioned later about the strange play, Culp's straight-faced reply was: "Don't ever tell me I don't know where to play hitters."

Tom Daly

Red Sox coach Tom Daly twice resorted to extraordinary measures to bring players down a notch. Buck "Bobo" Newsom was always going on about his pitching so one day Daly, a former catcher, challenged him, "Come on, Bobo," he said. "I'll warm you up bare-handed." And he did. His hand hurt for weeks, but he effectively silenced Bobo. He probably wouldn't want to try that with Pedro or Roger.

Then there was Wes Ferrell, who'd often state, "I can lick any man in checkers." Daly bought some books and studied up on checkers, then took Ferrell up on the challenge and beat him six games straight. Ferrell threw the checkerboard out the window.

Brian Daubach

Brian Daubach had played minor league professional baseball for nine frustrating seasons before finally signing a Red Sox contract. Brian is only the third left-handed Red Sox rookie to slam over 20 home runs; Ted Williams and Fred Lynn were the others. Ten of his home runs either tied the score or put the Red Sox ahead. All told, he had 27 game-tying and go-ahead RBIs.

✳   ✳   ✳   ✳

It is only fitting that Daubach is one of the famed "Dirt Dogs", blue-collar players with a down-and-dirty work ethic. His brother Brad worked on Fenway's ground crew during the 2001 season. They obviously have dirt in their blood.

✳   ✳   ✳   ✳

If you can picture China's Chairman Mao sitting down with Microsoft's chairman Bill Gates, if you can picture the proverbial lion laying down with the proverbial lamb, then maybe you can see Brian Daubach and Tim Wakefield hanging out together. Wakefield is a strong union man and the Red Sox union representative. Daubach, in some players' minds, is a scab, a hated "replacement player" who undermined the Major League Players Association back in the great strike of '95 (This is ironic because Brian came from a blue-collar background; his father Dale is a letter carrier for the U. S. Postal Service. Little wonder he has been delivering for the Red Sox ever since.) Why then were Daubach and Wakefield seen fraternizing like old buddies at a recent sporting event (well, actually a wrestling event) at the Fleet Center?

Daubach was there with his good friend Trot Nixon, another Red Sox "dirt dog" and several other players, including Wakefield. As *Boston Herald* writer Steve Buckley put it so very well, "Understand that Wakefield, in addition to being a knuckleball pitcher, is also a knuckle-fisted union man. He is John L. Lewis, Samuel Gompers and Marvin Miller rolled into one, yet he appears to have enormous respect for Brian Daubach, player, as well as Brian Daubach, person."

✳   ✳   ✳   ✳

For some reason, Daubach's career numbers against pitchers from Aruba (population: 62,000) now include at least five home runs. He has two lifetime dingers off Calvin Maduro and three off Sidney Ponson. Next challenge: those pesky pitchers from the Outer Hebrides.

Dom DiMaggio

"Dom could do it all. He ran the bases like a gazelle, he played a flawless center field, and he possessed a riflearm." —Ted Williams

Dom DiMaggio may well be the best player not in the Hall of Fame. According to a song that was popular in New England but less so in New York: "He's better than his brother Joe; Dominic DiMaggio!" Well, probably not. But Dom DiMaggio was still pretty darn good. The Little Professor, so called because of the spectacles he sported, was one of the premier center fielders in baseball history, and no less an authority than Ted Williams has actively campaigned for his induction into the Hall of Fame. Little wonder. DiMaggio was a tablesetter for Ted, who feasted on AL pitching and drove Dom home more often than Morgan Freeman chauffeured Miss Daisy in that direction.

✳   ✳   ✳   ✳

Dom's brother Joe holds the major-league-record hitting streak of 56, but in 1949, Dom set the Red Sox record by hitting safely in 34 consecutive games. Who knows how much further he might have gone had his hard line drive off Yankee pitcher Vic Raschi not been snagged by another agile center fielder. The center fielder's name? Joseph DiMaggio. Blood may be thicker than water but not where baseball is concerned. The headline in a Boston paper the next day screamed: JOE DIMAGGIO'S CATCH STOPS BROTHER'S STREAK. Explaining the catch to Dom after the game, the Yankee Clipper was almost apologetic. "If I had let the ball go through, it would have hit me right between the eyes," he said.

✳   ✳   ✳   ✳

DiMaggio was a true gentleman both on and off the field. A home plate umpire once called him out on some very borderline strikes. As always, DiMaggio kept his composure and didn't turn around to confront the man in blue. When he got back to the dugout, he rested for a moment with his knee on the top step, then removed his glasses and began methodically wiping them off. He gazed steadily out at the umpire and said in a calm, almost meditative voice: "I have never witnessed such incompetence in all my life." Manager Joe McCarthy, accustomed to slightly saltier language from his ballplayers, fell off the bench laughing.

*   *   *   *

Dom DiMaggio was a smaller, bespectacled version of his brother Joe. The "Little Professor" had more total hits than any other player during the years he played, 1940-52 (excluding war years) and only Williams and Musial had more doubles over that same stretch. Only Ted scored more runs than Dom in the same period. He averaged 104.6 runs scored per season over his career. He is the only player NOT in the Hall of Fame to have done so. In the HOF, only Lou Gehrig and Joe DiMaggio rank higher.

*   *   *   *

Player-manager Joe Cronin was very close to DiMaggio and was responsible for getting Joe's little brother to play for the Red Sox. "Dad was one of the first to convince him that he could play the game with glasses," recalls Maureen Cronin. "He was from San Francisco, played on the same sandlot that my dad had played on. Dad had known Dom through Joe. They grew up in the same neighborhood. That's why he was very quick to look at Dom." Dom himself said, "The greatest satisfaction I have in baseball is that I broke in wearing glasses, and in those days, an athlete wearing glasses was a no-no."

✳   ✳   ✳   ✳

"Being the lead-off man, Dom had the toughest job in the lineup," said Mel Parnell. "If he made an out he had to come back to the dugout where Ted Williams would grill him about where the pitch was, what the ball was doing, and what the pitcher had. He got the third degree from Ted."

Bill Dinneen

B ill Dinneen threw a no-hitter for the 1905 Red Sox, then known as the Boston Pilgrims. After his 12-year major league career was over, he worked for another 29 years as an American League umpire. This transition from player to umpire is rare enough but Dinneen is the only major leaguer to have both pitched and umpired a no-hitter. In fact, he umpired six no-hitters in his career.

Bobby Doerr

"Bobby Doerr is one of the very few who played this game hard and came out of it with no enemies." —Tommy Henrich

R ed Sox second baseman Bobby Doerr once handled 414 fielding chances flawlessly before committing an error—a streak that encompassed almost three months. But Doerr was much more than just another good-field, no-hit infielder. His hitting credentials were equally impressive. Although known for his ability to get on base for Ted Williams and other Red Sox big guns, Doerr also hit 223 lifetime home runs and drove in 1,247. His versatility at the plate and in the field carried him all the way to baseball's Hall of Fame.

✳   ✳   ✳   ✳

Bobby Doerr was a pitcher's worst nightmare. He broke up a no-hitter against Spud Chandler in front of 69,107 fans at Yankee Stadium on July 2, 1946. On two other occasions, Doerr had the only hit in games the Sox played against Bob Feller.

Doerr was the only Sox player to hit for the cycle twice—in 1944 and 1947. He also batted in over 100 runs in six consecutive seasons with the Red Sox. The Hall of Fame second baseman combined with Vern Stephens in 1948 to drive in 248 runs and in 1949, the dynamic duo knocked in another 268. In 1950, they plated 264 of their teammates.

Midway through his 13th season in the majors, right after throwing his third no-hitter, Bob Feller was asked to name the four toughest hitters he'd ever faced. Three of them were Red Sox: Feller named Joe DiMaggio, Ted Williams, Johnny Pesky and Bobby Doerr.

Patsy Donovan

Unlike Johnny Cash's "Boy Named Sue," Sox manager Patsy Donovan made no effort to compensate for his less than manly name by acting extra macho. Donavan hated obscenity. "Tish, tish," he told players, or "Tut, tut, boys, please don't say those words."

Lib Dooley

Lib Dooley was arguably the most loyal fan in Boston Red Sox history. Although obviously it is impossible to measure such things, her friend Ted Williams, who knows something about greatness, called her "the greatest Red Sox fan there'll ever be" and that's good enough for us. Lib was known among Red Sox management, players and fans as "The Queen of Fenway Park" and her distinctive broad-brimmed hats and bright, elegant clothing made her stand out in any company, let alone in a time-worn ballpark such as Fenway. Dooley saw more than 4,000 consecutive games at Fenway Park and was a close friend of many Red Sox players, past and present, including Johnny Pesky, Bobby Doerr, Williams, Dom DiMaggio and Nomar Garciaparra. She baked cookies for many of them over the years and continued to send Ted Williams—who she considered a brother—some of his favorite foods up to the year of her death.

She didn't forget the batboys or the home plate umpires at Fenway either. Lib always had a little tray ready on the wall that separated her front row seat from the field of play. On it, she placed little cookies and bite-size candy bars for the boys with the bats and the men in blue.

Dooley started attending games at Fenway Park during WW II and hadn't missed one until illness finally ended her consecutive game streak in 1999. It was a record for longevity that even Cal Ripken could envy.

Lib was modest about her father John S. Dooley's role in Boston baseball. He was one of the key organizers of one of the early booster clubs, the Winter League. At the turn of the century, when Ban Johnson was attempting to place an American League franchise in Boston, the team lacked a suitable playing field. Jack Dooley facilitated contact with the Boston Elevated Railway, which owned the old Huntington Avenue Grounds—then a dump—and helped bring both parties together. That field became the first home park of the team later renamed the Red Sox and served as site of the first World Series, played in 1903.

Mr. Dooley also played a role in having the ban on Sunday baseball in Boston lifted in the 1930s. Elizabeth Dooley came by her passion for the Red Sox as part of a family tradition. Her father, as a young boy, attended the first baseball game ever played under electric lights, in 1880.

Lib died at the age of 87—Fenway was just one year older than she—in June of 2000, just shy of 120 years after her father had been to that first night game in Nantasket. The baseball gods paid a strange tribute to her. The Red Sox went out that day and lost to the Yankees 22-1, the worst home loss in their history.

Patsy Dougherty

Ironically, it may have been a Boston writer who gave the arch-rival Yankees their nickname. The reference to "Yankees" was first noted in a *Boston Herald* article of June 21, 1904, regarding the trade of Patsy Dougherty to New York for Bob Unglaub. DOUGHERTY IS A YANKEE was the headline. Since this time, Red Sox fans have coined a lot of less printable names for their A.L. foes.

* * * *

Dougherty hit three triples in one game, September 5, 1903. He led the league in hits that year, then hit two home runs in Game Two of the first World Series. Dougherty, in 1904, led the league in runs (as he had in 1903) with 113—33 for Boston and 80 for New York.

Walt Dropo

Walt Dropo's former roommate was Red Sox south-paw Mickey McDermott. McDermott was 15 years old and 138 pounds soaking wet when the 6'5", 240-pound rookie first knocked on his door and introduced himself. "He was the biggest son of a bitch I ever saw in my life. I thought that the Ringling Brothers Circus truck must have broken down and Garantua was rooming with me. I said: 'You got any bananas with you?' I said: 'Hey Moose, when you die leave your head to the Elks Club so they can put antlers on it.'" Dropo went on to capture the AL Rookie of the Year award on the strength of 34 homers, a .322 average and 144 RBIs.

* * * *

Walt Dropo

Red Sox pitcher and part-time singer Mickey McDermott became Dropo's best friend on the Red Sox. One winter evening McDermott was performing in a Boston nightclub when Dropo arrived with a young lady on each arm. In order to make an impression on the lovely young things, Dropo had arranged for a table near the stage. Spotting his teammate, McDermott said: "Ladies and gentlemen, sitting in the front row is the great first baseman for the Boston Red Sox, Mr. Walter Dropo." Dropo glowed as he acknowledged the applause from the audience. "In fact," continued McDermott, "he's so good that they named a town here in Massachusetts after him. It's called Marblehead."

✳   ✳   ✳   ✳

The only major league player to ever hit a baseball over the Great Wall of China was Walt Dropo. Quite a number of years after his playing days were over, Dropo was working for a fireworks company and had occasion to visit China on business. Dropo told us, "About six months before I visited China, Bob Hope went over there and he hit a golf ball with a 9-iron over the Great Wall. I just took it on myself to bring a bat and a ball from the United States. I had my little niece throw me a pitch and I hit it over the Great Wall of China. The Wall wasn't that high." Was there anyone on the other side to catch it, hoping for a souvenir? "The Mongolians were over there."

✳   ✳   ✳   ✳

Dropo was Rookie of the Year in 1950, but he first played in Fenway Park way back in 1943, and his manager was none other than Babe Ruth himself! The game was an exhibition contest to raise money for the war effort. Dropo was 20 years old at the time, drafted out of the University of Connecticut and serving in the army at Fort Devens. "I played for the base team," the Moose from Moosup remembers. "They sent down a couple of us to that game to represent Fort Devens." He played first base, but went 0 for 2 while teammate Ted Williams (also playing for Ruth's squad) took left field, went 2 for 4 and homered, driving in four runs. Dom DiMaggio tripled and drove in two as Ruth's All-Stars beat the Boston Braves 9-8.

Dennis Eckersley

Dennis Eckersley had two stints with the Red Sox and became an instant fan favorite throughout New England. He was a 20-game winner his first year in Boston—1978—though he also led the league in home runs surrendered.

Would that another pitcher on the team had won just one more regular season game that year! His next year was equally strong, though the team was not.

*   *   *   *

In 1984, Eck and Mike Brumley were traded to the Cubs for Bill Buckner, but his greatest years were with the Oakland A's where he was *Sporting News* Fireman of the Year in 1988, 1991 and 1992. Eck also appears on that publication's list of baseball's 100 greatest players. In the 1988 playoffs, he actually saved every one of the four games the A's won. In 1992 he won the A.L. Cy Young and MVP awards. In addition he also boasts three All-Star Game saves.

*   *   *   *

Part of Eck's popularity was his style. With his trademark long flowing hair and mustache he looked more like Zorro about to skewer the bad guys than a major league pitcher. He was equal parts Errol Flynn and The Rock. His colorful language and enthusiastic mound demeanor only added to his heroic aura. He threw a no-hitter the year before he joined Boston, and as it came down to the final out of the game, The Eck recalled later,

Dennis Eckersley (Brace Photography)

"I was ready, but Gil (Flores) kept on stepping out of the box. I pointed at him, 'Get in there. They're not here to take your picture. You're the last out. Get in there.' I was pretty cocky back then!"

*   *   *   *

However, arrogance in an athlete is only bad if he can't back it up and Eckersley could definitely walk the walk. He had tremendous control, and in 1989 walked only three batters! In 1990 he only walked four in a total of 114 innings of relief work!

*   *   *   *

Once when Eckersley was in the midst of throwing a no-hitter for Cleveland against the California Angels, he got two strikes on the batter and turned to the on-deck circle, pointed at Jerry Remy and yelled, "You're next!" Later, Eckersley and Remy became teammates on the Red Sox.

*   *   *   *

Late in 2001, Eckersley became the national spokesman for Fire Prevention Week for the National Fire Protection Association. This wasn't just because he had been named "Fireman of the Year" three times. It resulted from a family incident when Eckersley's five-year-old son Jake registered his first save.

"It was December and my wife Nancy was working on making a cozy fire in our fireplace. Without warning, the fire shot back at her, and suddenly her hair was engulfed in flames." Eck wasn't home, but their son had learned a lesson he'd been taught at school. "My boy instinctively yelled, 'Stop, drop and roll,' and thankfully Nancy found the ability to respond through the chaos," Dennis explained. Nancy's hair was burned, but she was otherwise OK.

"We know of Dennis' reputation for saving games," said Meri-K Appy, Vice President of Public Education for NFPA. "Now we're excited that he is helping us to save lives."

*　　*　　*　　*

The Eck was worshipped in Cleveland, Boston, and Oakland, beloved for his style and flair, his performances and his colorful sayings. He was converted to a reliever a few years after leaving Boston. As Friend and Zminda wrote, "But with the attention and adoration came problems. He partied too hard, drank too much. In 1986, Eckersley decided to go into rehab and came out dry. That he stayed that way is probably his greatest save."

Eck-cetera:

Eckersley was responsible for coining a number of unique baseball terms, including the expression "walk-off home run." The Eck was inspired to utter the words for the first time after giving up a homer to Kirk Gibson in Game Two of the 1988 World Series. The term comes from all the players exiting the field as the winning run scores.

*　　*　　*　　*

Other unique words in the Eckersley vocabulary include "oil", which was his term for liquor, long before "Oil Can" Boyd arrived on the scene. Money was known to Eck as "iron." He called himself "the Bridge Master," and if he surrendered a home run he said that he'd been "taken to the bridge."

Howard Ehmke

You win some, you lose some, and some are snatched rudely from your grasp by the fickle finger of the official scorer. Howard Ehmke won a no-hitter in 1923 despite giving up a double. Slim Harris (the pitcher for the other team) hit a double but missed touching first on his way to second and was thus ruled out. It was the only hit (not!) of the game for Ehmke's opponents. His next time out, a week later, Ehmke probably pitched another no-hitter—that he didn't get credit for. The leadoff batter reached on a "scratch roller" off the third baseman's glove. The official scorer ruled it a hit, though many considered it an obvious error. Ehmke only allowed one other Yankee base runner, a walk. Thus was Ehmke denied the glory later accorded Johnny Vander Meer for his consecutive no-nos. The Red Sox got six hits and won the September 11 game, and Ehmke had three of the six.

Ehmke was a 20-game winner that year totaling almost a third of Boston's wins as the Red Sox finished last with a pitiful 61 victories.

Dwight Evans

Every Red Sox fan worth his salt remembers Carlton Fisk's dramatic game-winning homer in Game Six of the 1975 World Series. Without the heroics of right fielder Dwight Evans, there would probably have been no opportunity for such heroics. Evans' one-handed stab of Joe Morgan's apparent home run in the 11th inning kept the Red Sox's hopes alive. Evans whirled and threw a strike to double up baserunner Ken Griffey Sr. for the third out, setting the stage for Fisk.

✳   ✳   ✳   ✳

When Evans first came up to the Red Sox, Bill Lee was so impressed that he told reporters that the rookie might be the next DiMaggio. Two Boston radio hosts known for their negative approach to sports reportage commented: "Yeah, he'll be Vince DiMaggio."

✳   ✳   ✳   ✳

In 1986, a season that was to become infamous in Red Sox history, Dwight Evans swung at the very first offering of the campaign and drove it out of the ballpark—the only time that it had been done. Asked about it after the game, Evans was not impressed. "No big deal," he said. "We lost.

✴   ✴   ✴   ✴

Even Harry Potter isn't as superstitious as these major league muggles! When a game in Seattle went into extra innings, Red Sox players wore their caps backwards to inspire a rally. The hometown Mariners countered by wearing their chapeaus inside-out and backwards, bending the brims to make them more streamlined. Not to be outdone, some Red Sox taped batting gloves on the ends of bats and used them as fishing poles while other bench-warmers placed Dixie cups over their ears and lathered their faces in shaving cream.

When Dwight Evans homered in the top of the 14th inning and eventually won the game for the Red Sox, the efforts of the bench crew took prominence over Evans' on-field heroics.

✴   ✴   ✴   ✴

Dewey was infected by some of the same disease that gripped certain other players in the cramped, combustible Boston clubhouse. Con Chapman reports a pecking order established amongst the players. Newcomers who came over to Boston from other clubs noticed that batting practice pitchers threw fresh, white baseballs to the regulars and the more scuffed ones to the benchwarmers. When new utilityman Jack Brohamer moved to the post-game spread a little too quickly, Evans brusquely yelled, "You can't eat the spread until the regulars have had it." And Mike Greenwell took umbrage to rookie Mo Vaughn's lining up for batting practice ahead of Greenwell. Some pushing resulted, and Greenwell earned a black eye in the process.

✴   ✴   ✴   ✴

Evans hit 256 homers from 1980 to 1989, more than any other A.L. player during that decade. Other decade leaders were: 1900-09 Harry Davis—67; 1910-19 Gavvy Cravath—116; 1920-29 Babe Ruth—467; 1930-39 JimmieFoxx—4l5; 1940-49 Ted Williams—234; 1950-59 Mickey Mantle—280; 1960-69 Harmon Killebrew—393; 1970-79 Reggie Jackson—292; 1980-89 Dwight Evans—256; 1990-99 Mark McGwire—405 (mixed A.L. & N.L.); 2000-2009 Alex Rodriguez—435.

✳   ✳   ✳   ✳

Asked before the 1986 season to name the greatest highlight of his career in Boston thus far, Evans did not mention home runs, Golden Glove awards, or even his rifle throws to the plate to save a run. His number-one achievement? "Driving a car in Boston for 13 years without a dent."

Carl Everett

Like a nova that bursts into light and then fades, Carl Everett soared during his initial half-season with the Red Sox, even making the 2000 American League All-Star team. But then Everett crashed and burned so spectacularly that in just two years—to many fans it felt like 20—he had acquired the nickname C. Everett Kook and had earned himself a place on numerous "All-Bosox Wacko" teams.

This is not an easy list to make. With characters like Wade Boggs, Oil Can Boyd, Jimmy Piersall, Bill Lee, Ted Williams, Mickey McDermott, Sammy White, Babe Ruth ... the list goes on and on ... it's harder to crack than Richard Nixon's famous "enemies list." Everett did his darnedest and just may have succeeded.

✳   ✳   ✳   ✳

Blessed with amazing natural abilities and an admirable on-field work ethic, Everett quickly won over Sox fans with anti-Yankees remarks directed at his one-time team.

*   *   *   *

His pronouncement that he didn't believe in dinosaurs because he'd never seen one earned him the nickname "Jurassic Carl."

*   *   *   *

On July 15, 2000, the far from dormant Mount Everett erupted after umpire Ron (Mea) Kulpa re-established the batter's box and told Carl to stay within it. Carl went ballistic and before the argument was over, he head-butted the umpire and earned himself a 10-day suspension. Brian Daubach took Everett's place in the lineup and hit a three-run homer to win the game.

A number of other run-ins with manager Jimy Williams, the Boston media and even well-respected fellow players like Darren Lewis and Bret Saberhagen followed. In spring training, a frustrated Williams ordered the bus to actually leave on time one day, leaving a furious Everett behind.

The straw that broke the Sox GM's faith in Everett, though, came just a few days after the September 11 attacks on the World Trade Center when Everett showed up late for a workout, got in an argument with new manager Kerrigan, called Kerrigan a "racist" and earned himself another suspension. *USA Today* columnist Mike LoPresti called Everett a "national disgrace." In a time when the American people as a whole was focused on helping heal the nation, Everett—who was being paid at the rate of roughly $43,000 per game—couldn't manage to show up for work on time and then exploded when taken to task.

Ladies and gentlemen, boys and girls, Everett has now left the building!

Sherm Feller

Red Sox public address announcer Sherm Feller once intoned: "Will the fans in center field please remove their clothes?" After a brief pause, and to the delight of the large bleacher population, he quickly added: "From the railing."

*   *   *   *

On July 20, 1969, Sherm Feller informed a large throng at Fenway Park that Neil Armstrong had made history by setting foot on the moon. The effect on the crowd was stunning as patrons discussed the milestone event with their friends. The umpire finally called time. Baltimore Orioles' future Hall of Fame third baseman Brooks Robinson had not heard the announcement and approached the plate ready to hit. When the umpire gave him the news, he spontaneously dropped his bat and began to applaud the feat. Someone in the crowd started to sing "God Bless America," and soon, the whole ballpark was joining in the patriotic chorus.

*   *   *   *

Sherm Feller was a public address mainstay at Fenway Park for many years, and his measured voice was one of the most distinctive and recognizable in all of New England. On one occasion, however, it was Miller time in Boston and no one even knew. Jon Miller, the talented Baltimore Orioles and ESPN broadcaster and part-time mimic, was at Fenway covering the Orioles-Red Sox series. In the course of the game, Miller, a former Red Sox broadcaster, visited Feller to renew old acquaintances. When Feller had to leave the booth briefly on a matter of some undetermined urgency, Miller stepped into the breach and didn't miss a beat. Feller did a double take when he heard himself apparently speaking in his own absence and hurried back to the booth. He was so impressed and amused that he allowed the interloper to continue announcing players for the next three innings. No one in the ballpark knew they were listening to a sham Sherm.

The Ferrell Brothers— Wes and Rick

One of the great brother combinations in Red Sox history was Wes and Rick Ferrell. Rick was a catcher who made it to the Hall of Fame. Wes was a pitcher who once won 20 for the Sox, but he was also a feared hitter and actually recorded more career home runs than his brother.

* * * *

Wes Ferrell had his combative side as well. One time, he was so angered by a loss that he took a pair of scissors and cut his pitching glove into pieces. Another time, he punched himself in the head twice, knocking himself against the dugout wall both times until fellow players grabbed him and restrained him. His uniforms and caps also suffered occasional severe damage.

Rick Ferrell

On July 17, 1933, Rick Ferrell batted for Boston and faced brother Wes who was pitching for the Indians at the time. He told Dick Thompson, "In the second inning, I homered off Wes, and in the third inning, he homered off Hank Johnson. It was the first time in history that brothers homered while playing against each other in the same game. We laughed a lot about that, though Wes was upset that I hit mine off him. He didn't like that at all."

* * * *

Wes and Rick Ferrell (Brace Photography)

Just what we need, a new baseball stat—the quadruple triple. In 1934, Rick Ferrell was one of four Boston players to triple, all in the same inning. Part of a 12-run inning, Ferrell was joined by Carl Reynolds, Moose Solters and Bucky Walters—all of whom tripled. In the same inning, batting around, Ferrell also walked, Reynolds singled, Solters singled and Walters doubled.

*   *   *   *

The Ferrell brothers, Wes and Rick, were part of a robust farm family of seven boys who grew up in rural North Carolina. Living on the land they used to improvise baseball games on the pastures near their house. They devised a way to record the longest hit of the day by planting a stick in the ground at the point the ball eventually landed. It became a point of some family honor to go and move the stick beyond its present place and the last, furthest stick gave the hitter bragging rights for the rest of the day. This tradition was carried over to the major leagues—sort of. On that July day, Red Sox catcher Rick Ferrell hit a home run off his brother Wes, then pitching for the Cleveland Indians. As he was circling the bases he taunted his brother with a coded message. "Hey Wes," he said, "you'd better go put up a stick for that one." Rick may have been the only other person on the field who knew what the reference meant. Wes did not take the teasing well. He became very agitated and began to kick dirt around the infield.

The family feud was fought to a draw that day however, when Wes homered in the bottom of that same inning. As he crossed the plate he had the last word for that day. "Hey Rick, looks like you're going to have to move that stick back some."

Wes Ferrell

In August of 1936, Wes Ferrell was suspended for ten days and fined $1,000 by then-manager Joe Cronin after the temperamental pitcher left the mound in a huff during a game at Yankee Stadium. Citing poor defense behind him, the 20-game winner acted like a spoiled child, throwing his glove and cap into the air and stomping from the field in front the of the amused New York crowd. He had made a similar unauthorized exit just days earlier in Boston and Cronin had seen enough.

When he found out about the fine, Ferrell was beside himself with anger. "I'm going to slug that *&%* Irishman right on his lantern jaw," he is reported to have told teammates. Cronin was scarcely intimidated. "Fine," he told the handsome right-hander. "I want to see you when we get off the bus in the alley by the hotel." The manager was all too ready to duke it out with this malcontent; however, Ferrell failed to show up at the appointed time and place. Ferrell was an amateur astrologer and used the stars to guide his life decisions. Whatever he saw in the stars that night obviously prevented him from seeing many more stars later.

Dave "Boo" Ferriss

"He's the only man I ever knew in baseball who never has an unkind word to say." —Johnny Pesky

According to all reports, "Boo" Ferriss was the most clean-cut person that you could ever meet; a true southern gentleman. "Boo never used profanities, and the strongest words out of his mouth were: 'Oh shuckins!'" recalls former roommate Mel Parnell. Teammates used every trick in the book to try to get him to curse but with no success. Pitcher Mickey Harris used to switch his shoes so he'd have two lefts or two rights, and on one famous occasion nailed Ferriss' spikes to the floor in front of his locker. Ferriss got dressed and then slipped into the shoes and tied the laces. When he got up and tried to walk, he promptly fell on his face. His teammates howled with laughter. If ever there was time to abandon your principles and utter a few choice oaths, that time had arrived. Instead, Ferriss looked up dolefully at his roommate Tex Hughson and in his best Mississippi drawl said: "Tex, someone done done me wrong."

*   *   *   *

In his rookie year of 1945, Ferriss had an auspicious debut. His first 10 major league pitches were balls, but he recovered and won the game—a shutout. He finished the season at 21-10 and achieved a remarkable feat, particularly for a greenhorn: he beat every team in the league the first time he faced them.

Carlton Fisk

In the year 2000, Carlton Fisk was voted into baseball's Hall of Fame in Cooperstown, largely because of his performance in Game Six of the 1975 World Series. Fisk's 12th inning, game-winning home run at 12:33 a.m. on October 22 of that year was the most famous in Red Sox history and remains one of baseball's shining moments. Fisk hit Cincinnati pitcher Pat Darcy's first pitch directly at the left-field foul pole, using unforgettable body language to will it fair.

*   *   *   *

As a catcher, Fisk liked to challenge hitters, but Bill Lee was strictly a finesse pitcher. This led to some heated meetings on the mound. "I liked to experiment," says Lee. "I would throw a change-up when he didn't expect it, and he'd get really mad. It always embarrassed me that he could throw the ball back to me harder than I could throw it to the plate."

*   *   *   *

Neither rain nor snow nor sleet nor hail . . . Blame it on the post office. At the end of the 1980 season, in which he stroked 18 homers and batted .289, Boston's Hall of Fame catcher Carlton Fisk was expected to re-sign with the Red Sox. When his contract was not postmarked by the deadline date, however, he was free to

Carlton Fisk (Brace Photography)

Carlton Fisk

pursue other offers and eventually signed with the Chicago White Sox, where he continued to accumulate HOF stats until his retirement. Hired by Dan Duquette shortly before he was elected to the Hall of Fame, Fisk proudly wore his Red Sox cap during the ceremonies in Cooperstown and his #27 was retired by the Red Sox in ceremonies at Fenway later in the year.

Bill Lee was Fisk's battery-mate during much of his time in Boston and remains a close friend today. "Fisk had durability, he was tough. He was the runt of the litter of the Fisk family. His father is 87 and still cleans his flue, goes up on the roof. Fisk is the only prima donna in the bunch. It's ironic that it was all during the turmoil of Yawkey dying and Haywood [Sullivan] taking over and bringing his son [catcher Marc Sullivan] into the fold, that the Red Sox thought that Fisk was expendable. [Branch] Rickey always said that it was better to trade a player one year too early than one year too late, but in the Fisk case it turned out to be a decade too early."

Fats Fothergill

Fats Fothergill couldn't have been *too* fat. Before he came to the Red Sox from Detroit, he hit a home run at Fenway for the Tigers, rounded the bases and did a front flip, landing right on home plate. At 5'10 1/2" he weighed 230. Kirby Puckett was 5'8" and weighed 210 but you can bet no one ever called him "Fats." At least not to his face.

Fothergill sounds like a figure to mock, but his career average after 12 years in the majors was .325. Though he broke in at 230 pounds, as his career progressed his weight began to climb towards his average. In only three of his years did he bat below .300. Floyd Conner says Fothergill once bit umpire Bill Dinneen during an argument during a period when he was on a crash diet. "That was the first bite of meat I've had in a month," he explained.

Jimmie Foxx

Jimmie Foxx, the Red Sox slugger known throughout baseball as "Beast," had an intimidating effect on opposing pitchers. With arms like tree trunks and power to spare, he was a pitcher's worst nightmare. Yankee hurler Lefty Gomez once faced him in a key situation at Fenway. Gomez shook off the first sign from catcher Bill Dickey. He shook off the second sign and the third. Finally Dickey called time and strode purposefully to the mound. "I've gone through every pitch you have! What do you want to throw to him?" the Hall of Fame receiver demanded. "If you want to know the truth, Bill," said Gomez. "I was kind of hopin' he'd get bored and go home."

✶   ✶   ✶   ✶

Gomez once described a tremendous homer that Foxx had hit against him. "It went into the third deck at Yankee Stadium," he said with a hint of pride in his voice. "Why, you couldn't walk out there in an hour." When Yankee manager Joe McCarthy inquired about what pitch Double X had hit, the reply was: "It was the greatest pitch I ever threw—for the first 60 feet." Unfortunately, the distance to home plate is 60'6".

✶   ✶   ✶   ✶

Lefty Gomez once admitted: "Jimmie Foxx could hit me at midnight with the lights out."

✶   ✶   ✶   ✶

"Pitching to Foxx is easy," said Gomez. "I just give him my best pitch and then run to back up third base." Later in his starry career, Gomez admitted: "I'm throwing as hard as ever, but the ball isn't getting there as fast."

✶   ✶   ✶   ✶

Jimmie Foxx was known by his Red Sox teammates as a low-ball hitter and a high-ball drinker.

*   *   *   *

In 1938, Jimmie Foxx had a banner year at the plate, winning two-thirds of baseball's Triple Crown. He led the American League with a .349 average and drove in a league best 175. In most seasons, his 50 home runs would have made him a run-away leader in that category as well, but Hank Greenberg chose that same year to hit 58. In an early season game against the St. Louis Browns that year, Foxx was running a high fever and should have been home in bed. However, because the Red Sox lineup was decimated by injuries, Foxx agreed to play. He later admitted that he was barely able to see the ball, let alone hit it. But this was Jimmie Foxx, and luckily his reputation alone was worth something. In six trips to the plate, Foxx failed to offer at a single pitch and was walked six straight times, setting a major league record in the respect category. He walked a total of 119 times that season.

*   *   *   *

Even the great Ted Williams was in awe of Foxx's brute strength: "It sounded like cherry bombs going off when Foxx hit them. Hank Greenberg hit them pretty near as far, but they didn't sound that same way. They sounded like firecrackers when Mantle and Foxx hit them. At Fenway, I remember him hitting this long, long homer over the Wall into the teeth of a gale, and I remember look-ing at all those muscles as he trotted around the base and shaking that huge hand of his as he crossed the plate—and feeling almost weak. I was a skinny guy anyway, and I felt weak in comparison to Jimmie Foxx."

*   *   *   *

Lefty Gomez once suggested that Foxx "wasn't scouted—he was trapped."

*   *   *   *

Cleveland Indians pitcher Lloyd Brown had had enough of Jimmie Foxx. After Foxx hit a game-winning ninth-inning home run off Brown, the frustrated pitcher decided to take direct action against the man known as "The Beast." "That's the last time you'll ever do that against me," he threatened. "Why? Are you quitting the game?" replied Foxx.

Foxx, known as "The Beast," shared some of Babe Ruth's prodigious appetites. The day before Independence Day in 1940, a lifelong Foxx fan, retired sea captain Israel Blake from Orrs Island, Maine offered Jimmie a dozen lobsters if he hit a home run in the game that day. Blake had actually brought down 18 lobsters, one for each of Foxx's home runs to that point in the season. Foxx did hit a homer and later downed all the crustaceans at one sitting.

It was actually quite a game. The Sox had been down 10-3 before clawing their way back. Jim Tabor hit a three-run homer in the eighth, but Philadelphia came right back, scoring a lone run in the top of the ninth. Boston's last ups saw them down by a score of 11-6. After two runs had scored, Ted Williams took Chubby Dean deep for a game-tying three-run homer into the A's bullpen. Screwballer Nelson Foster was brought in and Foxx poked his second pitch into the screen just inside the left field foul pole—a walk-off home run followed by a feast fit for a beast!

*   *   *   *

When Yankees pitcher Lefty Gomez was watching Neil Armstrong's moon landing, his wife asked him what the white sphere was that the astronaut had just picked up. "That's the ball Foxx hit off me in New York in 1937," Gomez said.

Rich Garces

First came El Tiante, then the Yankees came up with El Duque. Rich Garces, from Venezuela, quickly became a true fan favorite in Boston soon after he joined the Red Sox in 1996. "El Guapo" (as he is called, a term essentially meaning in today's lingo, "the hottie") is listed as 255 pounds but most everyone realizes there's at least another 50 or more pounds on his portly 6'0" frame. He's piled up an enviable win-loss record with the Red Sox, 23-7, always in relief—a tribute to the number of times the Bosox have come from behind or broken open a tied game. As a result, "El Guapo" T-shirts became popular items in Boston.

El Guapo was the "bad guy" in the movie *Three Amigos* and the tag may have first been hung on Sr. Garces by Sean McDonough as a result, even though Garces is from Venezuela and not Mexico. One Fenway bleacher creature occasionally turns up costumed like the character in the film, in a sombrero and poncho.

$$* \quad * \quad * \quad *$$

In 2001, Manny Ramirez began wearing his pants so low and baggy that he looked certain to trip on them as he ran. He said he'd begun wearing El Guapo's pants.

When Garces showed up for spring training 2002, after losing 35 pounds over the winter, bringing him down to a reported 245 pounds, he said he'd had to buy a whole new wardrobe. Some of the other Red Sox were impressed at the still-not-svelte short reliever, and when someone asked Brian Daubach if he'd seen "Guapo" yet, Dauber said, "Yeah, what's left of him."

Nomar Garciaparra

Nomar Garciaparra was possibly the best thing to happen to baseball in Boston since the birth of Ted Williams. The young Red Sox shortstop is almost too good to be true. On the field, he is one of the game's brightest offensive and defensive stars. Off the field he is a poster boy for good behavior, the kind of kid you'd like to introduce to your daughter. He possesses the idealism and heroic naivete of Don Quixote and has the earning potential of Donald Trump. At the plate, Nomar has more moves than Don Juan and is more deadly than Don Corleone. Before each pitch, Nomar steps out of the box and tightens his batting gloves, adjusts his wristbands, repeatedly taps the toes of first one foot and then the other. He then whacks the bat once against his back before settling in to hit. He repeats the procedure between each pitch. But his superstitions go beyond the ball field. He listens to the same music while making his way to the ballpark—always via the same route. In the clubhouse, he invariably puts on first his right sock then the left, right stirrup, left stirrup, etc. "He'd have a hard time hitting me, "says Bill Lee of Garciaparra. "I'd make so much fun of his antics. Every time he'd come up. I'd be fixing my glove, fixing my shoes. We'd go back and forth, back and forth, and eventually the ump would call the game."

*　　*　　*　　*

"My routine really doesn't take that long," argues Nomar. "People think it takes forever because I stand right at the plate to do it. I always keep one foot in the box. That probably stems from college—there used to be a college rule where you had to keep one foot in the batter's box or you'd get an automatic strike called against you. The toe-tapping thing and the glove tightening I've done as far back as I can remember. As a little kid, I'd tap my toes. The reason I did that was because I just liked the feeling of my toes being at the end of my shoes when I was about to exert any energy. That's basically what I'm doing when I'm tapping them—getting my toes to the end of my shoes. People ask me if my shoes were too small when I was a kid, and I say it wouldn't matter how tight my shoes were, I just liked that feeling of them being in there. That's how I started tapping my toes. I don't do any set number. I don't know if it's a timing thing or not.

"I hit and I play the game on a lot of feeling. It's important how I feel when I'm about to hit. When I step out of the box, it's important how my feet feel. The way my hands feel is just as important to me. When I pull my gloves, I'm pulling down to get my hands to the end of the gloves so that it feels tight like I have nothing on. That way I can grip the bat better. Again, there's no set number of times. I just pull them until I'm ready. Some players call time and step out of the box and walk around thinking about the previous pitch or whatever. For me it's just: Now I'm ready. Let's go. It extends to what I do even before I get to the ballpark. I truly believe that baseball is such a repetitive game. You play this game *every day* and people ask me how you get better at it. Well, you take a lot of ground balls and you take a lot of swings—over and over and over . . . and over.

"I truly believe that I get into the routine because I expect to perform well every day. I'm going up against the best every day. There's no room to slack off. People expect you to play your best every day, and so I go through a routine to prepare myself—so that I know that I'm physically and mentally ready—prepared for the game. Where I can say to myself—*OK, I'm ready!* Every day!

"I don't like having excuses. I don't want to have to make any excuse for playing bad. I played bad because of this or that. I can just say I played bad because I was horrible today, and I've got to work on it tomorrow or do something to get myself better. That's why I have a basic routine. I think I know I'm ready and I have a job to do—this is my job. People expect me to go out there and play my best. They pay their money to see that. I really feel that if I stayed away or wasn't ready or prepared, I'm really doing them a huge injustice.

"When I first entered the league, opposing players and umpires would look at me and say: 'What are you doing?' They might make comments like: 'Are you ready yet?' It was funny, but now, after all the success I've had, they just seemed to decide: 'Well, I guess we'll just leave you alone.' "

★   ★   ★   ★

In his rookie year of 1997, Nomar put together a 30-game hitting streak, tying an AL record. He also set a major-league record for RBIs by a leadoff hitter and for homers by a rookie shortstop. He amassed 209 hits—most by a rookie since Johnny Pesky over 50 years earlier. He became the first unanimous choice for rookie of the year since Carlton Fisk in 1969. Jimy Williams was immediately impressed with the rookie. "The kid plays like he's been here before," he said. "I don't know when or who he's played with, but I swear he's been here."

*   *   *   *

On May 11, 1999, Nomar hit two grand slams in a single game and added a two-run homer, driving in a total of 10 runs! His first grand salami came on his first at-bat in the first inning; his two-run drive in his second at-bat in the third. In his final at-bat, in the eighth, Nomar hit his second bases-loaded homer, becoming only the third Red Sox player ever to hit two in a single game (the others were Jim Tabor and Rudy York). He also became the first Sox player to knock in 10 runs in a game since Freddie Lynn accomplished the feat.

*   *   *   *

In a backward sort of way, Nomar was named after his father. His name is his father's name spelled backward: Ramon.

*   *   *   *

Nomar loves the chemistry that exists on the current edition of the Red Sox. "In my rookie year, Jeff Frye and Jim Corsi had a mild disagreement in the clubhouse before a game with the Chicago White Sox. Nothing serious at all. So then the game starts, and we're ahead of the White Sox by a run, and they get a runner on second late in the game. The manager brings in Corsi in relief. He has to face Frank

Thomas *and* Albert Belle, so he's trying to psych himself up and get himself ready. We have a mound conference with the manager and Frye and me. As we're talking, Frye picks up the resin bag. First base is open, so we decide to walk Frank and pitch to Albert. Corsi's trying to pump himself up. He says: 'All right! All right! And he looks at me and Jeff Frye and says: 'We've gotta roll this up guys! Jeff, give me the resin bag.' And Jeff says: 'Hell no', and throws the resin bag on the ground and walks away like he's really mad. Then Corsi looks at me and says: 'Nomar, you've gotta turn this play for me, right?' I just shrug and say: 'Look Jim, I'm just a rookie. I've gotta stick with my second baseman. You're on your own.'

We were laughing as we ran back to our positions, and Corsi just stared at us in disbelief. He didn't even have the resin bag in his hand because Jeff had thrown it away. He was left standing there like a lost puppy dog. I'm sure he was thinking: *I'm about to face Albert Belle in a crucial spot in a big game and my second baseman and shortstop have just told me to screw myself.* It was like a mutiny.

"He walks Frank Thomas as planned and then makes the first pitch to Belle. Albert hits the ball in the hole, and I come out of nowhere to backhand it and throw off-balance to Frye. Frye grabs it out of nowhere, wheels and throws to first, and we turn the most unbelievable double play you've ever seen. As we're running to the dugout, Corsi says: 'Yeah! Yeah! Thanks guys!' And we say: 'That wasn't for you. Screw you! We wanted to win in spite of you.' It was just the funniest thing. Jeff and I almost died laughing. We messed with him and then went out there and made an unbelievable play for him. We have a great bunch of guys; we really do. Everybody gets along well. It just makes it so much fun to come to the ballpark every day."

✳   ✳   ✳   ✳

Somebody once asked Nomar what he thought of the curse of the Bambino. "I said: 'I'm from L.A., I don't know what the heck you're talking about.' Some things I guess it's just best I don't know. I just said: 'I play for the Red Sox NOW. We're going to start our own tradition here. And then you can talk about *us* in years to come.'"

*   *   *   *

If his first few years were any indication, Nomar probably couldn't wait for the next season to begin. In his rookie year of 1997, he batted .306 with 30 homers and 98 RBI. In 1998, he hit .323 with 35 HR (only the fifth player in major league history to hit at least 30 HR in each of his first two years) and 122 RBI. In 1999, he finished with a .357 average, 27 home runs, and 104 RBIs. If he hadn't missed 27 games due to injury, he would have exceeded 200 hits. He finished with 190. Individual statistics didn't mean much to this young man, however. "Every year I have just one goal in mind, and that's to win the World Series. That's it. And if I ever win it, then I'll say: 'You know what? My other fingers are a little bit lonely.'"

*   *   *   *

As a rookie, Ted Williams once said that his goal was to be able to walk down the street after his career was over and be acknowledged as the greatest hitter of them all. Did Nomar have similar career goals? "When it's all done, I would just like to be able to walk down the street and have people say: 'There goes Nomar—a great player who's just like us. One of those guys who really loved the game.'"

*   *   *   *

Even when he wasn't hitting, Nomar had a hot bat. Ex-teammate Jeff Frye completed hitting for the cycle Friday night August 17, 2001, for the Toronto Blue Jays—hitting a gapper and holding up with a single. It actually would have been a sure double, but Frye, at the urging of the first base coach, stopped at first to complete the rare hitting feat.

The Sox link? Frye was using one of Nomar's bats. Apparently on his last trip to Fenway he asked Nomar for a couple (Nomar gave him five) as he felt they would "have some hits in them." Apparently he was right.

✳   ✳   ✳   ✳

Nomar Garciaparra admires Derek Jeter's range and A-Rod's quickness, but his real hero is much more animated than any of those guys. "When I was a kid, I tried all the positions, and I enjoyed 'em all," he said. "Actually, catching was my favorite, because it's a position where you can be almost like a quarterback, seeing the whole field and running the game from behind the plate.

"Back then, my idol was Bugs Bunny, because I saw a cartoon of him playing ball—you know, the one where he plays every position himself with nobody else on the field but him? Now that I think of it, Bugs is still my idol. You have to love a ballplayer like that."
—Nomar Garciaparra, in *Diehard*.

Rich Gedman

R ed Sox fan Tim Savage, a former vendor at Fenway, writes: "My most enduring memory of Rich Gedman was that he was involved in an incident against the Tigers that remains the most bizarre play I ever saw. Gedman was catching and Lou Whitaker was on first, when Kirk Gibson ripped a gapper. Since Whitaker had to hold up for a moment to see if it might be caught, Gibson was right on his tail as he rounded third. The throw came in, Gedman tagged out Whitaker at the plate, and umpire Larry Barnett stepped into the baseline to make the out call. As he did so, Gibson came barreling in and smashed right into Barnett, knocking him out.

"Gedman was smart enough to step out of the way, and applied the tag on Gibson as he ran by. (Third base umpire) Ken 'King Kong' Kaiser came over, and seeing a ball on the ground that had apparently fallen out of Barnett's ball bag during the collision, ruled that Gedman had dropped the ball and Gibson was safe. Ralph Houk came out to argue the call, and he and Kaiser squared off while standing over Barnett's fallen body. It reminded me of all those scenes in the *Iliad* where the Greeks and the Trojans fight over the corpse of a slain comrade."

Gary Geiger

His name may have been Geiger but he was no counter. In a 1961 game at Fenway, the Red Sox were trailing the Los Angeles Angels 3-2 in the tenth inning. Chuck Schilling worked the pitcher for a two-out walk bringing Gary Geiger to the plate. Geiger came through with a hard drive to the outfield fence for a triple, scoring Schilling with the tying run. Unfortunately Geiger thought that Schilling represented the winning run and held up between third and home. He was caught in a run-down and was tagged out.

Dick Gernert

In June 1953, the Detroit Tigers visited Fenway Park, and the carnage that ensued was of biblical proportions. On June 17, sparked by first baseman Dick Gernert's two home runs and four RBIs, the Red Sox tamed the tabbies 17-1. But this was just the color cartoon before the next day's main feature. On June 18, the Red Sox once again scored 17 runs, only this time they did it in a single seventh-inning barrage! A total of 23 Red Sox hitters came to the plate in the record-setting frame, and 20 of them reached base. Gernert once again led the charge with a home run and four RBIs. The Sox added 11 singles, two doubles and six walks in this pitcher's nightmare, including a bases-loaded walk to Gernert. Gene Stephens recorded three of the record 14 hits in the inning, which dragged on for 48 minutes. The final score of 23-3 was more suited to the NFL's Patriots and Lions. Asked about his memories of this extraordinary series, the modest Gernert replied: "I remember that the next game they beat us."

★   ★   ★   ★

En route to the 1958 Most Valuable Player Award, Red Sox outfielder Jackie Jensen was complaining about being in a mild slump. Roommate Dick Gernert who was mired in a real slump was unsympathetic. "I'll settle for your slumps," grumbled Gernert, who was mired in hitting quicksand.

Don Gile

Like Ted Williams, Don Gile hit a home run in his last at-bat in the major leagues! Gile was on the Red Sox roster for every single game of the 1962 season—but did not get a single hit until the very last day. In fact, he sat on the bench the first 34 or so games without even making it to the plate. Then Manager Pinky Higgins put him in—against Whitey Ford, of all people! Gile struck out on four pitches.

The next time Gile was brought in to hit in a game situation, there were two outs in the ninth, and the runner got picked off. That day he played both halves of a double-header and managed only a weak single in the first. But in the eighth inning of the night-cap, he hit an eighth inning home run in his last major league at-bat. There is no report on whether or not Gile tipped his cap to the crowd.

Billy Goodman

Billy Goodman was a good-hitting second baseman for the Red Sox from 1947 to 1957, leading the American League in 1950 with a .354 mark. While in the field, he had the habit of chewing on blades of grass between pitches. "He ate so much of the infield around second base, the ground had a curve in it," claims Mickey McDermott. "One time I asked him: 'What do you do in the wintertime, farm yourself out?' His teeth were like a leprechaun's."

✳   ✳   ✳   ✳

In 1950, the year he captured the American League batting title, Billy Goodman had no regular fielding position and was called the "one-man bench." In the days before the DH, Billy Goodman couldn't readily break into the strong Sox infield. His third full season with the Red Sox was 1950. That year, the Red Sox had Walt Dropo at first. He led the league with 144 RBI in his rookie year. Bobby Doerr was, at that point, a veteran seven-time All-Star second baseman who hit .294 and led the league in triples that year, tied with Sox center fielder Dom DiMaggio. Vern Stephens played short and played in his sixth All-Star Game in 1950. Stephens hit .300. Not wanting to be overshadowed by the rookie Dropo, Stephens also knocked in 144 runs to tie for the league lead. Johnny Pesky held down the hot corner and sported a .312 average. The outfield didn't offer many openings either. The outfielders were Dom DiMaggio (.328), Al Zarilla (.325) and Ted Williams (a disappointing .317, after breaking his elbow in the All-Star Game.)

So what could Goodman do? A true utility player, he fit in where he could, when he could, and amassed 150 hits in 424 at-bats, for a league-leading .354. Not bad for a guy who didn't have a steady position.

Mike Greenwell

A fiery player who reportedly wrestled alligators in the off-season, Greenwell once irritated his teammates by calling them "a bunch of wimps and fairies." The man they called "Gator" even got into a fight with fellow Soxer Mo Vaughn behind the batting cage during batting practice. Most people would rather tackle the alligators. In 1996, he knocked in all nine runs in a Red Sox victory over Seattle.

*   *   *   *

Greenwell broke in with a bang. His first three hits in the major leagues were all home runs. If he'd kept it up, he'd have an even

1400 home runs—and the Red Sox probably wouldn't have let him go after the 1996 season.

*   *   *   *

One Boston writer said that whenever Greenwell looked in the mirror he saw Carl Yastrzemski.

Lefty Grove

Unlike the Yankees' easy going Lefty Gomez, Red Sox southpaw pitcher Lefty Grove was famous for his foul temper. Ted Williams suggested: "He was a tantrum thrower like me but smarter. When he punched a locker, he always did it with his right hand. He was a careful tantrum thrower."

*   *   *   *

When he threw punches at lockers, he threw them with his right hand so he wouldn't hurt his pitching arm. No matter how angry he was, he always protected that salary wing. Once, years later, he gave some free advice on the subject to Bill Werber, when the two were teammates on the Red Sox. Werber also possessed a fine temper, and one day he got so mad at himself that he kicked a full water bucket and broke his toe. "Never," advised Grove, "kick a full water bucket. Pick out an empty one. And never kick it with your toe. Kick it with your whole foot."

*   *   *   *

It has been said of Red Sox Hall of Fame pitcher Lefty Grove: "He could throw a lamb chop past a hungry wolf." Grove led the American League in ERA nine times.

*   *   *   *

"Gimme a blank contract," Grove would ask Yawkey. "I'll sign it and you fill in the figures."

*   *   *   *

Grove had exactly 300 career wins and led the league nine times in ERA, four of them when he pitched for the Red Sox in hitter-friendly Fenway. His six shutouts in 1936 also led the American League.

*   *   *   *

Double or nothing? On June 9, 1934, Lefty Grove gave up six doubles in one inning to assorted Washington Senators.

*   *   *   *

One spring in Sarasota, Lefty Grove tried to attach a firecracker to Ted Williams' auto engine, but broke a handle lifting the hood, and cut his pitching hand severely.

Creighton Gubanich

Catcher Creighton Gubanich had a brush with fame on May 2, 1999. On that day he became the first Red Sox player ever whose first major league hit was a grand slam home run. He was sent back to the minors without getting into another game. Called back up a while later, he managed 47 at-bats and a .277 average but never did hit another one out.

Devern Hansack

The right-handed pitcher had given up on baseball and take up work as a lobster fisherman in his native Nicaragua, but come to the attention of the Red Sox when he'd taken part in a tournament in The Netherlands—and was signed. On October 1, 2006, he stepped out of the Red Sox dugout to pitch the last game of the year—after a rain delay of three hours and 23 minutes. It was his second major-league appearance, and he didn't give up a hit. He pitched a complete game, it was a shutout. Every Oriole who came to bat was retired except for one who walked, and he was out in a double play. Hansack got the win, a complete game shutout with no hits—but it wasn't called a no-hitter. Can you guess why? No, it's not some obscure rule. There actually is no reason; only an arbitrary definition of a no-hitter promulgated by the Commissioner's office declared that a rain-shortened game (five innings, in this case) didn't count—even though it's in the books as a complete game.

Carroll Hardy

Carroll Hardy is probably best known as the only player to ever pinch hit for the great Ted Williams, which is like asking Snoop Doggy Dogg to go on for Pavarotti. Williams had fouled a ball off his foot and been forced to leave the game. Actually, it was one of three notable pinch-hitting assignments by Hardy. While playing for the Cleveland Indians in 1958, he also pinch hit for future record-breaker Roger Maris—and proceeded to hit his first major-league homer. In 1961, he was called to pitch hit for a promising but temporarily struggling newcomer named Carl Yastrzemski. And when Ted Williams hit a home run in his last at-bat in baseball, and left the game to a thunderous ovation, it was Carroll Hardy who replaced him in left field.

✳   ✳   ✳   ✳

Want to impress a pretty girl or get a free drink at any bar in the United States of America? Just tell them you once pinch-hit for Ted Williams. Of course, you may have to have some proof like Carroll Hardy does. Hardy, who played for the Red Sox from 1960-62, is best remembered as the only man to pinch-hit for Williams. Think about that for a minute. Ted Williams was a lifetime .344 hitter with 521 home runs and a .400 season under his belt. Hardy, a career .225 hitter with 17 home runs in eight major league seasons, was like another species when it came to hitting. So how did this event come to pass, you ask?

During the last part of the 1960 season, Ted Williams came to the plate in a meaningless game in Baltimore and fouled a ball off his instep. Williams was taken out of the game and immediately returned home to Boston. Red Sox manager Pinky Higgins sent Hardy, a utility outfielder, into the game to pinch-hit for Williams. It would be nice to report that this Hardy boy was so inspired by the notion of replacing Ted that he came through with a heroic home run. Alas, he hit into a double-play to end the inning, but the event did give Hardy some pretty exclusive bragging rights. When Ted met Hardy years later he greeted him with a grin and said, "Well, I guess I made you famous."

*   *   *   *

Hardy also pinch-hit for Carl Yastrzemski, making him the only hitter to pinch-hit for two of the biggest legends in Boston sports history.

Tommy Harper

Speedster Tommy Harper was the all-time single-season Red Sox stolen base king, with 54 swipes in 1973, before Jacoby Ellsbury took the crown with 55 swipes in 2009.. As he approached Tris Speakers previous record of 52, the Red Sox announced that when he stole his 53rd, the game would be halted and the base presented to Harper. "In that case," said Harper mischievously, "I'm going to try stealing home. I want to stand there while they dig it up." The Red Sox were probably pleased that the record steal took place at second base instead.

Ken Harrelson

Sporting Nehru jackets and love beads, Ken "Hawk" Harrelson was the Red Sox fashion plate and trendsetter in the late sixties. The Hawk, whose impressive nose resembled that noble bird's beak, reportedly had two hotel rooms, one for himself and one for his extensive wardrobe of mod clothes. Harrelson was also the first player to wear a batting glove, which was actually a converted golf glove.

Bucky Harris

One might think managers were above practical jokes of their own, but not always. In 1934, around the Fourth of July, Red Sox manager Bucky Harris once threw a cigar with a flaming "blue nosed" match stuck in it into a Pullman washroom where a card game was in progress. Players sometimes held card games in the washroom because it was larger than the berths on the train. The match flared up and the cigar looked to the six startled players like a big firecracker. The baseball men were playing in their BVDs due to the summer heat on the long ride to St. Louis, and they played with a cardboard "table" held on their knees. When they saw what they thought was a monster firecracker tossed into the room, everything went flying—chips, cards, and the like, as the participants bolted out of that washroom as fast as they could.

Scott Hatteberg

Baseball is sometimes a game of sin and redemption—and sweet revenge. August 6, 2001—the Red Sox were leading Texas 4-2 when they had a chance to break the game wide open in the bottom of the fourth inning. Catcher Scott Hatteberg came up with runners on first and second and nobody out. Hatteberg did the worst thing he could do in this particular situation—he lined hard, right into a triple play. The Rangers promptly scored five runs in the top of the fifth, giving them a solid 7-4 lead. In the bottom of the sixth, Hatteberg came up again with nobody out—this time with the bases loaded. Redeeming himself as well as anyone possibly could, he slammed a pitch into the Red Sox bullpen. No one had ever hit into a triple play and hit a grand slam in the same game. "From the outhouse to the penthouse," a happy Hattie said in a postgame interview.

Dave (Hendu) Henderson:
From Goat To Gloat

The Red Sox trailed the Angels 3 games to 1 in the 1986 American League Championship Series. The score was 5-4 in favor of the Angels with the Red Sox batting in the top of the ninth. With two out, reliever Gary Lucas was brought in to replace Angels starter Mike Witt. Lucas promptly hit Rich Gedman with a pitch. Angels manager Gene Mauch then brought in right-hander Donnie Moore to face Dave Henderson. With the count at 1-2, Hendu fouled off two pitches and then homered into the left field seats to give the Red Sox the lead and steal the game for the Red Sox. Henderson was wearing the goat's horns earlier in the contest as he had a ball go off his glove for a home run. Innings later, he won the ALCS game for the Red Sox with a dramatic HR.

Jim Henry

You work on this play for hours and hours in spring training and then something like this happens! On September 25, 1936 in a game between the Red Sox and Senators in Washington, Red Sox pitcher Jim Henry (career record of 6-2 with a 4.79 ERA over three ML seasons) found himself in a tight situation. The Senators were threatening to score in the bottom of the third with Joe Kuhel on third and Johnny Stone on first. Stalling for time, Henry walked behind the mound and picked up the rosin bag. While thus preoccupied, the Senators decided to pull a double steal on him. Glancing up, Henry was so surprised that he wheeled and threw the rosin bag to second base instead of the ball. Kuhel scored, Stone was safe at second, and when the dust had settled—and the laughter had subsided—the umpire ruled it a double steal. No error was charged to Henry, but just as his crimson face was returning to normal, Stone stole third on his very next pitch. Red Sox manager Joe Cronin had seen enough. He walked to the mound and sent the embarrassed pitcher to the showers—where presumably he threw in the towel.

John Henry

In February 2002, while waiting for the I's to be dotted and the T's crossed on his group's purchase of the Red Sox, new principal owner John Henry pulled up in a huge Florida Marlins bus at The Plantation Inn in Crystal River, Florida for the Ted Williams Hitters Hall of Fame dinner and induction ceremonies. Henry had sold the Marlins team less than 12 hours earlier, but explained he'd arranged to borrow the bus through the end of spring training so he could commute from his home in Boca Raton to the Red Sox spring training site in Fort Myers.

Henry got out of the Marlins bus all by himself—he was the only passenger—and carried his own overnight case and garment bag, walked down the drive and checked into the hotel without any retinue. Dressed in jeans and a light sweater, slight of stature, the unassuming owner probably wouldn't have known what to make of Roger Clemens' complaints that Red Sox players had to carry their own luggage—but the private bus idea is scary. Twenty-five players—25 buses?

Mike Herrera

Were the Red Sox the last major league team to sign a black player? Or were they one of the first? Did the Red Sox actually have a black ballplayer long before Pumpsie Green and 22 years before Jackie Robinson debuted with the Dodgers? Cuba's Ramon "Mike" Herrera totaled 276 at-bats in 1925 and 1926 while serving as a second baseman for the Red Sox (an even .275 batting average). He also played for Negro League teams both before and after his stretch with Boston.

Before joining the Red Sox, Herrera had played for Almendares in Havana, as well as with La Union, all Leagues and the (Cuban) Red Sox. The Boston Red Sox purchased him from their Springfield (Eastern League) club. The *Boston Globe* termed him a "splendid prospect" and he did go 2 for 5 in his first game.

Todd Bolton, asked about Herrera's history in the Negro Leagues, replied:

"In the pre-Negro League years he barnstormed in the U.S. with the Long Branch Cubans and the Jersey City Cubans. When the first Negro National League was formed in 1920 Herrera was a member of the Cuban Stars (West), one of the inaugural teams in the league. He stayed on with the team in 1921 when it became the Cincinnati Cubans. Herrera returned to the Negro Leagues for one final season in 1928 with Alejandro Pompez' Cuban Stars (East).

Photographs of Mike Herrera seem to show that he could easily "pass" for white, and for those who want to measure such things, he may have been more white than black. So did he have to "pass for black" when he was in the Negro Leagues? Not really, Bolton explains. There were a number of light-skinned players in the Negro Leagues and even "white" Cubans. These players were used to playing together in Latin America. It was only in the United States that they were segregated.

Butch Hobson

Before becoming the Red Sox's gritty but erratic third baseman, Butch Hobson had been a triple option quarterback for Bear Bryant at the University of Alabama. The first quarterback to play on Astroturf in Tuscaloosa, his elbows took a beating from blindside tackles. "That's why he could throw around corners, but he could never throw straight to first base," explains Bill Lee.

Brock Holt

There was an honorary "fifth Beatle" so it should be okay to have an honorary official fifth Killer B.

Brock Holt is known to appreciative Red Sox fans as "The Brock Star." He may well be the best utility man the Red Sox have had since Billy Goodman. That is high praise since Goodman played every position except catcher and pitcher for the Red Sox and was named to two All-Star teams. In 1950, he won the batting title with a .354 mark and was runner up for MVP.

To call Holt versatile is to slight him with faint praise. He has become an indispensable cog in the Red Sox roster. In fact, Holt is so versatile that writer Nik DeCosta-Klipa once referred to him as "the Red Sox human Swiss army knife."

*   *   *   *

On the FOX TV show Scream Queens, actor John Stamos plays a character known as Dr. Brock Holt. Is there any connection between the factual and fictional Brock? Brad Falchuk, the co-creator of the show hails from Newton, Massachusetts and is a rabid Red Sox fan. Not only that, but the show's second episode has three doctors dressed in the uniforms of the 1986 World Champion New York Mets being brutally murdered. If he can wreak revenge on the '86 Mets, Falchuk is more than capable of paying tribute to the popular Red Sox player.

*   *   *   *

In June of 2015, Brock became the first Red Sox player to hit for the cycle since John Valentin turned the trick in 1996.

Harry Hooper

Hooper is considered by many to be the greatest defensive right fielder who ever played the game. He was the first AL player to use flip-down sunglasses and also pioneered the sliding catch. No less an authority than the great Walter Johnson called him "the toughest out of all in a pinch." Hooper also stole 300 bases for the Sox.

Hooper was an integral part of the last Red Sox World Series champions of 1918, and he also contributed greatly to bringing the championship to Boston in 1912. In Game Eight (yes, Game Eight; Game Two was stopped on account of darkness) of the '12 Series, Hooper, with a little help from above, made one of the greatest catches in Series history.

With the score knotted at 1-1 in the ninth, Hooper was running to his position in right field. Seeing something on the ground, he knelt to pick it up and discovered that it was a small piece of paper with a picture of the Sacred Heart of Jesus and a prayer. "I read the prayer as I went out to my position," recalled Hooper years later. "Then I put the picture in my pocket."

New York Giant Larry Doyle laid into a pitch and drove it to the deepest part of right field. If it had fallen in, it would have given the Giants the lead and probably ended the game. Instead, the Divinely inspired Hooper made a sensational bare-handed catch to save a run and send the game into extra innings. The Sox went on to win the game in the bottom of the tenth. Hooper was quite willing to share the glory: "The way I caught the ball—how I was in the exact spot and position to catch it and how I caught it—was as if someone had placed it in my hand."

Harry Hooper (Brace Photography)

*   *   *   *

Harry Hooper is said to be the first American League player to make use of flip-down sunglasses. He was also one of the first to employ the sliding catch that has become such a common part of today's game. Hooper was a threat at the plate and on the base paths, stealing a total of 300 bases for the Sox and another 75 for the Chicago White Sox.

*   *   *   *

Considered by many to be the greatest defensive right fielder in the history of the game, Hooper, along with teammates Tris Speaker and Duffy Lewis comprised the best outfield in baseball. No less an authority than Walter Johnson called Hooper "the toughest out of all in a pinch."

*   *   *   *

When Hooper homered in the ninth inning of the fifth and final game of the 1915 World Series, it was the first time a Series had ever been decided by the long ball. Hooper actually hit two homers in that final game, the first breaking a 4-4 tie.

*   *   *   *

It was also Hooper who argued that Babe Ruth would be more valuable if he played every day in the outfield rather that just pitching every forth or fifth day. His argument was not accepted at first, but eventually agreed to when Hooper pointed out how crowds increased every time Ruth played. Hooper was placed in charge of teaching Ruth the outfield. Hooper took over center when Ruth was learning the ropes in right.

Hooper was the only Red Sox player to play on all four World Championship teams—1912, 1915, 1916 and 1918.

Ralph Houk

Ralph Houk, who would later go on to manage both the Yankees and Red Sox, was a rookie catcher for the New York Yankees in 1947. The Yankees were playing the Red Sox with fastball specialist Frank Shea on the mound for New York. With Ted Williams approaching the plate, Houk decided to try a new strategy. Knowing that Williams was a great fastball hitter and would be expecting the heater, Houk decided to try to fool him by calling for a change-up. Ted adjusted to the slower pitch and drove a blue-darter straight back through the box for a double, almost maiming Shea in the process. Later, in the Yankee dugout, manager Bucky Harris asked young Houk what the pitch had been. "It was change of pace," Houk sheepishly replied. "Well, he sure as hell changed the pace of it, didn't he?" said Harris dryly.

Tex Hughson

Some men dream of shapely women, but others dream of different kinds of curves. Tex Hughson talked in his sleep and roomie Boo Ferriss said that he would go over every pitch he threw, adding comments on what (in some cases) he should have thrown.

Bruce Hurst

Before Roger Clemens brought his fastball and winning ways to Boston, the Red Sox pitching staff got about as much respect as Rodney Dangerfield. The Red Sox teams of the late seventies and early eighties were blessed with great offensive players like Yaz, Wade Boggs, Jim Rice, and Dwight Evans to name just a few. Bosox pitchers were invariably blamed for the Red Sox's lack of success—sometimes with reason. Bruce Hurst, Bob Ojeda and John Tudor were all talented pitchers, but their confidence was somewhat shaken when a Boston newspaper referred to the trio as "Plague, Pestilence and Death." Hurst credits the arrival of Rocket Roger for changing all that.

Hurst felt so strongly about Clemens that when Roger got into an argument with an umpire at first base in 1986, Hurst hustled out of the dugout to defend his teammate and he wound up being ejected. The umpire said that Hurst used a profanity. Hurst is a devout Mormon and does not curse. 'That is one of the most ridiculous things I've ever heard,' Roger said at the time. 'He might have said, "gosh darn."'

Pete Jablonowski

Pete Jablonowski was one of those hurlers who didn't exactly shine with the Red Sox. In 1932, he went 0-3 with the Sox after coming over from the Indians. With the exception of pitching two innings for the Yankees in 1933, he was out of the majors until he reappeared in 1936 with the Senators, having changed his name to Pete Appleton. That one year, freshly named, he went 14-9 with a 3.53 ERA, but then returned to his formal level of mediocrity, ending his career with a 57-66 record. Perhaps he should have changed his name a second time—to Feller.

Jackie Jensen

One of Boston's best players, Jackie Jensen, had a fear of flying. In fact, it caused him to retire from the game on two separate occasions. While on terra firma, Jensen compiled some impressive figures, however. In 1958, he captured the MVP award in the American League by hitting 35 home runs and driving in 122.

✳   ✳   ✳   ✳

In June 1961, Jackie Jensen's fear of flying caused him to refuse to fly to Detroit for a game the next day. Instead, he drove 850 miles and still managed to be in the lineup for the first pitch.

*   *   *   *

Jensen holds the rare distinction of having played in the Rose Bowl, the World Series and the All-Star Game.

*   *   *   *

It has been said that Jackie Jensen was one-third of the most high-strung outfield in baseball history. It's a claim that's difficult to dispute. Jensen, who feared flying, was in right, Ted Williams was in left and Jimmy Piersall in center.

*   *   *   *

Jensen was a three-time A.L. RBI champ—in 1955, 1958 and 1959. Like many Red Sox stars before and since, Jensen was often the target for heckling and verbal abuse from the Fenway fans. The boos and catcalls bothered the sensitive outfielder more than he was willing to admit, despite the fact that most Red Sox fans were 100 percent in his corner. Jensen once described the science of crowd reaction. "Boos sound louder than cheers," he explained. "One boo carries a long way. Twenty or thirty can sound like the whole ballpark."

*   *   *   *

After his MVP season in 1958, the boos were replaced by cheers, and Jensen suddenly could do no wrong. Once in a game with the Baltimore Orioles, Jensen missed a pitch by a country mile. In earlier times this would have brought loud jeers from all corners of Fenway Park. Now there were only words of encouragement. When

Jensen stepped out of the batter's box to collect his thoughts for the next pitch, Orioles catcher Gus Triandos said very quietly, "Boo!" Jensen immediately saw the humor in the situation. "Thanks, Gus, that makes me feel at home." Thus relaxed, he promptly hit the next delivery over the Green Monster.

*   *   *   *

Jensen almost stole Ted Williams' biggest act. In 1959, while Ted was struggling through his worst major league season, Jensen was having another banner year. He was terribly homesick for his family, however, and still had a dreadful fear of flying. In August he announced that the '59 season might be his last. Because the Red Sox were well out of the pennant race, Jensen asked for permission to end his season one day early in order to return to his loved ones on the west coast.

His last game was a Saturday contest against the Washington Senators at Fenway Park. Jensen was battling Cleveland slugger Rocky Colavito for the A.L. RBI title. Coming to the plate in the bottom of the ninth with the Senators leading 4-2, he was trailing Colavito by two ribbies. With the bases loaded, Jensen doubled to left and a fan touched the ball, creating a ground-rule double that drove in two runs to tie the game and draw even with "The Rock". Then in the 11th inning, with two men out, Jensen hit a dramatic homer to win the game.

Colavito didn't drive in any runs that day. Jensen was up by one RBI—and he went home instead of playing the final game, saying, "It doesn't mean enough to me. I've had enough chances already. If we were fighting for fourth place, I'd stay." Colavito did play but again failed to drive in a run and thus Jensen won the American League RBI championship. There was a buzz in the press box as writers mumbled about the possible great exit that the homer represented if Jensen indeed decided to retire. Jensen did retire—at least for the entire 1960 season—only to return for one last season in 1961. His final at-bat came in the eighth inning of the final game. It was the game in which Tracy Stallard yielded Roger Maris' 61st home run. Jensen pinch-hit for Stallard and popped up. Boston lost 1-0.

✳   ✳   ✳   ✳

In 1954 when Jackie Jensen was traded from the Washington Senators to the Boston Red Sox for Mickey McDermott and Tom Umphlett, he reacted with uncharacteristic enthusiasm. "How do I like the trade? How do I like apple pie—duck soup—making a million dollars? Boy, I love the trade!"

Smead Jolley

The area in front of the 37' Green Monster in Fenway's left field once featured an incline known as Duffy's Cliff (named after Red Sox left fielder Duffy Lewis, who was particularly adept at playing there). One time, Red Sox manager Marty McManus spent hours trying to teach good-hit, no-field left fielder Smead Jolley to negotiate the treacherous piece of outfield. When Jolley tried to apply his newly acquired knowledge, he went up the incline smoothly, making a nice catch of the ball. Unfortunately, on the way back down he landed on his posterior, and the ball fell to the ground.

"For the love of God!" the frustrated McManus bellowed. "I spent all that time teaching you to climb up the cliff and then you screw it up."

Replied Jolley: "I guess you should have spent some time showing me how to come back down."

✳   ✳   ✳   ✳

La Notizia was a newspaper devoted to Bostonians of Italian descent. In the mid-30s, well before the Red Sox lineup featured any Conigliaros or Petrocellis, the paper's inventive sports editor converted Smead Jolley into a paisano by assigning him the humorous name of Smeederino Jolliani.

John Kennedy

John Kennedy was honored by the Boston Baseball Writers Association for his versatility filling in at second, third and shortstop—as well as for his timely hitting. Known as "Super Sub," the infielder with the presidential sounding name was playing in the right part of the country. When he was just three years old, his father was playing marbles with him on the living room floor. FDR had just died and the elder Kennedy asked John if he wanted to be president some day. "No, I want to be a ballplayer," the youngster replied, a fact his father entered into his baby book for posterity.

✳   ✳   ✳   ✳

From 1962 through 1974, JK played for six teams, winding up his career with four seasons in Boston. Rumor has it that like the president, he also lived in a white house, vacationed in Hyannisport, and once said, "Ask not what the Red Sox can do for you, ask what you can do for the Red Sox."

✳   ✳   ✳   ✳

Kennedy hit an inside-the-park HR his first time up as a Red Sox rookie.

Kevin Kennedy

The only player on both teams who did not play in Pawtucket's "Longest Game" was with the Orioles' Rochester Red Wings team at the time. It was Kevin Kennedy, later Red Sox manager and currently a Fox Sports TV commentator. This 33-inning game took 67 days to complete—it started on April 18, 1981 and ended on June 23, 1981. Actual playing time was eight hours and 25 minutes. Pitch count for Pawsox pitchers: 459. Pawsox hurlers struck out 34. Quite a number of major league ballplayers of note participated in the contest: for the Red Sox, Marty Barrett, Wade Boggs, Sam Bowen, Rich Gedman, Lee Graham, Roger LaFrancois, Julio Valdez, and Chico Walker all saw action; as did pitchers Luis Aponte, Joel Finch, Bruce Hurst, Bobby Ojeda, Win Remmerswaal, and Mike Smithson. Manny Sarmiento pitched for the Pawsox, but never made it to the Boston team, though he did spend parts of seven seasons in the big leagues. A prospect named Cal Ripken played third base for Rochester and went 2 for 13. Kevin Kennedy sat on the bench, maybe hoping for a pinch-hitting role if the innings reached the high 30s. During the game he had a lot of time to contemplate his future, no doubt concluding that if you can't get playing time in a 33- inning game, it may well be time to hang up the old spikes and turn to managing.

Marty Keough

How tough are Boston fans? In spring training 1960, Marty Keough was in a car crash that occurred well after curfew. The saying of the day was "Keough can't hit a curve with an automobile."

Henry Killilea

Killilea was the owner of the Boston Americans, forerunners of the modern day Red Sox. The Americans won the first modern World Series featuring the A.L. champion Americans against the Pittsburg Pirates, the best of the National League. The Americans won the eight-game marathon, becoming the first World Series champion. Cy Young even pitched in while not on the mound, helping sell tickets before the game. The Americans lost a few public relations points, though, when Pirate owner Barney Dreyfuss was forced to pay his way into the Boston ballpark.

Wendell Kim

The Red Sox have rarely been considered fleet afoot. Small wonder then that when late 1990s third base coach Wendell Kim sprinted across the diamond on the way to take his position, beating every Sox fielder out, some considered him the fastest runner on the team. Not surprisingly, Fenway crowds used to greet his mad dashes with appreciative applause.

Wendell Kim always enjoyed showing off his magic tricks at the beginning of the season and he was really quite good. His abilities even got him hired for professional engagements as a magician. Perhaps the popular Kim's biggest disappearing act was his quick exit from the Red Sox coaching staff after some highly questionable third base coaching decisions during the 2000 season.

Ellis Kinder

"Ellis Kinder was our closer," recalls former Sox teammate Billy Consolo. "That man was a man's man! He was the strongest human being. He was scared of nothing. He used to show up about the seventh inning and go to the bullpen. He knew he wasn't going to be playing until the eighth or ninth inning. That's the kind of man he was."

✳   ✳   ✳   ✳

Mickey McDermott was Kinder's teammate and drinking partner. "Kinder didn't know what water was," says McDermott. "He thought the Atlantic Ocean was a chaser. They said drink Canada Dry and he tried to do it."

✳   ✳   ✳   ✳

Ellis Kinder

"Old Folks," as Kinder was sometimes known, may have thought he was hallucinating, but it really happened: while he was on the mound at Fenway Park, a passing seagull dropped a smelt on him.

*   *   *   *

Kinder pitched under Red Sox manager Joe Cronin. Maureen Cronin recalls her father's frustration with the talented but un-disciplined pitcher. "I can't imagine being a batter and knowing the pitcher is drunk as a skunk and you trying to hit the ball. He was bombed while he was out there. I can't imagine anything worse. Can you imagine facing Roger Clemens or Randy Johnson after they'd had a couple of pops? Dad tried not to say bad things about people and when I asked him to write a book, he said he couldn't really say all the things he knew."

Jack Kramer

Jack Kramer was one of the most stylish players in Red Sox history. Known as "Handsome Jack," he reportedly changed clothes for breakfast, lunch and dinner. A finesse pitcher with little speed, fellow Red Sox pitcher Mickey McDermott claims: "When Kramer threw his fastball, three birds shit on it before it reached home plate."

*   *   *   *

The Red Sox have not always been one big happy family. Friction sometimes existed between players with different personalities and temperaments. Catcher Matt Batts and pitcher Jack Kramer were an example of this. As batteries go, they were negatively charged. Once, while Batts was warming Kramer up in front of a large Fenway Park crowd, he told teammate Mel Parnell to pay close attention. Batts then removed his glove and proceeded to catch

Kramer's next offering with his bare hands—the ultimate insult to any pitcher. Kramer was incensed, refusing to have Batts warm him up ever again.

Roger LaFrancois

T he last man to play with a major league club for an entire season and hit .400 was not Ted Williams, but a fellow Red Soxer, Roger LaFrancois. Roger used to go to Red Sox games as a kid. He signed with the Red Sox and came up in their system, even receiving instruction from Ted Williams during spring training at Winter Haven. In 1982, it all paid off. Roger made the club out of spring training as a backup catcher behind Gary Allenson and Rich Gedman and he spent the full 162-game season with the Red Sox, making every homestand and every road trip. He didn't miss a game.

Unfortunately, he also didn't get to play in that many of them. The first time he appeared in a game was May 27, and by that time the Boston papers had already begun to run photos of him with captions such as "Day 32: do you know who this man is?" Ralph Houk was from the old school and as, LaFrancois says, "played nine". He really didn't utilize his bench the way managers do today. LaFrancois appeared only very briefly and approaching the final day of the season had only been in seven games, with five at-bats and only a double and a single to show for it. Still, he was batting .400.

Then Houk gave him the opportunity to start the game, and Roger faced a dilemma like the young Ted Williams faced in 1941. Should he sit out the game and preserve his .400 average, or should he go for it? "There was a lot of pressure on me that last day, but I didn't want to sit on my average," Roger quips today. "I decided to play." It turned out to be an 11-inning affair against the Yankees in the Stadium. Roger hit a solid single up the middle earlier in the game but then saw his average sink to .333 as the game went into extra innings and he'd gone 1 for 4. In the top of the 11th, though, the young catcher jumped on a 1-2 Rudy May breaking ball and bounced it over the pitcher's head for an infield hit. Three batters later, LaFrancois scored what proved to be the winning run on a Rick Miller single. His average stands in the record books at an even .400 today.

Roger LaFrancois is now the hitting coach with the Binghamton Double A team in the New York Mets system.

$$* \quad * \quad * \quad *$$

Roger LaFrancois is perhaps the only ballplayer to play on the same team as his childhood idol, Carl Yastrzemski, and also his idol's son. LaFrancois played with Yaz on the Boston Red Sox in 1982 and with Michael Yastrzemski on the Durham ballclub in the Atlanta Braves system.

Bill Lee

Bill Lee will never make the Hall of Fame. Not unless some slightly warped visionary decides to open a wing for the flakes, free spirits and characters who have spiced up the grand old game over the years. If that unlikely event occurs, Lee will be first in line for admission to a ward that will also confine the likes of Moe Drabowsky, Mark Fidrych, Jay Johnstone, Mickey McDermott and Daffy Dean.

Lee was an above average pitcher—not Hall of Fame material but a solid major-league starter. Never a fire-baller, the crafty southpaw got by with a fine repertoire of curves and sliders, interspersed with a mediocre fastball. When the speed limit in Massachusetts was lowered, a Massachusetts TV ad advised drivers not to exceed Bill Lee's fastball—55 miles per hour.

Bill Lee was never a clown; never an Absorbine Junior-in-your jock jokester. Lee's brand of humor was slightly more cerebral. He was the thinking man's flake; a kind of lower class Yogi Berra with better diction. Lee was dubbed "the Spaceman" because in the conservative, buttoned-down world of baseball, he had an absolutely unique view of the baseball world. And he wasn't shy about sharing this perspective with anyone who'd listen. He once had his foot X-rayed and suggested to the doctor: "That

Bill Lee

loose thing's just an old Dewar's cap floating around." Lee was eventually traded from Boston to Montreal for Stan Papi, despite the fact that he was the third winningest left-hander in Red Sox history (after Mel Parnell and Lefty Grove.)

Lee and his manager Don Zimmer seldom saw eye to eye. The low point came when Lee labeled the puffy-cheeked Zimmer "the gerbil," a nickname adopted by some in the Boston media. "I was actually praising him when I called him a gerbil," argues Lee. "I had said that Yankees manager Billy Martin was a no-good dirty rat and Zimmer was not that way. He's given his life to baseball. His fatal flaw was that he was a manager in a city where, as a visiting player, he had a very difficult time with pitchers. Pitching is 90% of the game of baseball, and pitching happened to be the stuff that got him out 80% of the time. He was a .200 hitter, and that is what dictated the way he thought about pitchers."

*   *   *   *

The 1978 Red Sox blew a 14-game lead and ultimately lost a playoff game to the Yankees. When southpaw Bill Lee was subsequently traded from the Red Sox to the Expos at the end of the season, he was asked if he was upset to leave. His reply: "Who wants to be on a team that goes down in history with the '64 Phillies and the '67 Arabs?"

*   *   *   *

When his friend and soul mate Bernie Carbo was sold to the Cleveland Indians, Bill "Spaceman" Lee went on an unofficial strike—jumping the club and going home. He was finally tracked down by Red Sox president Haywood Sullivan, who informed Lee that he must dock him a day's pay, amounting to about $500. Lee's reply? "Make it fifteen hundred. I'd like to have the whole weekend."

*   *   *   *

Before the anticlimactic seventh game of the 1975 World Series, Cincinnati Reds manager Sparky Anderson boasted that no matter what the outcome of the game, his starting pitcher Don Gullett was going to the Hall of Fame. Bill Lee, the Red Sox starter, countered with: "No matter what the outcome of the game, I'm going to the Eliot Lounge." And he did.

*   *   *   *

Lee once charged that the California Angels "could hold batting practice in the lobby of the Grand Hotel (in Anaheim) and not chip a chandelier."

*   *   *   *

Lee won 17 games three years in a row, 1973 through 1975. He also was a self-appointed and outspoken social critic of sorts, a constant source of amusement who garnered attention and applause from Boston's left-leaning college crowd. When he termed Boston a "racist city" (by no means was he the first to do so), equally outspoken City Councilor Albert "Dapper" O'Neil fired off a letter. "Dapper" spelled several words incorrectly, giving Spaceman the opening to write back a polite letter advising the councilor that some semi-literate idiot had gotten possession of his stationery and was writing embarrassing letters over his name.

*   *   *   *

When asked by a *Boston Globe* reporter "what is your role with the Red Sox?" The Spaceman replied, "I'm George Scott's interpreter!"

*   *   *   *

Lee wore number 37 during his time with the Red Sox, but would have preferred number 337. "That way," he explained, "if I stood on my head people would know who I am"

An envious Bill Lee once pointed out that Tibetan priests had the ability to make a baseball disappear and then reappear in the catcher's mitt. "There's my idea of an ideal relief pitcher," he said.

✳   ✳   ✳   ✳

Lee used the English language to paint some vivid if abstract images. After the Red Sox defeated the Oakland A's, he said that the A's were "emotionally mediocre, like Gates Brown sleeping on a rug." Huh?

✳   ✳   ✳   ✳

Lee ran for president of the United States on the farcical Rhinoceros Party ticket. He was asked for his position on the highly controversial issue of drug testing in baseball: "My position on mandatory drug testing? I've tested mescaline. I've tested 'em all. But I don't think it should be mandatory."

✳   ✳   ✳   ✳

When a young Bill Lee first visited Fenway Park and looked out to left field, he could scarcely believe his eyes. For southpaws, having the Green Monster just 310' away is about as reassuring as having a buzzard perched on your shoulder. Ever the optimist, Lee thought that the Wall might all be some temporary structure. "Do they leave it there during the game?" he asked hopefully.

✳   ✳   ✳   ✳

Bill Lee and Carlton Fisk were a very effective battery for the Red Sox and they remain close friends. Nevertheless, they didn't always see eye to eye.

"I came up with Fisk, and he always thought he was the team leader. I wouldn't let him get away with that. I liked his attitude, but I knew I was smarter than him. He was tough as nails. We got along well but we were like brothers—we fought a lot, like in all sibling rivalries—about the way to handle the game and pitch to certain batters. He was more of a challenger and I was more of a nibbler. I would change up when he wouldn't expect it and he'd get really mad and throw the ball back at me hard. I made some mistakes. I'd hang a change-up in bad situations and he'd say 'I told you so'. When I made a bad pitch, it hurt me and not only did I have to suffer the direct consequences but I also had to suffer the wrath of Zimmer and the wrath of Fisk. I liked to experiment and baseball doesn't like experimentation."

*   *   *   *

Does Lee like the Spaceman label? "At first I didn't like it," he admits. "I'm not a spaceman, I'm more earth-oriented, very conservative toward the planet and liberal toward humanity. I'm so far left that I'm right. I'm a southpaw. My hand points to the south. We're laid out this way. I praise the powers that be that made me left-handed and that made me think the way that I do because I can always look in the mirror in the morning and say when things are going wrong around the earth, *Hey, it's not my fault.* You see, I'm an anarchist. I believe in pulling down boundaries and borders. I don't believe in the word sovereignty; I believe it should be stricken from the American language. I think what race, what color, what religion, what nationality you are—these are all obsolete terms in the 21st century. That's why I am the spaceman because I believe in open space."

Spaceman Communications:

"When I left Boston I said they'd find me floating face down in the Charles River with 11 stab wounds in my back and they'd say they were self-inflicted."

Bill Lee

＊   ＊   ＊   ＊

"Fenway Park is a shrine, but domed stadiums are sacrilegious. Playing in the Astrodome was like playing in an old pair of Adidas sneakers."

＊   ＊   ＊   ＊

"I'd be a great manager but major league baseball has never forgiven me. If I came in I'd look like John Brown, the guy they hung at Harper's Ferry. Fire in my eyes, my hair is long and my beard goes all the way down to my navel. They'd say, 'Who the hell is this guy, the lord of the rings?' And I'd say, "That's right, boys, if you play for me you'll all have rings—some in your noses."

＊   ＊   ＊   ＊

"The Red Sox were a Greek tragedy in the 2001 season. Pedro's arm fell off a few days after he made the comment about digging up the Babe."

＊   ＊   ＊   ＊

"I hope the Red Sox come back next year in great shape and with new ownership. I'll be the general manager and Stephen King will be the owner and Laurie Cabot [a Massachusetts witch] will be my pitching coach. It'll be a *real* horror show. We'll do just fine. Luis Tiant will be my third base coach, with the cigar in his mouth doing the signs and the whole bit. Bernie Carbo would be back for the Bible meetings on Sunday."

＊   ＊   ＊   ＊

"Frank Howard hit the hardest ball off me at Fenway. It probably one-hopped a flatbed truck and went to Pittsfield."

*   *   *   *

"I'm still playing competitive baseball but everyone I know from the Red Sox are either in rehab or smoking Marlboro Lights and drinking Diet Pepsi. I've got no friends anymore. I'm the only hippie-head esoteric thinker left."

*   *   *   *

Lee once ran for president of the United States on the Rhinoceros Party ticket. When told that he was considered eccentric—if not downright goofy—the former southpaw pitcher retorted that he was normal and it was the "northpaws" who were not.

The World According to Chairman Lee:

"*That's like having a Mercedes and hanging little dice from the rearview mirror.*" —Bill Lee, on the Red Sox installing a new electronic scoreboard in Fenway Park.

*   *   *   *

"*My first edict if I were Commissioner of Baseball would be to get rid of the designated hitter, to bring back the 25-man roster; to get rid of Astroturf, maintain smaller ballparks and revamp quality old ballparks. I'd outlaw video instant replays. I'd outlaw mascots. I'd put organic foods in the stands. I would make cold, pasteurized beer mandatory from small breweries located near the ballparks—no giant multi-national breweries. I would bring back warm, roasted peanuts. Just the smell of grass and those warm, roasted peanuts should be enough to make people come to the park. I would just try to reduce it to an organic game; the way it used to be.*" –Bill Lee

*   *   *   *

"My policy would be no guns; no butter. They'll both kill you. Tear down the defenses. Ted Williams will be my Secretary of Defense. He'll go out and tear down all defenses just like he did the Boudreau shift." –Bill Lee, on what he'd do if he were President of the United States.

*   *   *   *

Bill Lee on Carl Yastrzemski: *"He's a dull, boring potato farmer from Long Island who just happened to be a great ballplayer. But he was the worst dresser in organized baseball. He made Inspector Columbo look like a candidate for Mr. Blackwell's list of best-dressed men. He had the same London Fog raincoat during his entire career. We'd throw it in trashcans all around the league, and somehow it mysteriously made its way back."*

*   *   *   *

Bill Lee on pre-game habits: *"I told (reporters) that I sprinkled marijuana on my organic buckwheat pancakes, and then when I ran my five miles to the ballpark, it made me impervious to the bus fumes. That's when (Baseball Commissioner) Bowie Kuhn took me off his Christmas list."*

*   *   *   *

After the Red Sox lost Game Two of the 1975 World Series to even the Series at 1-1 with the Cincinnati Reds, starting pitcher Bill Lee was asked: "Bill, how would you characterize the World Series so far?" Reporters waited for fresh insights from the Red Sox Zen philosopher. His reply: "Tied."

*   *   *   *

When umpire Larry Barnett failed to make an interference call on hitter Ed Armbrister at home plate in a much-publicized incident that may have cost the Red Sox the '75 World Series, Bill Lee felt that Sox manager Darrell Johnson had not argued the call with sufficient vigor. "I'd have bitten Barnett's ear off," said Lee. "I'd have van Goghed him!"

*   *   *   *

Well-known lefty Bill Lee surprised no one when he pitched his hat into the ring in the 2016 Vermont gubernatorial contest as a candidate for the Liberty Union Party. The self-described "pragmatic, conservative, forward thinker" proposed Vermont strike an agreement with Canada's Maritime Provinces to bring Bay of Fundy tidal power to the Green Mountain State. With a Canadian wife, Diana, he also suggested the border between Vermont and Quebec be abolished to make travel easier. "My problem isn't getting into Canada; my problem is getting back into the United States."

Lee previously ran for president of the United States in 1988 on the Rhinoceros Party ticket. The fact that it is a Canadian party may have hurt his chances. His run for governor garnered only 2.80% of the popular vote, a great ERA but a disappointing election result.

Sang-Hoon Lee

Another Spaceman may have landed, at least briefly, at Fenway. Has Bill Lee, a practicing Buddhist, been reincarnated—while he's still alive—as his namesake, Korean lefthander Sang-Hoon Lee?

"Bill Lee was crazy. So am I," said the long-haired (orange colored tresses) Lee. Sang-Hoon Lee is nicknamed "Samson," and Red Sox GM Dan Duquette actually said in introducing him, "We think that with his long, flowing hair, he will be a good complement to Rod Beck in our bullpen."

Introduced to the media, Lee took the mound at Fenway Park early in 2000 and pretended to throw a few pitches over the plate for the benefit of photographers. The first "pitch" was apparently smashed high over the Green Monster, to see Lee's pantomimed look of distress as he followed the flight of the imaginary homer. Lee bowed to the Wall. On the second pitch, he quickly and playfully gripped his shoulder, faking an injury. As far as we know, he has yet to call his manager a gerbil or sprinkle foreign substances on his pancakes.

Lee was the first player to see duty in three different countries playing professional baseball: Korea, Japan and the USA.

Dutch Leonard

Hubert Benjamin "Dutch" Leonard pitched six years for Boston, including a stupendous 19-5 season in 1914, with a 0.96 ERA—the best ever in the 20th century. After six seasons with the Red Sox, his *highest* earned run average was 2.72. When sold to the Yankees by Frazee, he refused to pitch unless he was paid the full year's salary in advance. He never pitched for the Yankees; New York owner Ruppert was offended and sold him onwards to the Tigers.

Leonard must not have had a very good move to the plate. In the 15th inning of a 5-5 tie in 1913, three Cleveland players in a row stole home.

✳   ✳   ✳   ✳

On June 20, 1918, Leonard suddenly quit the team and took a job at the Fore River Shipyard in Quincy, Massachusetts, where he proceeded to pitch for the shipyard ball team. At the close of the season, Leonard was shipped out (by the Red Sox, not by Fore River.)

This wasn't the only mid-season career switch the Sox suffered. A couple of weeks after Leonard's move, Babe Ruth let it be known he was skipping the team to play for the Bethlehem Steel Company team in Chester, Pennsylvania. Ruth relented quickly, though, and returned, helping lead the Red Sox to their last World Championship. Otherwise, who knows, he might have been sold to U.S. Steel instead of the New York Yankees and . . . well, we guess U.S. Steel would have won all those World Series instead of the Yankees.

Jon Lester

J on Lester was a homegrown pitcher, a second-round Red Sox draft pick in 2002. He made the Boston team in 2006, but in late August was diagnosed with large-cell non-Hodgkin lymphoma. He was 22, and a true bright spot on the roster. Chemotherapy went on for the remainder of 2006 and well into 2007—but he returned on July 23 in time to go 4-0, and to become the winning pitcher in the clinching game of the 2007 World Series against the Colorado Rockies. "It was like he had climbed Mount Everest," said manager Terry Francona. It was maybe the ultimate feel-good story of the year.

In 2013, Lester was on his second world championship team, with a 4-1 record in the postseason, including wins in Game One and Game Five of the World Series against the Cardinals.

The Red Sox had let Francona go after the 2011 season, and—after offering Lester a contract well below market value—traded Lester at the July 31 deadline.

And in 2016, Lester did it again, helping the Chicago Cubs break a 108-year curse. Always pitching in suspense because of a bizarre mental block that prevented him from throwing effectively to first base, Lester was 19-5, with a league-leading .792 winning percentage, and then 3-1 in the postseason. He worked a solid three innings of relief in Game Seven against Francona and the Indians. Why can't the Red Sox get pitchers like Jon Lester?

Ted Lewis

E dward Morgan (Ted) Lewis (1872-1936), pitched for the Boston Nationals in the late 1890s and for the 1901 Red Sox (then the Americans) before quitting baseball at the age of 29 and becoming a professor of English at Columbia University. He later served as president of Massachusetts State College and then as president of the University of New Hampshire. "Parson" Lewis—born in Wales—was a good friend of Robert Frost, who was quite a baseball fan himself. It's said that the two "discussed poetry and played catch in Lewis' backyard." We are not sure if it was Frost or Yogi Berra who first said "When you come to a fork in the road, take it."

Grady Little

Do we *really* need to talk about Grady?

Dick Littlefield

Littlefield began his career with Boston in 1950 winning two and losing two but with a 9.26 ERA. In 1951 he was with the White Sox. In 1952, the Tigers. In 1953, he pitched for the St. Louis Browns. In 1954, he appeared in three games for Baltimore. Moving over to the National League, Littlefield was with the Pirates in 1955. In 1956 he played with the Cardinals and the Giants, after opening the season with Pittsburgh. Little wonder Littlefield was dubbed the "Marco Polo of Baseball."

Jim Lonborg

Jim Lonborg was one of the most stylish right-handed pitchers in Red Sox history. Gentleman Jim was best own for his league-leading 22 wins during the Red Sox 1967 drive to the American League pennant. He is also famous for his courageous effort in a losing cause in Game Seven of that year's World Series. Lonborg was pitching on just two days' rest. After the game, he was surrounded by reporters, curious about the mental strain of such an ordeal. "It has to be physical," insisted Lonborg. "That's why I'm soaking my arm now. If it was mental, I'd be soaking my head."

✶   ✶   ✶   ✶

Even in the midst of the pressure packed '67 pennant drive, the Red Sox maintained their sense of humor. Nothing and no one was sacred. Carl Yastrzemski used to annoy his pitchers by not even turning around to pursue sure home runs to left field. The Red Sox mound fraternity thought that to save them embarrassment, he should at least pretend that these long homers might be catchable. When Cleveland's Max Alvis hit a shot over the Green Monster off ace Jim Lonborg, Yaz didn't move a muscle. Back in the dugout at the end of the half inning, Lonborg cornered him. "You could at least make it look like you might possibly catch it," he suggested. Yastrzemski was unrepentant. "I might have if they moved the stadium back a hundred yards or so," he said.

✶   ✶   ✶   ✶

Gentleman Jim Lonborg was the ace of the Red Sox pitching staff during the 1967 pennant year. The stylish right-hander won 22 games that season and became the first Boston pitcher ever to capture the Cy Young Award. Blessed with a blazing fastball and pinpoint control, he struck out 246 opposing batters in anchoring the Red Sox staff.

Before the last game of the '67 season, with the pennant still very much up for grabs, Lonborg showed that he was not immune to superstition. Since he had been more successful on the road than at Fenway during the season, he decided to check into a Boston hotel to simulate the feeling that he was on the road. He says that he fell asleep reading *The Fall of Japan,* woke refreshed in the morning, and then proceeded to defeat the Minnesota Twins to bring the pennant back to Boston for the first time in 21 years.

Derek Lowe

Coming to Boston with Jason Varitek as part of the most lopsidedly-beneficial trade in Red Sox history (they only gave up Heathcliff Slocumb (who was 0-5 at the time), D-Lowe was both a successful starter and reliever (leading the league in 2000 with 42 saves, and then a 21-game winner in 2002). In the 2004 postseason, Lowe had the unusual distinction of having won the deciding games in the American League Division Series, the League Championship Series, and the World Series. Can you say "hat trick"? His playoff ERA was 0.00.

Larry Lucchino

Larry Lucchino, named in December 2001 as the new President of the Boston Red Sox, tells how famous Washington attorney Edward Bennett Williams gave him his entry into baseball. Williams was the owner of both the Baltimore Orioles and the Washington Redskins football team. He brought in the young Lucchino, a lawyer who'd worked with a number of attorneys, including Hillary Rodham Clinton, while with Williams' firm during the Watergate hearings. Lucchino remembers, "Edward Williams used to say to me, 'I love the Redskins, I'm crazy about the Orioles, but I'd take both of them and trade them for the Red Sox.' That's not made up. That's absolutely so. And I said, 'Of course, you're from Hartford.'"

Lucchino had strong Boston area ties before coming to the Red Sox. In 1985, when vice president of the Orioles, he was diagnosed with non-Hodgkin's lymphoma and he spent over five weeks at the Dana-Farber Cancer Institute undergoing an experimental (and clearly successful) bone marrow transplant that saved his life.

As President of the San Diego Padres, Larry and the Padres launched the Cindy Matters Fund, named for a youngster in the area who was afflicted with cancer. A couple of years ago, he told one of the authors of this book that he was very impressed with the work in pediatric oncology that he had observed at the Jimmy Fund, and he knew of the Red Sox/Ted Williams connection. "As a baseball person, I was very proud of it, so proud of it that we imitate it shamelessly out here in San Diego."

One suspects the Jimmy Fund will continue to be a favored charity of the Boston Red Sox as it has been for nearly a full half-century.

Sparky Lyle

Aside from being one of the best relief pitchers in major-league history, Sparky Lyle was famous for dropping his pants and sitting on birthday cakes. According to Bill Lee, that's what prompted one of the worst trades in Red Sox history. "He sat on (Red Sox owner) Tom Yawkey's cake, and Yawkey found out," claims Lee. "The next day Lyle is shipped off to the Yankees and here comes Danny Cater. All because of sitting on a birthday cake."

Fred Lynn

When former Red Sox center fielder Fred Lynn first came up to the big leagues in 1975, he was platooned against southpaw pitchers. The first game he ever played in Milwaukee, the left-handed batter hit a home run his first time up, a double the next time up and then was removed for a pinch hitter the next time up against a left-handed reliever. Recalls Lynn: "I thought to myself: *This is some tough league!*"

*　　*　　*　　*

In 1975, Fred Lynn became the first and only player to win both the Rookie of the Year and the MVP in the same year. On June 18 that year, he tied an American League record by hitting for 16 total bases. Lynn also set the new record for doubles by a rookie with 47.

Fred Lynn (Brace Photography)

*   *   *   *

In June of 1975, his rookie season, Red Sox centerfielder Freddie Lynn drove in 10 runs in one game. He hit three homers, a triple and a single in a 15-1 win over the Detroit Tigers. His first home run came in the first inning with one man aboard; the second was a three-run job in the second, and the third came in the ninth—another three-run shot. The 16 total bases that he amassed that day tied the American League mark. He finished with 21 homers, 105 RBIs and a .331 batting mark.

*   *   *   *

One year during the off-season, Lynn jokingly told a Los Angeles newspaper that he thought Jim Rice should be playing leftfield because he was sick of covering up for Yaz. Many readers took the statement seriously. Next season in Chicago, Yastrzemski came all the way into Lynn's territory to make a diving catch of a sinking liner. "Showoff," said Lynn. "Someone's gotta cover your territory, Freddie," replied a grinning Yaz.

Steve Lyons

When erratic, off-the-wall Steve Lyons was traded to the Chicago White Sox for soon-to-be Hall of Famer Tom Seaver, a Baltimore reporter dubbed the trade: "Cy Young for Psycho!" The *Boston Globe* headline proclaiming the trade was as follows: SEAVER FINALLY CHANGES HIS SOX. Lyons actually had four separate stints with the Red Sox.

*   *   *   *

Steve Lyons and teammate Marty Barrett once both slid into second base—from opposite directions—on a ball hit to the outfield. The center fielder was so startled he overthrew the ball into the dugout, allowing both runners to score.

*   *   *   *

Talk about the glamour of the Big Leagues. For a lot of his career, Lyons says, "I sat on the bench for most of the games and stared at gross puddles of chew-spit, sunflower seeds, and empty Gatorade cups all over the floor of the dug-out."

*   *   *   *

Steve Lyons played for the Red Sox in four different stints, where he gained notoriety in eating seeds and other heroic deeds. He is the only player in Red Sox history to play all nine positions and DH. He's one of only three players in major league history to play all nine positions in a game. He also claims the world's record for eating sunflower seeds in one game: five bags of David's Sunflower Seeds. But that was in Montreal, so we guess it's the National League record.

*   *   *   *

Lyons was traded from Boston to Montreal for Tom Seaver, but was then traded back for nothing. "The deal was probably that Duquette (GM for Expos at the time) would buy the next lunch when he and Red Sox General Manager Lou Gorman got together."

Sam Malone

He had Mickey McDermott's drinking habits, Bill Lee's wit, Mike Torrez' hair, Dennis Eckersley's sex appeal, and Heathcliff Slocumb's arm.

Everyone may know his name, but Sam "Mayday" Malone did not actually play for the Boston Red Sox. Nevertheless, the character portrayed so convincingly by Ted Danson on *Cheers* fits well into the Red Sox mystique—and if he didn't actually exist, he probably should have. His antics are not that much more outrageous than those of McDermott or the Spaceman, after all.

Sports Illustrated's Steve Rushin once did a straight-faced story *(SI,* May 24, 1993) about Malone in which his life was described in great detail and his entry in *The Baseball Encyclopedia* was reproduced in all its gory detail. (He is wedged in between Chuck Malone and Charlie Maloney). According to this source, Malone's career marks are not overly impressive. Born on May 1, 1948 (thus the nickname Mayday) in Sudbury, Massachusetts, the 6'3" 195-pound right-handed reliever played seven seasons with the Red Sox from 1972-1978. His record was 16 wins and 30 losses and he sports a 4.01 ERA.

Also included in the article was a "cover" from June 28, 1976 showing Mayday on the mound watching the ball exit the ballpark over the Green Monster. The caption reads "WHAM, BAM, THANK YOU SAM: Mayday Malone Watches Another One Fly Out of Fenway." Other pictures show him in the company of Carl Yastrzemski and fictional Coach ("I always thought they gave me that name because I never flew first class") Ernie Pantusso. He missed the 1975 World Series entirely, reports *SI* due to a "mysterious domestic groin injury."

Malone had a drinking problem that may have hampered his career significantly. He admitted to having hung out too many nights at the Eliot Lounge on Mass. Ave., presumably with Bill Lee. He even admitted to occasionally drinking during games. "Never on the mound," he quickly added. "It sets a bad example for the catchers." He was also a ladies man of great repute and his pitches in that department were much more effective than those from the mound. "The closest I've ever come to saying no to a woman," he once admitted, "is 'Not now, we're landing.'" *SI* claims that Sam once requested that the Red Sox install Call Waiting in the bullpen to advance his love life. Red Sox manager Don Zimmer, never a friend of pitchers, was not amused.

Malone's pitching staple was something called "the slider of death." The name was given to the pitch by teammates who were accustomed to watching it fly out of Fenway, mortally wounding the Red Sox hopes of victory. Yankees slugger Dutch Kinkaid homered against Sam every time he faced him.

In fact, Malone surrendered many tape-measure home runs, including one that almost punched out the "O" in the CITGO sign and another, in Memorial Stadium in Baltimore, which cleared the ballpark and landed in the parking lot, where a plaque marked the spot until the park was demolished.

Sam's sole moment of glory came in September of 1972, his rookie year. In his first mound appearance in a Red Sox uniform, Malone saved both ends of a crucial double-header against the Baltimore Orioles, throwing only seven pitches to seal the two victories. Both times, Orioles slugger Boog Powell was his final out. Fenway went wild and Sam was now "Mayday" Malone.

Sports Illustrated reported that Malone s last appearance in the major leagues came in April of 1978 in Cleveland. It was his only starting assignment. The Indians' Paul Dade doubled, Larvell Blanks walked, and then Sam gave up "back-to-back-to-back-to-back homers to Andre Thornton, Buddy Bell, Willie Horton, and John Grubb." Rattled, Sam then beaned Duane Kuiper before manager Don Zimmer made his trek to the mound. This, claims *Sports Illustrated,* explains why Sammy's ERA for 1978 is represented in *The Baseball Encyclopedia* by the sideways 8, the symbol for infinity.

After his baseball career, Sam decided to open a bar and the rest, of course, is history. His friends at Cheers remained in awe of the big guy though, as much for his sexual exploits as for his baseball skills. Norm Peterson, the bar's most loyal patron, summed it up nicely: "Next to Sammy's life, my life looks dull," he said, pausing for a sip before adding, "Next to a barnacle's life, my life looks dull."

Malone did little to refute Ted Williams' assertion that all pitchers are stupid. He once said that PBS was his favorite network and that he especially liked the "two guys who talk about the day's events."

"McNeil and Lehrer?" he is asked. "No," Malone replied, "Bert and Ernie ... Wait a minute. Unless-maybe that's their last names."

Still Mayday could show glimmers of great intelligence. Cliff Clavin once asked him if he had the usual ballplayer superstitions. He replied, "Yeah, I had a crazy little one. I never pitched to anyone named Reggie, Willie or the Bull."

In 1992, Sam, age 43, tried a comeback with the New Britain Red Sox, Boston's Double A affiliate. Norm Peterson was excited about the prospect of Sam's return. "Boy-oh-boy," he said. "The thought of Sammy out there on the mound, chuckin' 'em down.

What I wouldn't give to see that, huh?" When Cliff Clavin pointed out that New Britain was only a *$30.00* train ride away, Norm replied, "Well, that's what I wouldn't give."

Sam once tried his hand at sports announcing, anchoring a local supper-hour sportscast. In a desperate attempt to attract a younger audience, he tried rapping a sports item, the final line ending, unforgettably, with the words, "G-G-G-G-G-groin injury."

The Boston Red Sox retired Sam Malone's #20 jersey in a private ceremony and it rests today in a glass display case in The 600 Club at Fenway Park. Well, semi-retired it at least. They continue to let players use the number—witness Darren Lewis in recent years. Nevertheless, on a team with characters like McDermott, Lee, Piersall, Tiant, and Conley, the name Sam Malone fits in very nicely.

Frank Malzone

L eo Durocher was once asked if Red Sox third baseman Frank Malzone had any faults. "Dandruff maybe," replied the veteran manager.

Pedro Martinez

W hen Roger Clemens left Boston for Toronto, the Red Sox brought in right-handed pitcher Pedro Martinez, nine years his junior, from the Montreal Expos. Pedro promptly created his own legend in Beantown. Arriving amid the hoopla of a six-year, $75 million contract, the 5'11", 170-pound native of the Dominican Republic was immediately worshipped by the Fenway Faithful. What did the new millionaire do with his newfound wealth? A luxury car perhaps, or a mansion in the suburbs? Why, he built a church of course—The Immaculate Conception in his home village of Manoguayabo. "That was better than a Cy Young to me," said Martinez.

*   *   *   *

In the summer of 1999, Pedro Martinez achieved god-like status in New England. His appeal crossed all ethnic and religious lines. Late in the season, with Pedro leading American League pitchers in virtually every statistical category, the following story appeared in the *Boston Herald:* apparently a Jewish Red Sox fan went to his rabbi before Rosh Hashanah and said, "Rabbi, I have a problem. I know it's Rosh Hashanah, but it's Yankees-Red Sox and Pedro is pitching." The Rabbi replied thoughtfully: "It's not such a problem. It's for nights like this that God invented VCRs." Sox fan: "So, I can tape the Rosh Hashanah services?"

*   *   *   *

Even his teammates become wide-eyed fans when Pedro is weaving his mound magic. "When Pedro is pitching and striking out all those guys, it's amazing to watch," says shortstop Nomar Garciaparra. "Last summer (1999), he struck out 16 Atlanta Braves in an inter-league contest at Fenway. The trouble is you end up watching him and you become a fan as you're watching him. I remember everyone is cheering every strikeout he's making, and they're going crazy. It was kind of funny because if we made a play, they were kind of mad at us.

They wanted to see him strike out everybody. I remember we were winning, and the last hitter of the game hits a ball between short and third, and I didn't even move! And I think it took [John] Valentin a little bit of time to move—because we were almost hypnotized. But this play was so funny because the guy hit it, and all the fans went: "Awww ... he didn't strike him out." All the fans were upset—and I was the same way, going "Awww . . . too bad." Then all of a sudden I realized: "Oh shit, I've got to go and make a play." It was a good thing Valentin got it because I was nowhere to be found. He made the play for the final out and the game was over, but it was really strange. That's the way he was—amazing. You become mesmerized. "

*   *   *   *

In capturing the 1999 Cy Young Award, Martinez put together what many consider—in relative terms—the best pitching performance in the history of baseball. At the age of 28, Pedro dominated American League hitters like no other pitcher before or since. He won 23 games, lost only four and compiled a 2.07 ERA, more than one full run ahead of any other pitcher. He struck out 313 (over 100 more than the next best) and allowed only 37 bases on balls.

*   *   *   *

While on the mound, Pedro is dead serious, but in the dugout he is a different man. He has been known to patrol the dugout in a Yoda mask, and he directs a continuous stream of chatter toward opposing players and teammates. He has even coined a few original baseball terms. According to the Martinez dictionary, a "dog fart" is a bloop single, a "ding-dong johnson" is a homer, and an "underwater johnson" is a slow swing.

*   *   *   *

When the Chicago White Sox took issue with some of his dugout dialogue during the 1999 season, teammates Nomar Garciaparra, Damon Buford, Mark Portugal and Bret Saberhagen devised a plot to keep their ace under control. "Pedro Martinez likes to talk a lot when he's not playing," confirms teammate Nomar Garciaparra. "He gets very animated out there in the dugout. It's good ... but at times it's like: *All right already, Pedro! That's enough!* One day we were beating the Chicago White Sox pretty good, and he was talking to the White Sox players and messing with them. I was sitting there watching as he was leaning up against the dugout post, and I said to the guys: 'You know what? Why don't we just tape him to this post? Maybe that'll calm him down, and then at least he can't walk around all over the place. It'll keep him quiet.' So we just started taping and taping. We were going to keep it going. At first, he was unconcerned. Then as we kept taping, he started realizing that he really couldn't move. We didn't care; we just kept going. He was still talking, and I said; 'We've forgotten one very big thing. We've got to tape his mouth up, too.' And then we taped up his mouth. Finally the game was over, and we just ran out and left him there.

"The White Sox were really good sports about it. He wanted to come out and shake hands, but he couldn't. He was stuck there. The only reason we didn't leave him tied up was that he was scheduled to pitch the next day. Otherwise, I'll tell you what—you would have seen him in the same uniform in the same spot when they sang the National Anthem the next afternoon."

*   *   *   *

"Pedro's a funny guy. He really enjoys the game, but on days when he's pitching—as soon as the game starts—it's all business." —Nomar Garciaparra.

*   *   *   *

It was billed as the Duel of the Century; the Gun-fight at the OK Corral. Instead, when Pedro Martinez faced Roger Clemens in Game Three of the 1999 American League Championship Series, it turned out to be Cy Young vs. Cy Old; Don Larsen vs. Dawn of Time. Pedro was masterful, striking out a Red Sox-record 12 Yankees (including Derek Jeter and Paul O'Neill twice) en route to a 13-1 thrashing of the hated Yanks. It was baseball's dominant team vs. baseball's dominant player as Martinez handed the Yankees their only loss in 19 postseason encounters. Pedro allowed only two hits and no runs before being removed after seven innings of work. Many Red Sox fans took this victory as retribution against the traitorous Clemens, who had departed Boston for more money a few years earlier. What made the win especially sweet for Martinez is the fact that he had only one of his usual tools working for him on the mound. Hobbled with a strained muscle in his back, Martinez should not have been on the mound at all. His fastball, usually clocked in the 96-98 range, was well under 90; his change-up was mediocre; his curveball lacked its usual sharpness. Only his amazing pitching intellect allowed him to bamboozle Yankee hitters for seven innings and inflict the worst defeat the Bronx Bombers had absorbed in their proud history of postseason play.

*   *   *   *

When Pedro won the 1997 Cy Young Award, he presented it to his fellow Dominican and idol, Hall of Fame pitcher Juan Marichal.

*   *   *   *

Ask major league hitters and they'll all confirm that the prospect of Pedro Martinez improving is too awful to contemplate. In the 2000 season (he was injured for much of the 2001 season), Martinez won 18 games, lost six, and compiled a league-leading ERA of 1.74, almost a full two runs lower than the runner-up in the American League pitching ranks. He allowed just 42 earned runs in 217 innings of work, walked only 32 and held opponents to a puny .167 batting average, with a league-best 284 strikeouts. He captured his second consecutive Cy Young Award, winning all 28 first-place votes cast by the Baseball Writers Association of America. He also led the league in shutouts with four. Martinez is the first A.L. pitcher in history to win two consecutive Cy Youngs unanimously. He also won a Cy Young Award in the National League in '97 as a member of the Montreal Expos.

*   *   *   *

When Martinez first signed with the Dodgers, the 16 year old was 5'8" and weighed 120 pounds.

*   *   *   *

Martinez had a disastrous encounter with the baseball gods on August 29, 2000, as Pedro had a no-hitter against the Devil Rays going into the ninth. Baseball fans around the country had a chance to watch the final inning as ESPN broke into its regular programming to pick up the game feed. After a few pitches to former Red Sox catcher John Flaherty, the chain on a religious medal he was wearing around his neck snapped and Pedro tucked it in his back pocket. The very next pitch—bam! A clean single. Pedro's no-hit bid was finished.

*   *   *   *

There were signs that Pedro might be getting a tad tired of all the defeatist talk around Boston. He was once heard to observe, "One of these days Buckner's gonna catch that grounder." Apparently he was as sick as the rest of us of seeing that replay over and over.

*   *   *   *

Don't mess with the Curse of the Bambino. At least that would seem to be the message delivered to Pedro Martinez by the angered baseball gods during the 2001 baseball season. Frustrated by the never-ending talk of the supposed curse placed on the Red Sox by a departing Babe Ruth, Pedro blurted out the following: "I don't believe in damn curses. Wake up the damn Bambino and have him face me. Maybe I'll drill him in the ass." To put this outburst in further context, the statement was made by Martinez on May 30, 2001, after he had broken out of a five-game winless spell with a brilliant 3-0 performance against the Bronx Bombers. A reporter's reference to the Babe was the straw that broke the camel's back.

*   *   *   *

Was Pedro tempting Fate when he made the remark? Is God a Yankee fan as Mickey McDermott has suggested elsewhere in this book? When Pedro opened his mouth, the Red Sox, playing without superstar shortstop Nomar Garciaparra, had a record of 28-22, putting them in a virtual tie with the Yankees for first place in the A.L. East. Pedro had a record of 7-1 and Manny Ramirez was hitting as if he were playing Tee-Ball. Everything looked rosy for the Boston side. Let's consider what happened after. By mid-August the Red Sox had fallen six games out of first place and their wild-card lead had collapsed like—well, like a deck of wild cards. The Red Sox fired manager Jimy Williams who was a manager of the year candidate everywhere but in Boston. And they chose to fire him on the 53rd anniversary of the death of Babe Ruth. The Red Sox proceeded to lose their next seven consecutive games against Babe's Yankees.

Most importantly, Pedro, who was 7-1 with a 1.44 ERA on May 30, fell lower than the Babe's belly. After his controversial remarks, he suffered a rotator cuff injury and was only able to start seven more times, failing to win another game all year long. During this stretch as a mortal, his ERA ballooned to 4.54 (although his season ERA was still a brilliant 2.39.) Just to put this in perspective, Martinez had not gone seven games without a win since the first seven games of his career.

When pitching coach Joe Kerrigan took over, his first words were, "It's one of the best jobs in sports for me to be able to come in here and chase away The Curse. I look forward to the challenge." Just don't knock the Babe, Joe.

Carl Mays

Ray Collins (1914) and Carl Mays (1919) both won two games in a single day. This is the same Carl Mays who killed Ray Chapman with a beanball after he was traded to the Yankees.

The Red Sox lost a lot of games to the Detroit Tigers in 1915, and manager Rough Carrigan asked his pitching staff who among them thought he could defeat the Tigers. Carl Mays declared that if he didn't win the ball game in Detroit, he'd walk back home to Boston. He won, on his own hit, 2-1 in the ninth inning, thereby saving considerable wear and tear on his spikes.

Mickey McDermott

Mickey McDermott

When fuzzy-cheeked teenager Mickey McDermott first came up to the Red Sox, the management tried to protect the young man from the temptations of the road. One day, he was called into manager Joe Cronin's office. Cronin explained that McDermott had been seen in a nightclub drinking with veteran pitcher Ellis Kinder, also known as "Old Folks." "You cannot be seen with Kinder in nightclubs!" lectured Cronin. "You've got your whole future ahead of you." McDermott denied that he had been at a nightclub the previous evening. Cronin told him to go look in the mirror. When he did, he saw that his tongue was completely green from drinking grasshoppers. "You look like a %$#&ing leprechaun," said Cronin.

*   *   *   *

Aside from being an above-average pitcher, McDermott was also a talented singer. Once, he pitched 16 innings against Cleveland, but in the 16th he faltered, loading the bases. Birdie Tebbetts, who had just been traded from the Red Sox to the Indians shouted from the dugout: "Sing your $%#*ing way out of this, McDermott!"

*   *   *   *

The Red Sox sent McDermott to live with Johnny Pesky, hoping that the stability of family life would have a calming effect on the young pitcher. It didn't work. "They gave him a car one time as a tribute on Pesky Day," recalls Mickey. "I borrowed it that night and I got some broad, and I kicked the window out trying to get laid in the back seat. He was going to kill me. I said 'Why didn't you have it open? I'm 6'3"; you're only 5'11".'"

*   *   *   *

McDermott thinks that he deserves to have his name associated with a Fenway landmark, just as Johnny Pesky does on the right field foul pole known as Pesky's Pole. "What about putting my %$#& name on the Wall? Batters hit the *&^%ing Wall ninety million times thanks to me. I threw it, they hit it, and I ain't got my name on it or nothin'. I didn't even get a trophy, and Pesky got a freakin' pole named after him! I put Joe DiMaggio in the Hall of Fame. I threw it, and he hit it. I went to Joe one time and said: 'You owe me fifty thousand dollars.' 'For what?' he said. I said: 'You son of a bitch, I put you in the Hall of Fame.' So he autographed a ball to me saying: 'To Maurice, thank you for all the nice fastballs at Fenway Park.' Because of me, he killed three people on the Charles River rowing a boat."

*   *   *   *

Mickey McDermott: *"I once pinch-hit in Chicago, and on the mound was Virgil Trucks. Ted Williams could hit Trucks after midnight so he said: 'C'mere, bush. Listen, look for his slider.' I walked to the plate, and Trucks threw three fastballs right down the middle of the plate and struck me out. I walked back to the dugout and I said: 'Listen, Theodore, let me tell you a little story: my name is NOT Ted Williams.' He said: 'You know, bush, you're finally getting smart.'"*

*   *   *   *

Boston's ace left-hander Mel Parnell was McDermott's roommate on the Red Sox. Parnell once confided to manager Joe McCarthy: "We'd been on the road for a year, and I haven't seen him yet. I'm rooming with his suitcases."

*   *   *   *

After six years in Boston and two with the lowly Washington Senators, McDermott was traded in 1956 to the New York Yankees where he played under the legendary Casey Stengel. On a road trip to Boston, McDermott was quick to return to his old watering holes. Returning to the Kenmore Hotel at four in the morning, McDermott thought that he could use his intimate knowledge of Boston hotels to sneak past his ever-vigilant manager. More than a little inebriated, he sneaked into the basement of the hotel and used the service elevator to reach his floor. Unfortunately, McDermott forgot that Stengel had played and managed in Boston and also knew the city like the back of his hand. When the elevator door opened, there stood Stengel. The two faced each other eyeball to eyeball. Finally Stengel said in disgust: "Drunk again!" Staggering past him down the hallway, McDermott hiccupped loudly and replied: "Me too, Skip!" Stengel was so amused he allowed the infraction to go unpunished.

✱　　✱　　✱　　✱

McDermott was like a son to manager Joe McCarthy. Proud Irishmen both, the wayward pitcher and stern disciplinarian established an immediate rapport. One day, McCarthy called the 18-year-old McDermott into his office. "Maurice, do you have a girlfriend?" he asked. "Yes, sir," replied the young southpaw. "Did you ever hear of Lefty Gomez?" the manager continued. Again McDermott replied in the affirmative. "Well," said McCarthy, "don't become Lefty Gomez! He left his fastball in the sheets." McDermott was puzzled. "I was only 18; I didn't know what he was talking about. I wondered what the hell he'd leave his fastball in my sheets for. I was looking for it for three days."

✱　　✱　　✱　　✱

A few years ago, McDermott was visiting the Ted Williams Museum in Hernando, Florida, for the annual Hitters' Hall of Fame induction ceremony. The Splendid Splinter was entertaining his good friends and honored guests President George Bush and wife Barbara. As McDermott was walking past the rostrum, Ted called out: "Maurice, come on over here." He then proceeded to introduce him to the President. "Well for chrissake, George, how the hell are you?" said McDermott. Embarrassed, Ted stammered: "I can't believe you addressed the President of the United States as George." McDermott replied: "Wait a minute, Theodore. He played against my friend Walt Dropo when he was at Yale and Walt was at Connecticut. Right, George?" Laughing at Williams' discomfort, Bush gave McDermott a high five.

*   *   *   *

McDermott sees some interesting parallels between baseball and marriage. "All my wives became umpires. They all said: 'Out!'"

*   *   *   *

According to the authors of *The Great American Baseball Card Flipping, Trading and Bubble Gum Book,* McDermott is: "the only player in the history of the Poughkeepsie, New York, public school system to be chosen unanimously by his high school graduating class as the man most likely to be found dead in his hotel room."

*   *   *   *

"Bob Neiman could hit me with the lights out," recalls McDermott. "His first two at-bats in the major leagues he hit homers off me. You could throw .306 bullets up there and he'd hit them, especially if you were a leftie. I went to Washington and we were good friends so we went out to dinner and he said, 'Tomorrow I'm going two for three off you'. I said, 'No, you're not!', and we bet $100 on it. First time up, I hit him right in the kneecap and then went into the clubhouse while he was in the whirlpool and took the $100 right out of his wallet while he was watching me. Not only was he a hundred bucks lighter but he wore (American League President) William Harridge's signature on his leg for a week."

Mickey McDermott

*   *   *   *

McDermott played for both the Red Sox and the Yankees, but there is no doubt where his allegiance lies. He is a diehard Red Sox fan. "During the 1949 pennant drive we had to win one, and instead we lost two at Yankee Stadium. See, God is a Yankee fan. There was a ball hit to right field and there was a guy named Cliff Mapes playing there. Pesky is on third, and if he scores we win. And I'll be a son of a bitch if a duststorm doesn't come up in right field! In right field! And Pesky can't see the ball to know if Mapes caught it or not. As it cleared, Pesky tagged up, and they tagged him out at home." Ah well, at least He didn't bother hitting us with the plague of locusts.

*   *   *   *

People who saw Mickey McDermott pitch thought there was no way that the native of Poughkeepsie, NY ("Poughkeepsie is a cemetery with lights," explains McDermott) could miss being a Hall of Famer.

The skinny (170 pounds) 6' 3" southpaw had blazing speed and a blazing wit. Despite his awesome potential, it is his wit that he is better known for today, and if there were a Hall of Fame for baseball characters, McDermott would be among the first enshrined there.

*   *   *   *

Bill "Spaceman" Lee after learning of a recent operation undergone by McDermott, quipped: "Mickey McDermott and I are identical twins. The only original body part McDermott has left is his brain." Lee said a mouthful. A more original baseball brain is hard to imagine: Here are some examples of this wondrous organ at work:

*   *   *   *

"Hitting for me was a gift. I didn't ask for help from Williams or anyone. Ted once took me aside and asked: 'Kid, are you copying me?'"

*   *   *   *

"The goddamned Yankees were the best hecklers. That goddamn white rabbit, Eddie Lopat, the great left-hander. I was pitching one game and they had a man on first and Lopat was screaming and hollering and raising hell. So I wound up and I made a move to first and threw it right at him in the f—ing dugout. He said, 'You still haven't got control. You missed me by a mile.'"

*   *   *   *

"I hit a triple once with the Red Sox. I was running like hell and I slid into third and I had been smoking down in the dugout before I came up and I'd put a pack of matches in my back pocket and when I slid they caught fire and there was smoke coming out of my ass and the third baseman said, 'You son of a bitch, you can really run!' The smoke was going like a flamethrower and I was yelling 'Yoww!' I had a f—ing blister on my a—like an apple."

Sam Mele

While in Boston, Sam Mele played under legendary disciplinarian Joe McCarthy, who would not abide alibis or excuses of any kind. One bright, sunny day in 1949, Mele was playing Fenway's right field, an infamous "sun field," when a line drive was hit in his direction. The ball took a bad bounce, and Sam ducked as the ball caromed over his head. As he came to the dugout at the end of the inning, Mele made his second and more costly error—this one with McCarthy. "Oh geez, the ball got lost in the sun, and I didn't have time to pull my sunglasses down," he whined. "You know something, my boy?" replied Marse Joe. "They play all night games in Washington." Mele finished out the year where the sun never shone—with the lowly Senators in the basement of the American League.

Oscar Melillo

They were on the right track but the wrong train. On July 4, 1937, trains carrying the Boston Red Sox and the Philadelphia Athletics train both left South Station at midnight for games in different cities. In the middle of the night it was discovered that two Red Sox players, Eric McNair and Oscar Melillo were in the right berths, but the wrong train. At first, Athletics players assumed that a secret trade had taken place, and were relieved when the two intruders were let off at Providence.

Lou Merloni

The names have been omitted to protect the guilty, but the Red Sox's Lou ("The Igloo?") Merloni reports that while certain teammates were busy on the field, an unnamed Red Sox player used to put their sneakers in a freezer in a pan of water. After the game, while that player was in the shower, the frozen sneakers were placed in front of the player's locker, resulting in Red Sox and blue feet. The same cold-blooded perpetrator would also take players' clothes, roll them up, wet them and then freeze them before returning them to the players' lockers.

*   *   *   *

Merloni's best buddy on the Red Sox was Nomar Garciaparra, and while Lou never achieved the level of success enjoyed by the young shortstop, they both shared a great enthusiasm for the game. "Lou is an unbelievable player," said Nomar. "An absolute riot and a great person in the dugout. The kind of person every team needs. The best comment I heard—and it's so true—is what Jimy Williams said about him. He said: 'Your friend over there plays like he's trying to get to another level. He doesn't realize that this is as high as you can get.'"

*   *   *   *

Lou Merloni has lived out the dream of many New England youngsters. Born and still residing in Framingham, Massachusetts, he began his major league career in 1998 with the team he loved as a kid—the Boston Red Sox. Called up to fill in for his pal Nomar Garciaparra, who had suffered a slight right shoulder separation, Merloni flew to Kansas City and arrived around 9:30 or 10 p.m. the night before the game. He realized when he got to the airport that "nobody had told me the name of the team hotel." Should he go to the park? He called Nomar's cellphone, but the evening's game was in progress, and Nomar was in the dugout. After sitting awhile at the airport, and calling from time to time, he finally reached his pal.

He didn't get to the plate in the next three games, but collected his first hit—a single—on May 14. The Red Sox then flew home to host the Royals with Boston mired in a four-game losing streak. Lou's proud parents were in the stands for his Fenway debut, and were also celebrating their 33rd wedding anniversary. Lou's first home appearance came in the second inning, with two men on base. How did the native son handle the pressure of playing in front of friends and family? He homered into the left field screen— a three-run shot off Kansas City Royal pitcher Jose Rosado! The blast provided all the runs the Sox needed, as they beat KC 5-2. One Fenway at-bat, one Fenway homer—instant folk hero.

The *Boston Globe* called it "one of the most electrifying home-town debuts since a 19-year-old kid from Swampscott homered on the first pitch he saw at Fenway in 1964." Conigliaro hit the first pitch; Merloni was working off a 3-2 count. He doubled later in the game and then walked, going 2 for 2.

Lou's second homer was almost an entire season and over 200 at-bats later, on October 2, 1999. He was to wait even longer before he'd achieve #3. He didn't hit a single homer in 2000 and it wasn't until September 28, 2001 that he hit his third—it was a pinch-hit ninth-inning home run in Detroit, in a game Boston lost 4-1.

The Monday after that, though, Boston was in Tampa Bay, and Lou hit two more—both in the same game. In one game, he'd equaled his career output between May 15, 1998 and September 27, 2001!

"It was Lou Merloni Night," manager Joe Kerrigan said. "He had a great series [6 for 9 with two home runs, two doubles, and four RBIs]." No, manager Joe Kerrigan did not put Merloni in the cleanup slot the next night. He had his hot-hitting shortstop take the night off.

Doug Mirabelli

Catching any knuckleball requires a bit of artistry for a catcher, and catching Tim Wakefield's was a challenge. From 2001 through 2005, he benefitted from the personal touch of backstop Doug Mirabelli – but Mirabelli was traded to the Padres for Mark Loretta after the 2005 campaign. Josh Bard was asked to catch Wake, but he struggled – badly. After ten passed balls in seven April games, the Sox decided to make a move and hastily traded Bard and pitcher Cla Meredith to San Diego to bring back Doug. He arrived in the nick of time on May 13, just 13 minutes before first pitch, actually changing into his uniform in the back seat of a State Police cruiser that whisked him to Fenway from the airport. There is no separation of baseball and state when it comes to the Red Sox in Boston. Mirabelli later admitted he'd risked a lot that day; he'd played the game without wearing a protective cup.

Dave Morehead

Dave Morehead threw the last no-hitter in Fenway Park. It happened more than a third of a century ago, on September 16, 1965. He'd just turned 23 a few days earlier and was coming off a 1964 season when he was 8-15 with a 4.97 ERA. The game took two hours exactly and boosted Morehead's record to 10-16. No one would have anticipated a no-hitter from the young rightie, especially since he was pitching for a Red Sox team that lost 100 games that year. Only 1,247 fans even bothered to show up at the park that day.

Later that same evening, after Tom Yawkey gave Morehead a thousand dollar bonus, General Manager Pinky Higgins was released and replaced by the capable Dick O'Connell. The move had been planned for some time, and couldn't be deferred despite the awkwardness of announcing it almost literally during the celebration over the no-hitter. It was the third no-hitter for Sox pitchers in four years. Both Earl Wilson and Bill Monbouquette had thrown no-no's in 1962.

Morehead's no-hitter was near the tail end of a lackluster—well, let's face it, dismal—season for the Red Sox (62-100, 40 games out of first.) His next time out he got bombed, and some wit in the crowd yelled, "Atta boy, Vander Meer!" in mocking reference to the only pitcher to throw back-to-back no-hit games.

✴   ✴   ✴   ✴

One 1966 evening in Lakeland, Florida, Morehead went out with fellow pitcher Earl Wilson and another player to get a drink at a local club called Cloud 9. Seeing Wilson, a black man, the barman said, "We don't serve niggers in here," so the party got up and left. Sox GM Dick O'Connell told the players to stop going there, but when the Boston press reported the incident, they ignored the bigger story of racial discrimination to chide the trio for going out to drink.

Ed Morris

R ed Sox pitcher Ed Morris (42-45 lifetime; 419 ERA) was stabbed to death at his own farewell party as he prepared to leave for spring training in 1932.

Daniel Nava

I t was the sort of dream any 9- or 10-year old boy has, and the fantasy came true for Daniel Nava of the Red Sox. He didn't come up the usual way; he was never drafted, but Red Sox scout Jared Porter signed him out of independent league baseball. On June 12, 2010, Nava had been called to the big leagues and he found himself at Fenway coming to bat against Joe Blanton of the

Philadelphia Phillies. The bases were loaded. The first pitch he saw, BAM! A grand slam home run. The only thing that could have been better is if he'd done it again his second time up – and the situation presented itself the very next inning: bases loaded. He struck out. Daniel led off the fifth and proved his hitting hadn't entirely been a fluke, as he doubled to deep center field. By the end of the season, he'd hit .242, with 26 RBIs, but not added another homer.

Bobo Newsom

Bobo made more moves than a hobo—and held a job about as long. Bobo played for 17 different teams in 20 years, some of them more than once. The peripatetic pitcher played for the Senators in part of 1935, all of 1936, part of 1937, the beginning of 1942, the end of 1943, the end of 1946 and start of 1947 and lastly, for ten games in 1952. During his travels, he cruised through Boston and won 13 while losing 10 in 1937.

Newsom "kept a hutch of rabbits in his room just for the company. But he forgot about them when he went on the road and they ate their way through the hotel furnishings. Manager Joe Cronin was presented the bill, and soon thereafter Bobo was sent packing."— Okrent & Wulf.

You can bet that Jimy Williams would have had him out of there by the fourth inning, but unhampered by any pitch count, Newsom threw 181 pitches and walked ten batters, and *still* managed to win a 1937 game by the score of 3-2.

Trot Nixon

Humiliating rookies is a practice as old and honored as the game of baseball itself. On Sunday, September 19, 1999, the Red Sox, in the midst of an AL East pennant race with the hated Yankees, were hosting the Detroit Tigers at Fenway. In the top of the eighth, with the Red Sox up 7-3, the near-capacity Fenway crowd broke into spontaneous applause. Savvy fans knew what was up. Glancing toward the out-of-town scoreboard they saw that the Yankees were losing to Cleveland 7-6—and in a pennant race, that's more than enough to get a Boston crowd excited. Newcomers to Fenway, however, might be a bit confused—even those in uniform.

Red Sox right fielder Trot Nixon, a promising rookie who had homered in his previous at-bat, had no idea what was going on. As the applause grew in intensity, veteran center fielder Damon Buford explained that the fans were paying tribute to him for the home run he'd hit and that it was traditional to acknowledge such a tribute with a tip of the hat. Not wanting to appear ungrateful, Nixon reluctantly obliged. Not until the end of the inning did he realize that he had been had. "What happened to the camaraderie?" the embarrassed freshman moaned to reporters. "Love in the outfield? There's no love there! Next time I won't even listen to him."

*   *   *   *

Trot Nixon was the most recent in a lengthy list of players who've started in right field for the Red Sox. The Opening Day right fielder changed 14 years in a row.

1988	Mike Greenwell
1989	Dwight Evans
1990	Kevin Romine
1991	Tom Brunansky
1992	Phil Plantier
1993	Andre Dawson
1994	Billy Hatcher
1995	Mark Whiten
1996	Rudy Pemberton
1997	Troy O'Leary
1998	Darren Bragg
1999	Trot Nixon
2000	Darren Lewis
2001	Trot Nixon

There have been numerous cases of players being hit in the cup, but usually it doesn't end up as a ground-rule double. On August 8, 2001, with both teams battling for the American League wild-card berth, the Red Sox were playing the Oakland A's in Oakland. In the third inning of that contest, Sox right-fielder Trot Nixon was confronted with a perplexing situation. With Frank Castillo on the mound for the Red Sox in the third inning, Oakland hitter Johnny Damon (now with the Red Sox) lined a shot down the first base line and into the right-field corner. The area was strewn with refuse, and when Nixon went to retrieve the ball he found it firmly lodged in the bottom of a discarded beverage cup. Damon steamed around the bases taking advantage of Nixon's momentary bewilderment. Quickly assessing the situation, Nixon motioned urgently toward the cup, asking for an umpire's ruling. After a long huddle, the umpires ruled it a ground-rule double, despite arguments from Oakland manager Art Howe that it should have been at least a triple.

"I reached into the cup a couple of times and couldn't pull it out," said the right-fielder later. "I gave it a couple of good shakes, and it still wouldn't come out, so I threw the cup with the ball in it into the stands." Where presumably it became a unique souvenir for some lucky fan.

Several months later, Trot told a dinner audience, "Something told me not to mess with it. I did get on TV because of it, though. I wonder how much money we could have made on eBay with that cup!"

Russ Nixon

Russ Nixon was traded twice to the Red Sox in 1960. First for Sammy White, then later with Carroll Hardy for Marty Keough and Ted Bowsfield. In 1962, Nixon hit two pinch singles in one inning for the Red Sox.

In a case of premature adjudication, Nixon, catching for the Red Sox against the Yankees, mistakenly thought there were two outs instead of one. When he caught a ball in the dirt on a third strike, he flipped the ball to the batter, Yankee Phil Mikkelson, and trotted back to the dugout. The whole Red Sox team, responding to Nixon's gesture, started to run in as well. Mikkelson tossed the ball into fair territory, towards the mound, and ran all the way around to second before the Sox recovered. Mikkelson later scored.

Hideo Nomo

Not only did Nomo pitch a no-hitter for the Red Sox in 2001, their first since Matt Young threw one in a losing effort in 1992, but he also was the strikeout king of the American League that year with 220. He had previously won the K crown in the National League in 1995 with the Los Angeles Dodgers.

Buck O'Brien

In 1912, pitcher Buck O'Brien shared accommodations with his catcher Bill Carrigan and Red Sox shortstop Heinie Wagner. One day they were facing the Cleveland Indians and their star, Nap Lajoie. After two quick strikes, O'Brien tried to brush Lajoie back, only to have him poleax the ball to the furthest reaches of centerfield and plate two runs. Next time up O'Brien again got two strikes on the Frenchman and then called for a mound conference with his battery-mate.

"What do you want to throw to him?" asked Carrigan. "I think I'll throw an old-fashioned roundhouse curve," came the reply. "I've never tried that on him before. It should catch him by surprise." Lajoie was so surprised that he lashed a bullet straight at Wagner at short. It caught him on the hip and caromed into the outfield. The three roomies gathered at the mound to discuss these events. "Buck," said Wagner, " If you throw that Frenchman any more like that, you'd better find somewhere else to sleep tonight."

✳   ✳   ✳   ✳

O'Brien was 20-13 with a 2.58 ERA for the Sox in 1912, helping them win the pennant. The World Series was rough, though. The Red Sox beat the Giants 4-3 in Game One, then struggled to a 6-6 tie in Game Two, called after 11 innings on account of darkness.

Game Three was a 2-1 squeaker, but O'Brien took the loss. Boston won Games Four and Five, but O'Brien gave up five runs in the first inning of Game Six—and the Red Sox lost, 5-2. O'Brien was 0-2, and it was rumored that he was beaten up by his teammates after the game! The Red Sox denied the reports. The Sox eventually won the Series, but O'Brien—who had been 5-1 in 1911 and won 20 in 1912, sunk to 4-9 in 1913 and was traded to the White Sox later in the year.

Troy O'Leary

In Games Four and Five of the 1999 Cleveland-Boston series, first John Valentin and then Troy O'Leary drove in seven runs in back-to-back games. In O'Leary's case, he taught Indians manager Mike Hargrove a little bit about respect in the process. Because red-hot Nomar Garciaparra had homered in the first inning, Hargrove elected to walk Nomar in the third, despite the fact that the strategic ploy loaded the bases. O'Leary promptly hit the first offering out for a grand slam home run. In the seventh, Hargrove again decided to walk Nomar to pitch to Troy. Similar result—a three-run homer to win the game for the Red Sox. A few days later, Hargrove was out of a job. R-E-S-P-E-C-T! Sox it to me!

Gene Oliver

It was said of weak-throwing former Red Sox catcher Gene Oliver that he had an arm like the Venus de Milo.

Johnny Orlando

When longtime Red Sox clubhouse man Johnny Orlando died, it was widely rumored that his friend Ted Williams scattered his ashes over the left field grass at Fenway Park. Supposedly, Orlando's will stipulated that his remains be spread on the ground where Williams had played. Authorities at

Fenway Park apparently objected, and so Williams discreetly went out and carried out his friend's wish.

David Ortiz

Tom Verducci wrote in *Sports Illustrated*: "David Ortiz never walks alone. People—teammates, opponents, officials, fans, even Yankee fans—are drawn to the perpetual sunlight that is his personality." He led the league in RBIs two years running—2005 and 2006—and his 54 homers in '05 not only led the league but set a franchise record. That September he was presented a plaque by the owners of the Red Sox, calling him "The Greatest Clutch History in the History of the Boston Red Sox." The list of his clutch hits is too long to detail here, but two of them on the same calendar day will never—ever—be forgotten by those who lived through the 2004 American League Championship Series. After the Sox had lost the first three games to the Yankees and were facing elimination, up came David Ortiz in the bottom of the 12th inning of Game Four. It was after midnight on October 18. Manny Ramirez had singled to left to lead off the inning, and on a 2-1 count, Big Papi homered to win the game, 6-4. That evening, Game Five ran even longer—tied 4-4 in the 14th inning. Two of those four runs had been driven in by David. A strikeout and a walk, another strikeout and another walk put men on first and second with two outs. On a 2-1 count, Ortiz singled to center field scoring the speedy Johnny Damon from second base for his second straight walkoff hit. Ortiz drove in 11 runs in the seven-game ALCS.

He was a sparkplug again in the postseason, batting .714 in the 2007 ALDS, and .333 in that year's World Series sweep of the Colorado Rockies. Four games, four runs batted in for "Big Papi." In 2013, he hit a dramatic grand slam in the bottom of the eighth of Game Two of the ALCS against the Tigers, a hit forever immortalized by a well-positioned photographer who captured the upturned legs of the Tigers' Torii Hunter spilling into the Red Sox bullpen in a vain effort to catch the ball, paired with the upraised arms—in a victorious "V"—of a Boston city policeman stationed in the pen. The slam turned a 5-1 Detroit lead into a tie game and set up a walk-off win in the bottom of the ninth. Ortiz then, in the next round of the playoffs, hit for a nearly unbelievable .688 batting average, with six RBIs, in that year's World Series win over the St. Louis Cardinals. It was no surprise that he was named World Series MVP.

Big Papi acknowledges cheers from the Fenway Faithful in his last year as a Red Sox.

Pretty good for a guy the Minnesota Twins put on the scrap heap. They didn't even trade him. In December 2002, in a move that will forever haunt the franchise, they just released him. Fortunately, it appears that Pedro Martinez urged the Red Sox to snap him up, and new GM Theo Epstein did just that, signing Ortiz the following month, in January 2003. All he did that year was hit 31 homers and drive in 101 runs and help the Sox get to within a game of the World Series.

His infectious smile and larger-than-life "Teddy Bear"-seeming personality has long been a magnet for young children (not to mention young-at-heart older folks). He has made countless charitable appearances and visits to the Jimmy Fund clinics and elsewhere. The David Ortiz Children's Fund has literally saved the lives of as many as 500 children both in New England and his native Dominican Republic.

In 2011, Ortiz received the prestigious Roberto Clemente Award, Major League Baseball's highest honor, presented to "those who best represent the game of baseball through their positive contributions on and off the field." But if there is one moment that stands out, it was in his bonding with six-year-old Maverick Schutte, who had been born with a congenital heart defect and undergone 40 (yes, forty!) surgeries in his very young life. Ortiz taped a video for Maverick saying he'd try to hit him a home run. He did, and Maverick sent him a video back saying, "Big Papi, you never let me down, and you're the best player ever in the Red Sox game." When Maverick was finally able to come to Fenway Park (from Cheyenne, Wyoming), the moment he saw Ortiz and shouted an excited "Big Papi!" was also captured on video, and it's yours to see and enjoy, thanks to the Internet.

Ortiz also had a very serious and resolute side, which he showed one day at Fenway Park—using a bad word that in the moment offended almost no one. It was after the 2013 Boston Marathon bombing when two jihadists killed a seven-year-old boy with a homemade bomb, and two young women as well. The city of Boston responded with the "Boston Strong" slogan—helping hold an emotionally-shaken city together. Before the first game the Red Sox played at home after the bombing, Ortiz took the microphone and declared, "This is our f****ing city!" He told NESN's Tom Caron, "We are entertainers. We are superheroes for some kids. We are on TV. We are famous, whatever. But we are also human and citizens just like everybody else. And when it comes to what happened at the Marathon, they did it to all of us."

In his final year, the 20th of his career, Ortiz just kept going. He led the American League with 127 RBIs, led the league in slug-

Mel Parnell

ging percentage, and was the only player in the league to top 1.000 in OPS (on-base-percentage plus slugging), with a 1.021 mark. He hit 38 homers. This all won him—for the second time—the league's Hank Aaron Award for the top offensive player in the league. He had won it before in 2005. Pretty good for a guy in his retirement year—arguably the best season ever for a player leaving the game on his own terms.

Mel Parnell

Mel Parnell was a left-handed Red Sox pitcher (1947-1956) and two-time 20-game winner. In 1953, he shut out the Yankees four times, and on July 14, 1956, at the age of 34, he pitched a no-hitter—a 4-0 shutout of the Chicago White Sox, the first for the Red Sox since 1923. The 1956 gem was the only no-hitter that a pitcher ended with an unassisted put-out. On the last play, the ball was hit back to Parnell on the first base side of the mound. He came off the mound and made the play and continued on to first base to record the final out. Red Sox first baseman Mickey Vernon said: "What's the matter, fella, you don't have any confidence in me?" Replied Parnell: "Mickey, I have all the confidence in the world in you. I just didn't have any in myself—I may have thrown it away."

✷　✷　✷　✷

The 1948 playoff-game loss to Cleveland is among the most disappointing games in Red Sox history. No one was more disappointed than southpaw ace Mel Parnell, who was expecting to start the game. Just before game time, manager Joe McCarthy told Parnell he had decided to go with right-hander Denny Galehouse instead. When the manager informed Galehouse of the change, Parnell says that the surprised pitcher "turned ghostly white." The Indians defeated the Sox 8-3 to capture the American League pennant.

Dustin Pedroia

L isted at 5-foot-9, but clearly two or three inches shorter, Dustin Pedroia has an outsized sense of his own baseball worth. The first time he met *Boston Globe* sportswriter Peter Abraham, he asked Pete, "Have you got any kids?" Pete responded that he did not. Pedroia came back: "You gotta get some so when they grow up you can tell them you covered me." He backed up his braggadocio with deeds: in 2007, his first full year, he hit .317 and won the Rookie of the Year award. He was the first batter up for the Red Sox in Game One of the 2007 World Series and hit a laser over the left-field wall, giving the Sox a lead they never relinquished.

Only later was it learned that Pedey had played the final two months of the season with a cracked hamate bone in his left hand. What did he do for an encore? Only become the Most Valuable Player in the American League in 2008, with a mere 81% of the

Dustin Pedroia goes airborne to avoid a sliding Yankees runner.

vote. The man who somehow became known as "the Muddy Chicken" led the league in runs scored in both '08 and '09, and hit .307 while winning his second Gold Glove in 2011.

Pedroia is seemingly always the first Red Sox player in uniform and out on the field before games, sometimes sitting alone with his bat on the dugout bench four hours before the game. It helps that he lives just a block or two from the ballpark. Red Sox ownership instinctively grasped how important his gameness and spirit were to the Red Sox. In midseason 2013, they signed the Sox second baseman to an eight-year, $110 million deal. It was Pedroia who had approached them the year before, saying he wanted to stay in Boston—even though he still had three years left on his original deal. The Sox stepped up to the plate. It was a win for both sides.

Eddie Pellagrini

Like Tony Conigliaro and Lou Merloni, another local who homered in his first Fenway at-bat was Eddie Pellagrini. The year was 1946. The date was April 22. Pellagrini recalls that Ted Williams congratulated him, but warned, "Eddie, that's the worst thing you could have done, because now they're going to pitch you like they pitch me!"

✳   ✳   ✳   ✳

Pellagrini had 1,423 major league at-bats, but knocked only 19 others out of parks around the leagues, hitting .226 in his career. His main claim to fame, to hear him tell it, was the year he "led the league in stolen towels."

Johnny Pesky

To many fans across New England, Johnny Pesky is Mr. Red Sox. In Game Seven of the 1946 World Series, Pesky was unfairly accused of holding the ball too long, allowing the St. Louis Cardinals' Enos Slaughter to dash home with the winning run. During the off-season, Pesky returned to his home state of Oregon to escape the unwanted attention from Boston fans and media. As part of his "therapy," he attended a college football game between Oregon and Oregon State. The two teams fumbled the ball throughout the sloppily played game, and the crowd became somewhat loud and abusive. Enjoying his anonymity, Pesky felt relaxed . . . until he heard a fan shout: "Give the ball to Pesky; he'll hold on to it."

*   *   *   *

Mel Parnell claims that he was responsible for naming Fenway's right-field foul pole "Pesky's Pole." "Johnny didn't have great power, but he had great bat control and could spray the ball around," says Parnell. "This made him a great number-two hitter hitting behind DiMaggio because if Dom got on, Johnny could move him around, either by bunting or by placing the ball. But every once in awhile he'd hit one out, curving it around that pole. I said: 'Johnny, that's your pole. That's Pesky's pole.' And it stuck."

*   *   *   *

Johnny Pesky achieved 11 straight hits in 1946—one short of the record held by two other Sox, Pinky Higgins and Dropo—and didn't realize it. When he came up the 12th time in a close game with George Metkovich on first base, Pesky decided to lay down a hit-and-run to protect him and move him over. The next two times up, Pesky got hits each time. Managers Joe Cronin and Joe McCarthy both gave Pesky the chance to call his own plays.

*   *   *   *

Pesky is one of two players who were in uniform for the only two American League sudden-death play-off games—in 1948 and 1978. Pesky played third base for the Red Sox in their 1948 loss

Johnny Pesky

to the Cleveland Indians and occupied the first-base coaching box in the 1978 loss to the Yankees. The man on the winning side on both occasions was Bob Lemon, who was a pitcher with the Indians in '48 and manager of the Yanks in '78.

*   *   *   *

On the last day of the season, Yaz sneaked into the clubhouse and cut up coach Johnny Pesky's clothes. Pesky had to fly back to Boston from Detroit wearing his uniform. Johnny got him back good, though, and quickly. Yaz caught a plane later that day and headed back to his home in Florida. His luggage, however, accompanied the team back to Boston. Johnny was waiting and grabbed Yaz's bag as the luggage was unloaded. He opened the bag and began passing out Yaz's clothes to passersby, shouting: "Here's a Yaz souvenir!" People began grabbing them and soon they were all gone. When Yaz eventually opened his suitcases, they were empty. In the mail some days later he found a Polaroid shot of Pesky with the clothes. Confronting Johnny with photographic evidence of his largesse, Johnny told Yaz: "I'm trying to take them back from the people."

*   *   *   *

Johnny "Needle Nose" Pesky set the major league record for the most runs scored in a game, with six on May 8, 1946.

*   *   *   *

Pesky's 1942 rookie record of 205 hits stood unchallenged until Nomar Garciaparra topped it in 1997 with 209. Pesky totaled over 200 hits each of his first three years in the majors, 1942, 1946 and 1947 (he lost the intervening three years to war.) No one has ever totaled 200 or more hits in each of their first five years in the majors, and Johnny might well have done it for six if the war hadn't intervened.

*   *   *   *

Johnny was no Ted Williams in the slugging department, however, and never tried to be. Fortunately, Pesky knew his role and played it to perfection, seldom going for the long ball. That didn't stop "Needle Nose" from doing some needling now and again. Johnny wore #6 on his uniform and Ted wore #9. Every so often, Johnny would do a handstand on the field and crow, "Look at me now! I'm Ted Williams!" as his inverted jersey read "9".

*   *   *   *

Johnny's principal job was to be one of the table setters for slugger Ted Williams and, indeed, in his first six years he scored over 100 runs every year. Johnny was discouraged from trying to stretch a single into a double, nor was he to steal second once on first: in either case, he'd be leaving first base open with Ted Williams coming to the plate.

Johnny Pesky and Ted Williams are the only two players in ML history to score 100 or more runs in each of their first six years in the majors. Both Earl Combs and Derek Jeter did it six or more consecutive years, but both played a few games the year before their streaks began.

*   *   *   *

In 1950, Billy Goodman was a super-sub supreme. He had no regular position, and Manager Steve O'Neill moved him around where needed. Goodman clocked considerable playing time in left after Ted Williams broke his elbow in the All-Star Game. The ultimate utility man began to accumulate hits. Late in the season, it became clear that he actually had a shot at the batting title, but with Williams coming back on September 15, and the DH not yet devised, what place was there for Goodman to occupy? The infield was made up of such stalwarts as Walt Dropo (that year's rookie of the year with a .322 average and 34 HRs), Bobby Doerr (.294 average), Vern Stephens (.295 and 30 HRs) and Pesky, who was hitting over .310 at the time. The outfielders were all hitting a ton as well.

Rico Petrocelli

Johnny Pesky approached O'Neill and volunteered to yield his position at third base so that Goodman could have a place to play and get the necessary at-bats to qualify for the batting crown. O'Neill took him up on the offer, and Billy Goodman earned himself a batting title. It should be no surprise that it was sometimes said Johnny Pesky led the majors in Most Friends.

Rico Petrocelli

Rico Petrocelli is one third of the answer to a great trivia question: There are three American League players—all former Red Sox—with ten or more letters in their names who have hit 40 or more homers in a season. Can you name them? (Answer: Tony Conigliaro, Carl Yastrzemski, Rico Petrocelli).

Jimmy Piersall

Jimmy Piersall arrived in Boston in 1952 with the reputation as a great fielder with some eccentricities. Teammate Mel Parnell recalls: "I remember pitching a game in Chicago, and I could hear a roar from right field. I turned to look, and all I could see was the number on Jimmy's back. He was facing the stand, leading a locomotive cheer of P-I-E-R-S-A-L-L. If the ball had been hit to right field, he would never have been able to make a play on it."

✴   ✴   ✴   ✴

When former Red Sox center fielder Jimmy Piersall hit the 100th home run of his career while with the Mets, he celebrated by running around the bases backward—perfectly legal at that time but totally unorthodox.

✴   ✴   ✴   ✴

The Red Sox sent Piersall to Birmingham, and apparently his reputation for erratic behavior preceded him. Teammate Mickey McDermott recalls one particular incident: "The umpire called him out on a bad pitch, and he didn't holler, he didn't say nothin', he just reached in his back pocket and pulled out a water pistol and shot the umpire with it. The umpire fainted dead away. After all the stories he'd read about Piersall, he said later: 'I thought the sonofabitch was going to kill me.'"

*　　*　　*　　*

After his hospital treatment at Westborough State Hospital for mental illness, chronicled in his book *Fear Strikes Out,* Piersall couldn't recall anything from over a year of his life. During that time, he played extremely well but was involved in fracas after fracas—fistfights, arguments and all sorts of shenanigans. He had to read news clippings about them later, much to his own mortification. He played to the crowd, taking melodramatic bows in center field after routine plays. He did calisthenics in the field. He ran in from his position behind Dom DiMaggio, imitating the Little Professors distinctive trot on the way back to the dugout. He waved his arms like a chicken when Satchel Paige was pitching. He made oinking pig sounds. He agitated Paige so much that he lost his concentration and wound up surrendering a grand slam to Sammy White. White, for his part, joined in the clowning and crawled the last 10 feet to the plate, kissing it to make contact as the Sox won 11-9.

*　　*　　*　　*

It was a cold and rainy April day at Fenway Park, and the game was delayed several times for pitching changes and sporadic downpours. During one such halt in proceedings, Piersall collected various debris thrown from the bleachers—popcorn containers, programs, newspapers and the like—and piled them behind the old center field flagpole. He then set them ablaze and warmed himself by the fire.

Jimmy Piersall

Jimmy Piersall

*   *   *   *

Jimmy Piersall's reputation as a flake began with his very first major league at-bat. The nervous rookie outfielder entered the game as a pinch-hitter facing Gene Bearden, the crafty pitcher for the Washington Senators. In his book, Piersall describes the result. (Bearden threw a) "baffling knuckle ball … and I was so scared that I threw the bat over the third-base dugout and into the grandstand the first time I ever swung at a ball. Imagine my embarrassment when I found myself standing at the plate without a bat in my hand." Piersall tried to look nonchalant as he strode to the on-deck circle and quietly asked Bill Goodman, "What do I do now?" Goodman gave Piersall a word of encouragement and his bat. Piersall responded by singling to right on a 3 and 2 count.

*   *   *   *

Piersall's career was interrupted by institutionalization and successful treatment for mental illness. He later commented. "Probably the best thing that ever happened to me was going nuts. Whoever heard of Jimmy Piersall until this happened?"

*   *   *   *

Asked about the time Piersall sat on second base while Ryne Duren was batting during a game at the Stadium, he said, "Someone said to Casey Stengel, referring to me, 'Is he really Goofy?' Casey said, 'He's the only guy in the park who knows where to play Duren.'"

*   *   *   *

Piersall also said, "I was always a Red Sox fan. I hated the Yankees from the day I came out of my mother's womb."

*   *   *   *

One day Piersall went 6-for-6 at the plate, still tied for the American League nine-inning record, while the great Ted Williams had an off day, going 0-for-4. Piersall could hardly sleep that night, anticipating the glowing reports of his feat in the morning sports pages. "The headline in the paper the next day was that Williams went 0-for-4 for the first time in two years," groans Piersall.

*   *   *   *

Asked to talk about the time he sat on Babe Ruth's monument in Yankee Stadium, Piersall says: "It was the second game of a double-header and we had about eight pitchers walking in and out of the bullpen. So I got tired of that and sat on Babe's monument. I didn't want to make a farce of things, but we were having such a bad day. When the game resumed, the umpire came out and told me I couldn't sit on the monuments. I said to him, 'I'm talking to the Babe.'"

Eddie Popowski

When Eddie Popowski died in 2001, he'd been with the Red Sox for every one of his 64 seasons in pro ball. He'd been a player (stuck behind Bobby Doerr, he never made it to big league play), a coach (1967-74, 1976) and even interim manager of the Red Sox twice—in 1969 and 1973. "The first 50 years were the toughest," he used to say. Since 1975, he'd been a special assignment instructor along with Johnny Pesky and Charlie Wagner.

Way back in 1931, he'd quit driving an ice truck and taken a job playing with the House of David touring baseball team—and was once stopped by police in Ohio who were searching for John Dillinger. Easy mistake to make: both Dillinger and Popowski were driving Packards. With the House of David, he played against the likes of Babe Ruth and Lou Gehrig, and against Negro League clubs featuring such stars as Josh Gibson and Satchel Paige.

In the 1960s, after Ted Williams had retired, he and Pop were watching a prospect in the batting cage and they differed on his potential. They placed a little one dollar wager, Williams betting the kid would get three hits in that day's game. Instead he struck out three times. Ted tugged a dollar out of his billfold and provided Pop with an instant keepsake: a one dollar bill inscribed, "I lost, Ted Williams." Pop kept that dollar with him until his dying day.

*   *   *   *

In the fall of 2001, the Red Sox lost Pop, with 64 years of service, switchboard operator Helen Robinson, with 60 years of service and long-time scout Joe Stephenson, who had served the team for 53 years.

Dick Radatz

Dick "The Monster" Radatz stood 6'6" and tipped the scales at 240 pounds. The relief specialist was that rarest and most beloved phenomenon in Boston—a Yankee killer. Many Red Sox fans have an enduring image of Dick Radatz, arms raised straight up in a victory salute, walking off the mound after saving another game against the hated Yankees. He was also very cocky. In 1963, Red Sox pitcher Earl Wilson was leading the Yanks 2-1 in the ninth, but proceeded to load the bases. After a brief mound conference, Wilson let manager Johnny Pesky know that it might be time to bring on the Monster. Pesky brought in the fire-balling reliever to kill the New York rally. As the two pitchers met briefly at the mound, Radatz said to Wilson: "Why don't you crack me a beer? I'll be right in." Ten pitches and three strikeouts later, Mickey Mantle, Roger Maris and Elston Howard had been retired on strikes and Radatz was sharing a cool one with his appreciative teammate.

*   *   *   *

One of the best relievers of his or any era, Dick Radatz struck out 478 batters in 414 innings over a three-year span. Even more impressive, over a four-year period from 1962 to 1965, he played a significant role in 149 of Boston's 286 victories! "I was a one-pitch pitcher," said the fireballer from Detroit. "Either hit it or get out. I literally thrived for that one-on-one confrontation. I had to have that challenge like I needed three square meals a day."

Now a radio talk show personality in Boston, the man they called "The Monster" never lost favor with the fans at Fenway. In four-plus years with the Sox, from '62 to the start of the '66 season—some of the most depressingly dismal years in recent Red Sox history—Radatz won 49 and lost 34 for Boston. He was one of the first specialty relievers in the game, often brought in day after day. Twice he led the league in saves, no mean feat for a team that was often in or near the American League basement. More importantly to Boston fans, he was a Yankee killer, mowing down the heavy hitters from the Bronx with apparent ease.

Mickey Mantle had a particularly hard time with The Monster. Mantle faced Radatz 63 times. He managed just one hit—a home run—(yes, that's a .016 average) and struck out 47 times.

Radatz was a mediocre 3-7 in the three years after he left Boston and he credits the atmosphere in Fenway Park for making the difference. "Fenway Park is so intimate it's like playing a slow-pitch game in your neighborhood. And when you're on a roll, the fans are with you. And because I knew the fans were with me, it put a couple of extra inches on the fastball."

Manny Ramirez

Red Sox fans had been all over diminutive Craig Grebeck (5'7", 155 pounds) in 2001 because of his hitting struggles, but the utility infielder quietly played a part in two of the most memorable hits in Fenway Park's recent history.

Frustrated by a string of splintered bats, Manny Ramirez asked Grebeck if he could borrow a few of his bats prior to a Saturday game against Toronto. The results were unforgettable. Ramirez promptly hit a pair of tremendous home runs that together traveled an estimated 964 feet.

On June 23, 2001, Manny Ramirez slugged two home runs at Fenway in a 9-6 loss to the Toronto Blue Jays. Both were powerful blasts. In the first inning, Manny hit a 463-foot homer off the light tower above the fence in left-center field. Ramirez came up again in the third and launched a massive drive high up on the light stanchion behind the Green Monster that fell 12 inches short of glory.

It was estimated as a 501-foot drive, which would make it the second longest in Fenway Park history, trailing only a 502-foot blast by Ted Williams, hit in 1946, and which is memorialized by the famous red seat high up in the right field bleachers.

Many took note of the fact that Manny's home run was judged to have fallen short of matching Ted's record by just one foot. Both were indeed powerful drives, Ted's easily measured, Manny's necessarily estimated. The greater power may well have been that of Red Sox reverence for tradition, and sentiment—when you're an icon like Ted Williams, it's worth at least a foot on the old measuring tape.

✳   ✳   ✳   ✳

"Manny being Manny"—so the saying went, fondly—until he wore out his welcome in Boston by quitting on his teammates, not to mention bullying traveling secretary Jack McCormick by knocking the 74-year-old to the floor for not promptly arranging complimentary tickets for Manny's guests. He was often the good-natured butt of the boys at the start of games; when everyone was supposed to run out together to take their positions before the game, many times the other Sox held back, leaving Manny running out all by himself. One memorable time, he initiated it. The day after he was sworn in as an American citizen, he ran out to take his position carrying a small American flag while the sound system played "I'm Proud To Be An American".

Once in left field, one never knew quite what to expect. It looked as though he was the most casual of outfielders, more than once seen with a plastic water bottle in his hip pocket, and another time falling onto the ball he was supposed to be fielding. He caught some baserunners by surprise, though, and led the league in outfield assists in 2005, with 17. He was the World Series MVP in 2004, despite a dismal fielding percentage of .750: two errors in eight chances.

Then there was the time in 2005 when he disappeared into the wall on left field on July 18. It was a 1-1 game, in the top of the sixth. There were two outs and the bases had just been loaded on a walk. A mound conference was convened, and Manny took a moment to duck into the wall. When Wade Miller wound up and threw home, Manny was fortunate that Tampa Bay's Joey Gathright took the pitch – he had only just emerged from inside the Green Monster. On the next pitch, Gathright singled in two – with a hit to left field. Miller was later befuddled when asked if he hadn't checked to see that all his fielders were in the outfield. "Why would I check?" When Manny was asked what he was doing during his break, he said he had peed into a cup. "I'm just glad he came back," said Sox skipper Francona.

Jim Rice

Jim Rice was the Red Sox's best right-handed hitter since Jimmie Foxx and, also like Foxx, one of the strongest men in the major leagues. On more than one occasion he checked his swing and snapped the bat in half. Asked how he would position his outfield against Rice, Kansas City manager Whitey Herzog once said: "What I'd really like to do is put two guys on top of the CITGO sign and two in the net."

✳   ✳   ✳   ✳

The number 406 holds double significance for Red Sox fans. Any fan worth his salt knows that in 1941 Ted Williams hit .406 to become the last man in major-league history to bat .400 for an

Jim Rice

entire season. But Jim Rice also achieved a 406 milestone. In 1978, the Red Sox strongman accumulated 406 total bases, the first to reach the 400 level since Hank Aaron managed exactly 400 in 1959. Rice became the first American Leaguer to hit this elusive mark since Joe DiMaggio did it 41 years earlier. Rice had 213 hits, including 46 homers and 15 triples, and led the majors in both categories. He also led in RBIs (139) and slugging percentage (.600) while batting .315. He was named AL MVP.

★　　★　　★　　★

Rice was the first player ever to amass over 200 hits and 35 home runs in three consecutive seasons ('77-'79.)

There was no wasted motion in Rice's powerful swing. One of strongest men ever to play the game, he boasted that he never lifted a weight. "Anyone who has to doesn't have a chance," he said. When that strength was uncorked with his short stride and flick of his bat, the results were often explosive. Rice loved his golf as well and had equal power in his drives. U.S. Open champion Lou Graham once said that Rice could hit a golf ball farther than anyone on the pro tour at the time.

★　　★　　★　　★

Jim Rice set a major league record by appearing in 163 regular-season games in 1978. Those of you who don't know why there were 163 games in 1978 are suffering from selective amnesia and are no doubt living happy and productive lives wallowing in this blissful ignorance.

★　　★　　★　　★

From the moment when Ted Williams began playing left field in 1940 (he played 1939 as a right fielder) through Yaz's years and then Rice's which ended in 1987 (as the regular left fielder), just those three Red Sox legends roamed Fenway's left-field grass for 48 years, nearly half a century, save for the years Ted was off at war.

$$* \quad * \quad * \quad *$$

In 1999, many Red Sox fans were outraged when Red Sox ace Pedro Martinez was snubbed for the MVP award in favor of Ivan "Pudge "Rodriguez, the great catcher for the Texas Rangers. Those Red Sox fans with a longer memory, however, were more philosophical, recalling that in 1978 the situation was reversed. Jim Rice captured the '78 MVP title over Yankee pitcher Ron Guidry who won 24 games for the Yankees, lost only three and compiled a microscopic 1.72 ERA. Rice finished the campaign with a .315 batting average and led the league with 213 hits, 46 home runs, and 139 RBIs.

$$* \quad * \quad * \quad *$$

Jim Rice, in *My Greatest Day in Baseball,* gives credits to his teammates: "When you come to my house, my wife's got pictures of Fenway Park, she's got pictures of me sitting on the bench when a guy was doing a photograph session. Everything else in my house—you see books, it's all golf, no baseball. Baseball was more of a team thing. Even the things that I accomplished are because of the team getting me in certain situations. But if you come to my house you'll see all golf books."

Dave Roberts

It's quite a thing to be lionized forever for traveling 90 feet in one game. Okinawa native Dave Roberts came to the Red Sox in midseason 2004. He hit .256 and drove in 14 runs during the second half of his season, once he came to town. But it was "The Steal" which made him famous forever. The Sox faced elimination in Game Four of the '04 ALCS. After being bounced from the playoffs by the Yankees the year before, they'd lost the first three games of the LCS, the third one by a humiliating 19-8 score. In Game Four, they fell behind 2-0 and were still down by a run, 4-3, after eight innings. And only the greatest closer of all time – Mariano Rivera – was on the mound for New York. Kevin Millar walked to lead off the ninth. When Terry Francona told Roberts to pinch-run, the entire baseball world knew Roberts had been charged with stealing second base, to get himself into scoring position. He did. And scored, when Bill Mueller followed with a single to center. The game was tied. It took until the bottom of the 12th to resolve matters. Big Papi homered. Boston lived, for another day. Roberts never had an at-bat in the Series, but he did score another run – the very next night. Again pinch-running for Millar, who had again walked while the Sox were down by one run – this time in the eighth inning - he advanced around the bases and scored the run which tied the game and ultimately sent it into extras. Those were his only two appearances of the ALCS, and he never had to be called upon in the World Series.

Si Rosenthal

Outfielder Si Rosenthal was a Boston native who broke in late in 1925 and enjoyed one solid season with the Sox in '26, hitting .267 with 34 RBIs. A foot injury held him back from a more fruitful major league career, but he did go on to log a .333 average over the next nine years in minor league play. Rosenthal's son Irwin joined the Marines in World War II and was killed in the Pacific on Christmas, 1943. Si himself signed up in the Navy, at age 40. Assigned to the minesweeper *U.S.S. Miantonomah,* Rosenthal was seriously injured in an explosion caused by a German mine off the coast of France and was rendered paraplegic. A few years later, the Red Sox held a "Day" for him and raised money to buy him a specially fitted house.

*   *   *   *

When Si first signed with the Boston Red Sox organization, Hugh Duffy was the manager. Si told the story like this: "Duffy wanted me to change my name to Rose because it would fit easier in box scores. But I told him that I wouldn't do it. I was born with the name Rosenthal. It won't make any difference if my name is Rose, Rosenthal or O'Brien. I'll rise and fall on my own name." A rose by any other name. . . .

Red Ruffing

Red Ruffing won 39 games and lost 96 (including 25 in 1928 alone) for the Red Sox—and still made it into the Hall of Fame! It was his good fortune to be traded to the Yankees, where he then won 231 while losing only 125. As a Red Sox pitcher, Ruffing had been 1 and 14 against the Yankees, but playing well in New York always seems to help in Hall of Fame voting. Ruffing had lost four toes on one foot in a coal mining accident and had to wear a special shoe. It was off Ruffing that Ted Williams hit the ball to the famous "red seat" at Fenway, more than halfway up the right-field bleachers.

Pete Runnels

Only five players have ever won two batting titles and still manage to hit under .300 lifetime. A pair of them won two titles for the Red Sox: Pete Runnels (1960 and 1962, lifetime .291) and Yaz (1963, 1967 and 1968, lifetime .285.)

*   *   *   *

Billy Consolo remembers the battles between Runnels and teammate Ted Williams. "Every time Pete Runnels got a base hit, Ted Williams would just follow him, and Ted had less at-bats so he was going up two points when Runnels would go up a point. That's how he won [the batting title]. Runnels hit probably two or three home runs a year. Runnels finally hit a home run and so all of us on the bench said, "OK, now Runnels has got it. I mean, he's *hitting?*" He hit a gut shot out of the ballpark in Washington and Ted Williams followed him with a gut shot over the right field fence. Topped him with every thing he did! If Runnels hit a double, Ted Williams would follow him with a double. It was back and forth. In those days, they didn't have the electronic scoreboard so somebody behind the scoreboard was putting up these numbers. The guy must have been multiplying behind the scoreboard, to the tenth of a point."

Babe Ruth

When Babe Ruth first came up to the Red Sox it was as a pitcher, but even then he liked to hit. He insisted on taking his cuts in batting practice. One day, he arrived at the ballpark to discover that all his bats had been sawed in half by resentful teammates. Despite this setback, Ruth went on to have a rather respectable hitting career.

* * * *

When Ruth was sold to the Yankees and moved from the pitcher's mound to the outfield, his former Red Sox teammate Tris Speaker offered the following words of wisdom: "Ruth made a grave mistake when he gave up pitching. Working once a week, he might have lasted a long time and become a great star."

* * * *

On July 16, 1918, the Boston Red Sox and the St. Louis Browns were tied 1-1 in the bottom of the ninth. With a runner on first, Babe Ruth hit the ball out of the park to win the game. However, in those days, the game was declared over when the winning run scored, therefore Ruth was credited with a triple and not a home run.

* * * *

Babe Ruth

After Red Sox owner Harry Frazee had sold Babe Ruth to the New York Yankees, Bostonians were justifiably outraged. One frigid January evening, Frazee and some friends from the theatrical world were out on the town. Frazee wanted to show that he was a man of some importance in the city. So, dressed in his best tuxedo, he hailed a cab and instructed the driver to proceed to Fenway Park. The cabbie overheard part of the backseat conversation and deduced who his passenger was. When they arrived at the ballpark, the driver asked: "Do you own the Red Sox?" Frazee replied proudly: "Why yes, my boy. Yes, I do." The cabbie promptly knocked Frazee on his ample posterior, shook his fist at him and said, "Then you're the %$&% who sold Babe Ruth to the Yankees." With that he drove off with the other passengers, leaving the dazed and bewildered owner sitting in a snow bank.

*   *   *   *

In 1919, Red Sox pitcher Babe Ruth set the baseball world on its collective ear by poling an unheard-of 29 home runs—more than the rest of the American League combined!

*   *   *   *

Ruth has had many nicknames in his colorful career, but the one that fit him best was coined in the September 9 issue of the *Boston Post* when they called him "the Prince of Whales" because of "the way you've been whaling the ball all season." He was also referred to as "the mastodon [sic] of hitters, Babe—the dinosaur of slam artists. If you lived in the Stone Age, you'd doubtless be swinging an elm tree at every boulder they pitched to you." Other quotable quotes from that same newspaper account of Babe's exploits include a couple of hyperbolic gems:

"You are the only *20th Century Express* in Baseball, Babe. You never make local stops at second or third. The only place you stop for water is the dugout after you've gone all the way around."

"We'd have a medal struck out for you, but we know you wouldn't care for anything that's been struck out!"

* * * *

In January of 1920, when Babe Ruth had been sold to the Yankees, the *Boston Post* sub headline was: RUTH TERMED A HANDICAP AND NOT AN ASSET BY THE RED SOX.

* * * *

What pitcher has the best lifetime record against the New York Yankees? Answer: Babe Ruth, 17-5 for the Red Sox.

* * * *

On July 11, 1914, pitcher Babe Ruth won his first game for the Red Sox, 4-3. Ruth struck out the first time up and was lifted for a pinch hitter in the seventh. Looking back on Ruth's later successes, can you imagine lifting Babe Ruth for a pinch hitter?

* * * *

The record for Sox shutouts by a southpaw in a season is 9. It is held by Babe Ruth, a mark he established in 1916. Righties Cy Young and Joe Wood each had 10; Young did it in 1904, Wood in 1912.

* * * *

Babe Ruth's daughter, Julia Ruth Stevens, threw out the first pitch in Game Four of the 1999 ALCS vs the Yankees. She was asked why she was cheering for the Red Sox, instead of the Yankees where her famous father had spent most of his career.

"Because I think they deserve a break," she said firmly. "Well, they do. They've had a lot of tough breaks. And the umpires certainly haven't made it any easier for them, I must say." Now that Red Sox ace Pedro Martinez has suggested drilling the Babe in the rear end with a pitch, we wonder if Ms. Stevens' allegiances have been altered.

Gene "Half-Pint" Rye

Gene "Half-Pint" Rye, who for some unknown reason changed his name from his birth name of Eugene Rudolph Mercantelli, came to the Red Sox from Waco in 1931. He arrived with stunning credentials, having hit three home runs in one inning for the Texas team. In the big leagues, the 5'6", 165-lb Rye was not nearly as potent. In 17 major league games he managed seven hits in 39 at-bats for a watered down .179 batting average. Who knows why? Who really cares? The more interesting question is why he changed his name to Rye in the midst of Prohibition.

Ray Scarborough

Not many ballplayers win an argument with an umpire, but Red Sox pitcher Ray Scarborough did. Obtained from the Washington Senators, Scarborough brought with him a well-deserved reputation as the best bench jockey in baseball. He could get on guys and really run them ragged. At that time, Bill McGowan was considered the number-one umpire in the American League—at least by himself. One day, while umpiring behind home plate, he had missed several close pitches.

From the Sox dugout, Scarborough kept up a constant stream of verbal abuse. Finally, McGowan came over to the dugout and had a few choice words for his tormentor. Scarborough responded with a few choice words of his own. Things got so heated that

McGowan ended up throwing his balls and strikes indicator at the mouthy pitcher. The indicator went under the players' bench, and Scarborough went down on all fours to retrieve it. When he finally found it, McGowan demanded that it be returned to him immediately. "Like hell," said Scarborough. "You can get it back from the league president." McGowan received a two-week suspension from the American League.

✳   ✳   ✳   ✳

Ray Scarborough's hometown was Mt. Olive, North Carolina and he spent his winters working as a pickle salesman. No, really—honest to God—he really did.

Curt Schilling

Through 2007, Curt Schilling had the best ratio of strikeouts to walks (4.38 to 1) of any major league pitcher since 1900 who had thrown at least 2,000 innings. He also held the record for the highest winning percentage in the postseason among pitchers with 10 or more decisions. Schill was 11-2, for an .846 winning percentage. Other pitchers had more wins, but no other had a higher percentage of wins.

His most famous outing came in the 2004 ALCS. After suffering one of his two postseason losses in Game One, when he was hammered for six runs in three innings by the New York Yankees. It was clear something was badly wrong, and it turned out he had suffered a serious injury to the ligament in his right ankle. After first experimenting on an anonymous cadaver, team doctor Bill Morgan surgically attached Schilling's ligament to the outside of his ankle. As he pitched in the game, blood seeped through his no-longer-sanitary stocking in what became known as the "bloody sock" game. It was the symbolic opposite of an Achilles heel, and served as a red badge of courage representing the Red Sox' will to win.

George Scott

George Scott

Red Sox first baseman George "Boomer" Scott introduced a new name into the already-rich baseball lexicon. He called home runs "taters." It quickly caught on and was adopted by the likes of Reggie Jackson and other notables.

*   *   *   *

Scott used to wear a strange necklace strung with irregular shaped white objects. When a curious teammate asked what the objects were, the menacing Boomer replied: "The teeth of American League pitchers."

*   *   *   *

Bill Lee on George Scott: "I remember George Scott was in taking a shower, and Eddie Kasko was in taking a shower at the same time. George was lathering himself up with Head & Shoulders shampoo, and he had a big froth of it on his hair. Kasko, who was completely bald, looked over at George and said: 'Boy, I used to use that product quite a bit too!' Scott wasn't long rinsing his hair out."

*   *   *   *

When the Red Sox sent Sparky Lyle to the Yankees for Danny Cater, many fans felt it was the worst trade in Red Sox history. Cater was at-bat in spring training, and a pitcher knocked him down—hit him in the bill of his cap and sent him spinning into the dust. Lying there, writhing around in real or imagined pain, he cried: "I can't see, I can't see!" Boomer Scott leaned over him and suggested: "Well, open up your eyes!"

*   *   *   *

When Scott was traded to the Milwaukee Brewers, he almost won the Triple Crown. When he was traded back to Boston in 1977, however, he had lost much of his bat speed. Throwing batting practice for the Red Sox, coach Harvey Haddix threw out a challenge. "Boomer," he said, "I can throw nine fastballs in a row by you—up and in." Scott smirked: "Yeah, sure." Haddix, who was approaching sixty at the time, threw seven in a row past him before Scott finally fouled one off. Boomer said triumphantly: "See, I told you you couldn't do it!"

*   *   *   *

George "Boomer" Scott, Red Sox slugging first baseman, once explained the difference between a streak and a slump: "When you're hitting the ball, it comes at you looking like a grapefruit. When you're not, it looks like a black-eyed pea."

*   *   *   *

Red Sox manager Dick Williams on George Scott's eating habits: "He looks as though he ate Christmas dinner every night of the week." Williams didn't respect Scott much, and wrote in his autobiography: "Talking to him is like talking to a block of cement."

*   *   *   *

"It wasn't that George Scott was really that funny," says Bill Lee. "It was just that he came from Greenville, Mississippi, and it's like anyone that comes from Mississippi—you know they're going to rank number 49 or 50 in any category. Boomer was the same. People from Mississippi just thank God that Alabama is down there, too."

*   *   *   *

Moe Berg's assessment of rookie George Scott in a 1966 interview with a UPI reporter: "I believe there are fortunes to be made by the contractors who replace the walls he will tear down by the force of the baseballs he will hit."

∗   ∗   ∗   ∗

Billy Gardner was known as "Slick" because of his great hands at second base. Mike Barnicle says that while coaching a young George Scott, Slick told Boomer the reason he was so quick was that his father used to "drive golf balls at him from ten yards away and it was either catch the golf ball or die." Whether the gullible George bought that one or not, we can't say.

Eddie Shore

On June 23, 1917, Red Sox relief pitcher Eddie Shore tossed a perfect game against the Washington Senators. This is amazing enough on its own merit, but consider this: Shore wasn't the starting pitcher for the game; Babe Ruth was. After walking leadoff man Ed Foster, Ruth became involved in a heated dispute with the umpire and was ejected. Advising manager Jake Stahl that he "had nothing" that day, Shore nevertheless warmed up quickly and entered the game in relief of Ruth. Right away, Foster was gunned down at second in a steal attempt. Shore was flawless for the next 8⅔ innings and was officially credited with a perfect game because he was on the mound for all 27 outs.

Reggie Smith

A switch-hitter, on four different occasions Reggie Smith hit homers from both sides of the plate in a game for the Red Sox. A very powerful player, Smith once picked up Yankee Thad Tillotson during a fight and held him over his head. He then threw him like a medicine ball—and he landed on his feet. Tillotson was listed as a 195 pounder.

Tris Speaker (Brace Photography)

Tris Speaker

Tris Speaker was one of the greatest center fielders in baseball history. Outfield defense was the forte of "The Grey Eagle," who recorded 35 assists in 1912. In 1915, a slim (6'2,", 198 lbs.) young Red Sox pitcher named Babe Ruth dubbed Speaker "a fifth infielder" because he played incredibly shallow at his position. The grateful Babe had witnessed Speaker throw out runners at first on more than one occasion. Five times he made unassisted double plays by grabbing low liners on the first hop and then stepping on second base and throwing to first.

✴   ✴   ✴   ✴

When does a Speaker not speak? Tris Speaker and Duffy Lewis didn't speak to each other for years after the day Lewis threw a bat at Speaker and hurt him; the balding Lewis was reportedly angry at Speaker for pulling his cap off during batting practice.

✴   ✴   ✴   ✴

Speaking of Speaker, he started his career as a pitcher but moved to the outfield to take advantage of his talents as a hitter, foreshadowing Babe Ruth's similar migration from the mound to the outfield. Cy Young used to hit him fungoes every day to help him develop his fielding, and Speaker always credited Young for the help. Speaker seemed to have a number of talents. One day, he bested Will Rogers during a roping exhibition put on before a benefit game for a Boston sportswriter's widow.

✴   ✴   ✴   ✴

The Red Sox bought Hall of Fame ballplayer Tris Speaker from the Cleburne, Texas, club for $400. There could have been bidding competition from the Pirates, but Speaker smoked cigarettes, and this didn't sit well with Bucs owner Barney Dreyfuss, who passed on Speaker.

*   *   *   *

As the Red Sox ace pitcher, Ruth especially admired Speaker for his hitting skills. Ironically, the man who would later become the most feared hitter in the game depended on the Gray Eagle for most of the Red Sox offense. Speaker finished his career with a lofty .344 batting average.

Tracy Stallard

After Roger Maris hit his then-record 61st regular-season home run off Red Sox Tracy Stallard, the rookie pitcher was besieged by reporters' questions. "I have nothing to be ashamed of," he replied. "He hit 60 others, didn't he?"

Bob Stanley

In 1986, reliever Bob "Steamer" Stanley was going through a rough time. Cursed with a sinkerball that no longer sunk, he was booed mercilessly by the Red Sox fans but still managed to keep his sense of humor. He told teammates that his actual name was Lou Stanley and that actually fans were chanting "Lou, Lou," when he walked to the mound.

*   *   *   *

When "Steamer" prowled the home bullpen in the late 1980s, he developed a great rapport with the fans—the infamous "bleacher creatures." Anytime a beach ball landed on the field, Stanley would ceremoniously place the ball on the ground and, as if performing a sacred sacrifice, use a ground crew rake and pop the ball, throwing the deflated remains back to the cheering bleacherites.

*   *   *   *

Stanley was very active with the Jimmy Fund and did his best to brighten the lives of children stricken with various forms of cancer.

"One time, I went to visit this boy who wouldn't come out of his room because they had taken his eye out. I brought him one of my jerseys from the 1983 season when I had set the Red Sox record with 33 saves. I also brought him a bat and a ball, and I gave them to him, and we talked for awhile. When I got home, the doctor called. 'I don't know what you did, but he's running down the hallway with your jersey as a night shirt.' He was only 10, and the thing was down to his feet. A couple of weeks later, I ran into his father, who was a security guard at the racetrack. I asked him about his son, and he told me that he had died. He said they had buried him with my jersey." After Stanley retired in 1989, his own nine-year-old son, Kyle was diagnosed with a similar kind of cancer. Kyle recovered due to advances made in those few intervening years—advances made in no small part due to the wonderful work of the Jimmy Fund.

Dave Stapleton

Sox fans are still upset that manager John McNamara did not put Dave Stapleton into Game Six of the 1986 World Series as a late-inning defensive replacement for Bill Buckner, a role he had so often assumed during the regular season. Who can say how that one simple act might have altered Red Sox history?

He may have saved the day (and helped Boston win the World Series) had he been at first base. It would probably have been a routine play and no one would remember it today. Or maybe the ball would have skipped between *his* legs and Stapleton would now be living in seclusion in Idaho instead of Buckner. One thing is certain—his NOT replacing Buckner has made him a rather large footnote in Red Sox history. Fans probably wouldn't otherwise remember Dave Stapleton, even though he did get two hits in three World Series at-bats. Ironically, Stapleton is remembered for the play he never got the chance to make.

*   *   *   *

Stapleton played his entire major league career with the Red Sox (1980-1986), but after that fateful World Series, he never got another chance to play major league ball. An odd quirk, which may explain his early exit from major league competition, is that his batting average declined each and every year of the seven seasons he served the Sox.

> 1980:   .321
> 1981:   .285
> 1982:   .264
> 1983:   .247
> 1984:   .231
> 1985:   .227
> 1986:   .128

Can any other player boast such a steady, unceasing seven-year decline? Stapleton was clearly going, going, gone. ... Another couple of years and he could have been the batboy—or even worse, a pitcher.

Vern Stephens

In 1953, during batting practice at Fenway, St. Louis Browns shortstop Billy Hunter stroked a line drive that hit a pigeon in center field. The pigeon fell to the ground but quickly recovered and flew off, prompting Red Sox shortstop Vern Stephens to comment: "That's a sure sign, Billy. When you can't knock out a bird with a line drive, it's time to start looking for another job."

✱   ✱   ✱   ✱

Junior Stephens was a free spirit but a dedicated ballplayer. The night before a twin-bill in Cleveland, some mobsters tried to get him drunk in order to influence the outcome of the games. After a night of carousing with his newfound friends, Stephens hit three home runs and drove in 11 in the next day's doubleheader, foiling the plans of the gamblers.

Jerry Stephenson

Talk about having a bad day! On May 9, 1968, with Jerry Stephenson on the mound for the Red Sox, Ed Stroud of the Senators bunted safely, then stole second. Stephenson balked and Stroud strolled to third. Stephenson finally recorded an out, but then threw a wild pitch and Stroud scored safely. All on a 15-foot bunt.

Dick Stuart

If any man was born to be a designated hitter, it was Dick Stuart, alias Dr. Strangeglove and the Boston Strangler. Unfortunately, Stuart came along before the DH rule came into effect in the American League. Stuart possessed amazing power and could win a ballgame with a single swing of the bat. He also was a threat to give up as many runs as he produced. The kindest description of his play at first base is erratic. Even Hank Aaron addressed him as "Stonefingers," and it was rumored that his glove was not made by Spalding or Rawlings but by the Portland Cement Company.

His defensive technique was sometimes referred to as the "¡Olé!" approach—he waved his glove at the ball as it passed by, like a matador with his red cloth. One day, after yet another miscue had led to yet another opposition score, Stuart was given a standing ovation at Fenway for successfully scooping a hot dog wrapper that had blown across the infield.

*   *   *   *

Dick Stuart (Brace Photography)

Before he came to the Red Sox, Stuart played for the NL's Pittsburgh Pirates. One day, the announcer gave the usual pre-game announcement to the Forbes Field crowd: "Anyone who interferes with a ball in play shall be ejected." The Pirates' beleaguered manager Danny Murtaugh grumbled to no one in particular: "I hope Stuart doesn't think that means him."

★   ★   ★   ★

Not only was Stuart inept as a fielder, his base-running skills also left much to be desired. He was always missing or misreading his coach's signs. He once suggested: "When I get on base, why not just point to the base you'd like me to go to?"

★   ★   ★   ★

The press loved Stuart because he provided great newspaper copy. Once, at a Boston postseason baseball banquet, he got up to speak and noted that his manager Billy Herman was in the audience. "Hope you have a great winter, Billy," said Stuart as Herman nodded his thanks. "Because you had a horseshit summer," he continued after a short pause.

★   ★   ★   ★

Stuart was once stopped by a Boston police cruiser. The officer pointed out that Stuart still had 1963 license plates on his car despite the fact that it was now 1964. "I had such a good year that I didn't want to forget it," he explained.

★   ★   ★   ★

Dick Stuart, who hit 66 HRs one year in the minors, is the only first baseman in major-league history to have three assists in one inning. Dr. Gold Glove, perhaps? More like Dr. Jekyll.

*   *   *   *

Dick Stuart once hit an inside-the-park homer at Fenway when the ball hit the Wall, then glanced off a fielder's Adam's Apple.

*   *   *   *

Stuart, who hit 66 HRs one year in the minors, is the only first baseman in ML history to have three assists in one inning. Despite this aberration, he was a klutz in both major leagues. "Dr. Strangeglove" led the league in miscues by first basemen in each of his first seven years, including his rookie year of 1958. That year he played in only 64 games but used the opportunity to commit an impressive 16 first-base errors for the Pittsburgh Pirates. Once he had established his reputation, he built on it throughout his five years in Pittsburgh and then packed his porous glove for the trip to Boston where he topped American League first sackers in errors for two more years.

*   *   *   *

The Red Sox first baseman was so bad in the field that it is difficult to exaggerate his level of incompetence. In 1963, he recorded 29 errors at first base, *three times* that of his nearest "rival."

Despite his pathetic fielding, Stuart was an above-average major league hitter. After hitting 35 homers for the National League's Pittsburgh Pirates in 1961, his output fell to just 16 dingers in 1962. Traded to the Red Sox, he assaulted American League pitching for 42 homers in 1963, making him the first player to hit more than 30 homers in each major league.

According to former Red Sox manager Dick Williams, Stuart's clumsiness was matched only by his selfishness. Williams claims

Dick Stuart

that Stuart was once hit by a pitch with the bases loaded and awarded first base by the umpire, scoring a much-needed Red Sox run. Stuart, wanting another chance to hit, denied he was hit, and despite an obvious bruise on his forearm actually succeeded in having the call reversed. Stuart then struck out, ending the Sox rally.

*   *   *   *

Dick Stuart may have been a one-dimensional player, but that one dimension was power, and he exhibited lots of it in his Red Sox career. Like most power hitters, Stu was always looking for an edge. It is reported that he used to hammer little tacks into the barrel of his bat in order to tighten it up. His teammates were skeptical at best. Carl Yastrzemski laughingly recalls: "If it was a day game and the sun was out, you could see the reflection off the bat from the nails." Even the blindest of umpires couldn't miss that one.

Jim Tabor

Ted Williams' archenemy in the press corps was Dave "The Colonel" Egan, he of the poison pen and nasty disposition, and Ted's battles with Egan were legendary. They were, however, strictly of the verbal and written variety. It took teammate Jim Tabor to actually try to court martial the colonel. While Tabor was in the hospital with appendicitis, Egan had taken a cheap shot at him, suggesting in print that the team was better with him out of the lineup. The bruising and bruised third baseman was in no mood for such jibes. While Tabor was convalescing, he watched the games from the press box at Fenway—which put him in dangerous proximity to his tormentor.

On one famous occasion, Tabor grabbed Egan by the throat and pushed him against the railing beyond which was only an abundance of air and then the screen behind home plate. Before the colonel was thus demoted, General Manager Eddie Collins intervened and saved Egan from a possible fall to earth. There is no truth to the rumor that Ted Williams was on the field, egging Tabor on.

Birdie Tebbetts

Like most catchers, Birdie Tebbetts was notoriously slow of foot on the basepaths. In fact, he was even slow by catchers' standards. They measured his speed to first base with a sundial, and once on first there was little chance of advancement other than by a hit. That's why it was somewhat incredible that Tebbetts stole five bases during the 1948 season.

One of those five stolen bases came at the expense of Cleveland Indian catcher Jim Hegan, and Hegan was understandably upset by it. "Gene Bearden was pitching," recalled Tebbetts in the *Chicago Daily News,* "and neither he nor Hegan paid any attention to me. I took a pretty good lead and finally lit out. I got to second easy; they didn't even try a play. Somebody doubled and I scored. As I went across the plate Hegan looked at me and said, 'I never came closer to quitting baseball in my life than when you did that.' That's what they think of me on the runways!"

*   *   *   *

Ted Williams was noted for the intensity of his concentration. Pitchers and catchers alike would try whatever they could to crack it. Once when he was catching for the Tigers, Birdie tried to do so by telling Ted a long, drawn-out story during an at-bat. Ted listened through strike one, and then through strike two. Tebbetts was working up to the punch line when—BAM!—Ted hit the next pitch out of the park. As Ted trotted across the plate, he slowed up briefly. "And then what did she say?" he asked Tebbetts.

*   *   *   *

Birdie's obituary on the www.thedeadballera.com website reads, in part: "There ought to be a second-string or Junior Hall of Fame for guys like me," he once said. "I had a lifetime average of .270 and I'm proud of it. I poured my life's blood into it. I clawed and scrambled and fought and hustled to get it.

Birdie Tebbetts (Brace Photography)

"My whole world is wrapped up in baseball," he said, "and that means I must live the loneliest of lives. I can't discuss my problems with my friends or the newspapermen or the players or the coaches or my wife." His wife, the former Mary Hartnett, understood. One winter night during his days as a manager, the usually talkative Tebbetts was silent as he stared into the glowing fireplace of his home in Nashua, N.H. "What inning are you playing now, dear?" she said.

George Thomas

Red Sox utility man George Thomas (1966-71) was no Ted Williams. He finished his 13-year major-league career with a .255 batting average and a paltry 46 homers. In 1970, he got a rare starting assignment and responded with three doubles. When reporters gathered around his locker after the game, he deadpanned: "I'm exhausted. Please tell (manager Eddie) Kasko that he can either bench me or trade me."

Luis Tiant

"Luis Tiant is the Fred Astaire of baseball." —Reggie Jackson.

Red Smith once described Luis Tiant as follows: "He is a joy to watch; this swarthy, ample gentleman of 34 going on 44. Black-bearded and sinister, he looks like Pancho Villa after a tough week of looting and burning. He is a master of every legal pitch, and he never throws two consecutive pitches at the same speed." One of the most enduring images for Red Sox fans is that of Luis Tiant in the middle of his corkscrew delivery: back to the batter, eyes rolling skyward as if seeking divine intervention. As Joe Garagiola once said; "How can you hit a guy who doesn't even look at you when he goes into his wind-up?"

*   *   *   *

Luis Tiant (Brace Photography)

Luis Tiant's father, also named Luis, was considered one of the greatest pitchers in Cuba's storied baseball history. He had pitched against and defeated several touring major-league teams. The younger Tiant pitched for a year in the Cuban League in 1960-61, then he left revolutionary Cuba for Mexico and eventually the United States, never to return to his native land. Luis Sr. had never seen his son take the mound in the major leagues, but in 1975, Fidel Castro gave him special dispensation to visit Boston, where he threw out the first pitch at a game late in August. It was the first time father and son had seen each other in eight years. When his first attempt was a little low and outside, he motioned for the ball again and the old man fired a perfect strike right over the plate. Luis Tiant Sr. and his wife both passed away that winter.

*   *   *   *

An avid fisherman, Carl Yastrzemski once brought a prize catch into the Red Sox spring training club house in Florida to show it off. Predictably, Luis Tiant saw an amazing resemblance between the fish and his favorite target, Tommy Harper. "It's got teeth like Harper's," he shouted gleefully. Later, when the unsuspecting Harper entered the clubhouse, he was greeted with a stony silence. Spotting his Red Sox uniform on the floor by his locker, he bent to pick it up. To his surprise, a large and rather ugly fish was already "wearing" it, its grinning mouth propped open with tongue depressors and a Red Sox cap atop its head.

*   *   *   *

Stopped for speeding by a Massachusetts state trooper, Tiant explained to the officer, "I was bringing some heat." The cop, obviously a Red Sox fan, let him off without a ticket.

*   *   *   *

For the entire 1974 season, Luis wore nothing but white, save for his Red Sox uniform. He said it was his personal tribute to God.

* * * *

Pitchers are especially notorious for their superstitions. Luis Tiant used to smoke cigars in the shower after a game. Boston's one-time pitching coach Lee Stange claimed that Tiant also wore strands of beads and a special loincloth that he wrapped around his waist under his uniform to ward off evil spirits.

* * * *

Tiant was obviously a cock-eyed optimist. Steve Dillard recalls him in spring training one year, after someone had smashed one of his pitches to straightaway center field, yelling: "GO FOUL! GO FOUL!"

* * * *

Bill Lee, himself no stranger to humor, claims: "Luis Tiant was by far the funniest guy I ever played with. He just had an uncanny sense of humor with his broken English and the way he expressed himself. He and Tommy Harper just kind of went back and forth with each other. He'd call Harper 'liver lips,' and he'd bring in a picture of a big-lipped chimpanzee, and he'd look at it and say: 'I love you, Tommy.'

"Whenever he went in to take a shit, he'd flush the toilet and say: 'Goo bye Tommy!' They were just at each other's throats all the time."

* * * *

After weeks of the "Goo bye Tommy!" stuff, Harper finally struck back. Tiant was always on guard while he was in the bathroom stall, apprehensive after playing so many tricks on others. One

Luis Tiant

time, Yaz noticed Luis wasn't as vigilant as usual and helpfully alerted Harper, even supplying a bucketful of cold water. Harper climbed up onto a sink, walked along the row of sinks and positioned himself perfectly. When the flush began and Tiant was in the middle of his "Goo bye Tommy!", Harper suddenly poured the full bucket over Luis, to the delight of the 23 other players who had gathered to watch the drama unfold.

*   *   *   *

Like many baseball couples, Tiant met his wife Maria at the ballpark—but in this case, he was the fan, and she was the player. On an off night in Mexico City where he was playing for Los Tigres on his way from Cuba to the majors, he attended a girls softball game and was smitten with the attractive left fielder.

*   *   *   *

When Luis Tiant went to the Yankees from the Red Sox, he signed on with the Ball Park Franks company as a radio spokesman for their fine hotdogs. It was hard for Red Sox fans to hear El Tiante intone in his best Cuban accent: "It's great to finally be with a wiener!"

*   *   *   *

In the game of June 14, 1974, Boston at California, Luis Tiant pitched a complete game of 14.1 innings and lost 4-3 on a Denny Doyle RBI double, while Nolan Ryan went 13 innings and struck out 19 while walking 10. Cecil Cooper was 0 for 8 in the contest. Doyle became a Red Sox teammate in 1975. Tiant allowed three runs in the fourth and then pitched 10 scoreless innings until the 15th.

*   *   *   *

Bill Lee once shared the four-man rotation with Tiant. "Luis Tiant would wind up and throw it, and in the middle of his delivery he'd change it and drop down and throw a slider and do this and that—it was a dance. Luis was just Luis. Every day was a revelation."

✳   ✳   ✳   ✳

Fellow hurler Bill Lee likened a Tiant performance to a concert. "The orchestra comes out and everything starts banging and it shakes the place. Then it comes to the middle part of the symphony and things get very calm and sweet, and you want to kind of fall asleep. Then, all of a sudden, you sense that the end is coming. Everyone starts getting noisy again. The whole gang is letting out with all the instruments. Then, boom! The whole show is over. That's Tiant! Hard at the start, a little sweet, slow stuff in the middle, and then the big explosion at the end."—from Bruce Shalin's *Oddballs.*

Shalin himself added, "Luis knew exactly when to turn a bus ride into something out of *Saturday Night Live.*"

✳   ✳   ✳   ✳

Luis' eccentric rotating windup was perhaps first developed in Cleveland. He called it "The Jaw Breaker."

"My head stops seven times. First I look up; then I look down; then my jaw points toward second base; then toward third. Then it points at the centerfield corner; behind my back; and then—just before I pitch the ball—I point it upstairs near where Mr. Yawkey is sitting."

✳   ✳   ✳   ✳

Dwight Evans on Luis in the 70s: "The one thing that impressed me about those games—and Luis was really the one behind that whole

Red Sox era—as soon as he was done warming up and that lever came up from that gate, there was dead silence, and as soon as that latch opened he got a standing ovation all the way to the mound. It was exciting for us to see that, and it got us all going, too. It was a tremendous thing." —Bruce Shalin, *Oddballs*.

*   *   *   *

Luis told us: "We used to get Aparicio with rubber snakes. One day I remember we put one in his pants. He ran all the way from the inside out of the clubhouse out all the way to the field! He had his pants hanging down. He's lucky he didn't fall down and get injured."

*   *   *   *

In 2002, Luis begins work as pitching coach for the Red Sox Single A Lowell Spinners. Now that he's no longer throwing smoke, he's begun to market it. Always known for his trademark cigars, in 2001 Luis launched El Tiante cigars—23 to a box! Twenty-three was Luis's uniform number with the Red Sox. The wrapper depicts Luis in uniform and the cigars—maduros and rosados—are manufactured by Tabacalera Perdomo in Nicaragua.

"I'd smoke a cigar in the shower, sure. It takes practice. So many years. The water would hit your face and your hair but not hit my cigar. I'd smoke a cigar all the time in the whirlpool."

*   *   *   *

In the spring of 1988, Luis Tiant pitched for the Red Sox old-timers against the Equitable Old-Timers. He ran into trouble in the first, giving up four runs on a series of bloop hits.

In the dugout between innings, his teammates were waiting for his reaction. He didn't disappoint them. "That was some weak shit," he said, to everyone's amusement. When some players began to rub his arm, Luis quipped: "My arm is fine," he said, turning his rear end to this teammates. "Massage this."

Bob Tillman

In his rookie year, Bob Tillman told a radio reporter, he "couldn't hit a curveball with an oar." Which left him up the proverbial hit creek without a paddle.

*   *   *   *

Former Red Sox catcher Tillman had a reputation for using the old bean, his own and others. Here are two examples of his heads-up play:

1. With John Wyatt on the mound, a man on first and three balls on the batter, Wyatt pitched to the plate and the runner on first broke for second. The ball was outside—ball four. Wyatt dropped his head in disappointment. However, the catcher, Bob Tillman, caught the ball and pegged a dart toward second base, nailing Wyatt in the side of the head.

2. Needing a baserunner to start a rally, Dick Williams scouted around the dugout for a pinch hitter. Tillman jumped up promising he'd get on base. Williams sent Tillman up to pinch-hit. When the pitch is thrown, Tillman leaned into it, catching it on the side of his helmet-less head and took first on the HBP.

John Valentin

Besides being a steady third baseman and a fine clutch hitter, John Valentin is the Red Sox player currently most active with the Jimmy Fund. John's agent concedes that it was originally a self-serving strategy to assist him in salary arbitration, but the more he became involved with the kids, the more he wanted to contribute to the cause. When a young cancer patient named Lucas Bartlett expressed a Christmas wish to meet Valentin, John and his wife Marie agreed to stop by for a few minutes. The few minutes turned into four hours and regular contact until the boy's death the following August. For the rest of the season, Valentin wore Lucas' name in his cap and has worked to preserve his young friend's memory through various noble deeds.

*   *   *   *

The 1999 American League Divisional series pitted the Cleveland Indians against the Boston Red Sox. The Sox lost the first game in Cleveland 3-2 when ace starter and shoe-in for the Cy Young Award Pedro Martinez was forced from the game with a pulled back muscle. Game Two was even worse as the Sox were unraveled by the Indians 11-1.

Back in Boston for Game Three, the Red Sox finally came alive, winning 9-3. Game Four was even better as the Sox massacred the Indians 23-7 to set several postseason records for runs scored. John Valentin had alternated between hero and goat in the first three games, committing egregious errors and hitting dramatic home runs. In Game Three, he made a costly throwing error only to redeem himself with a game-winning homer. Tapping into recent Red Sox history, Fox sports announcer Bob Brenly commented that Valentin had gone "from Bill Buckner to Carlton Fisk in a single game."

*   *   *   *

Before Garciaparra arrived in Boston, Valentin was the regular Red Sox shortstop. If ever there was cause for dissension in the ranks, this surely offered that potential. The Boston media sharpened their pens to record the gathering storm. So how do the two infielders get along? "I love the guy," says Nomar. "He's taught me so much about playing shortstop and about playing baseball. People would naturally think he'd be the last one to help me. There is just one word to describe John: class. A complete class guy. He's always been that way to me. We've gotten really close, and we're great friends."

* * * *

My most embarrassing moment, by John Valentin:

"During spring training of my rookie year, the club went up to Baseball City to play the Royals. I had been told that I would be starting and that the game was to be televised. Oh my, I was so excited. I called my folks, brother, aunts, uncles, cousins, friends, etc. and told everyone that I was playing and to tune in. Just about every television set in northern New Jersey was watching me. I was playing short when a ground ball was hit to me. It was a routine grounder; really a good one that I could handle with ease looking real cool in the process. I fielded the ball and made the toss to first. Since there were two outs I continued after the throw to trot back to the dugout feeling on top of the world. I could just hear Mom say, 'That's my Johnny, atta boy.'

"When I got to the dugout, I finally looked up. You see, because I was on TV and a rookie, I was playing it super cool. You know, make the play and trot off the field. Maybe they would even show the play again in slo-mo. The only problem was that there was one out. Not only was I the only player trotting off the field, but the TV camera followed me all the way to the top step. When I reached the dugout, there was nowhere to hide. Turning bright red, I turned around and trotted back to short. The KC crowd gave me a standing ovation. I wanted to replay the last 45 seconds of my life. I wanted to crawl under the turf and hide. Fortunately, no one ever said anything about it ... not!"

* * * *

In one 23-month stretch spanning three seasons, John Valentin established himself as perhaps, in the words of Sox fan Steve Mastroyin, the "single most prominent one-game phenomenon

John Valentin

player in the history of the Sox." On July 8, 1994 with runners on first and second, the Mariners' Mark Newfield lined sharply to Valentin at short. Val stepped on second, doubling off Mike Blowers, then tagged the oncoming Kevin Mitchell, who was speeding from first base to second. It was only the tenth unassisted triple play in the history of major league baseball. But Valentin wasn't finished.

The following June, Val had a spectacular day at the plate, going 5-for-5 with three home runs. In the process, he became the first shortstop to hit for 15 total bases in one game, and only the eighth Boston Red Sox player to hit three home runs in a game. And there's more.

A year after that, on the 6th of June, 1996, Valentin hit for the cycle in a game against the White Sox. John made his mark in the postseason as well, on October 10, 1999, when he hit two home runs and drove in a total of seven runs, setting a postseason RBI mark.

During the 1999 ALCS, Valentin drove in five RBIs in Game Three against the hated Yankees. The previous weekend against Cleveland in the Division Series he had hit two home runs in Game Three and drove in seven in Game Four. As only ballplayers can, teammate Bret Saberhagen gave all the credit to superstition. "We ate dinner at the same place, Saraceno's in the North End," he said. "We sat at the same table. Marie [John's wife] wasn't there last night, but we left her seat open, and I ate the same stuff. If Marie had been there, he wouldn't have been two RBIs short."

✳   ✳   ✳   ✳

Seton Hall Alumni 8, New York Yankees 0. In a May 2, 1995 game between the Yankees and Red Sox, former Seton Hall teammates John Valentin and Mo Vaughn each hit grand slams for the Red Sox, Valentin in one inning and Vaughn the very next inning. The final 8-0 score represented the only time in history that two grand slams had accounted for all the scoring in a major league baseball game. V for Victory!

✳   ✳   ✳   ✳

Valentin had big shoes to fill when he finally made the Red Sox. But ironically he knew the shoes very well thanks to one of baseball's little ironies. "I had an interesting omen occur while I was playing A ball," explains Valentin. "Major League guys often take collections for the minor leaguers. They throw in a box of old spikes, gloves, wristbands, and T-shirts and donate them to the minor league players. A box arrived and the clubby gave me a pair of spikes. They were Luis Rivera's. Two years later when I got called up, I played short replacing Luis Rivera." When Valentin was moved to third base to make room for rookie sensation Nomar Garciaparra, he just had to know! "I asked Nomar if he had received a pair of spikes from me!"

Jason Varitek

Jason Varitek was shortstop on the 1984 U.S. Little League championship team, but by the time he got to Georgia Tech, a skinny kid named Nomar replaced him at short and Tek was sent behind the plate. Varitek thrived at his new position and was chosen to catch for the U.S. Olympic team at the 1992 Barcelona Games. In 1993, he was named *Baseball Americas* College Player of the Year.

✳   ✳   ✳   ✳

Varitek was acquired by the Red Sox along with Derek Lowe for Heathcliff Slocumb and Boston fans still wonder what the Seattle Mariners were thinking when they made the deal. Or indeed if they were thinking at all. On a team renowned for its bad trades, it was one of the most beneficially lopsided trades in Red Sox history. Slocumb had been a disastrous 5-15 with Boston—and looked even worse than his record indicated! He won only seven more games before his career came to a merciful conclusion. Lowe did tremendous work for the Red Sox, including a league-leading 42 saves as a reliever in 2000, before suffering a crisis of confidence throughout most of the 2001 campaign. Meanwhile Varitek blossomed into one of the league's top offensive and defensive catchers.

The Captain, Jason Varitek.

With hard work and dedication, Jason Varitek has become Boston's regular catcher and his work ethic and hard-nosed style reminds some fans of Carlton Fisk. Among his other talents Jason's training at shortstop initially earned him the job of designated catcher whenever knuckleballer Tim Wakefield took the mound. The "rambling Tek from Georgia Tech" revealed his secret to catching the knuckler: "Pick it up when it stops rolling."

Varitek was named team captain of the Red Sox in December 2004, and thereafter wore a "C" on his jersey. He was their third captain since 1923. Carl Yastrzemski was "Captain Carl" from 1969-83, and Jim Rice had been the last captain before Tek, 1985-89.

One little appreciated aspect of Varitek's work behind the plate is the fact that he ranks first among major-league catchers for the number of no-hitters he called. They were:

Hideo Nomo (April 4, 2001)
Derek Lowe (April 27, 2002)
Clay Buchholz (September 1, 2007)
Jon Lester (May 20, 2008)

In July 2015, Phillies catcher Carlos Ruiz caught his fourth, tying Varitek for first place in calling officially recognized big-league no-hitters. But Varitek did catch a hitless game thrown by Devern Hansack on October 1, 2006. It only lasted five innings, due to rain, but it's in the books as a complete-game shutout against the opposing Orioles. A major-league rule says this complete-game win with no hits was not a "no-hitter" for Hansack, but we say that defies logic.

Mo Vaughn

The "Hit Dog" was one of the most active Red Sox players ever in the Greater Boston community and founded the Mo Vaughn Youth Development Center, which has helped significant numbers of inner city kids. Brian Wilson, a childhood friend of Mo's since age 9, heads the Center. Mo's parents were often seen at Fenway. Both are teachers, and his father is also a school principal.

While with the Red Sox, Mo befriended young Jason Leader, a Jimmy Fund patient seriously ill with cancer. The boy asked Mo to hit a homer for him, and Mo said he'd try. That day, he did hit one and made all of Boston—and especially one young boy—happier for one day. Jason later died, but Mo, his parents and the Leaders have maintained an on-going friendship.

*   *   *   *

Ted Williams, who knows something about both hitting and fan abuse, felt some sympathy for Mo Vaughn when he struggled early in his Boston career. "Mo wasn't welcomed to Boston with open arms. Despite his superb collegiate career at Seton Hall, Vaughn heard lots of boos when he first came up with the Red Sox. I know first hand how tough Boston fans can be. They take no prisoners and they can drive you out of town unless you are equally tough. Once they are in your corner, however, they are the most loyal fans in the world."

*   *   *   *

Mo was a fan favorite in Boston, though he seemed to wear out his welcome with some fans. Red Sox management seemed not to want him, and Mo got the message—though he was hurt and wore it on his sleeve a little. Those who reviled him pointed out how he'd become an habitue of a "gentleman's club" called the Foxy Lady. One night he overturned his car while returning home from the club at 2 a.m. Red Sox fans got on his case as only they can do, calling him "Mo' Money" after he signed for $80 million with the California Angels despite telling a Boston sports talk radio show, "It isn't about the money."

*   *   *   *

Harking back to Clemens' ride on police horse Timothy in 1986, when the Sox clinched a spot in the playoffs in 1995, Mo Vaughn was talked into riding a Boston Police horse. "I'll never ride a horse again," Vaughn later vowed. "Everybody was saying, 'You gotta ride the horse, you gotta ride the horse. The horse is good luck.' The horse is not good luck—I was zero for 14 in the playoffs." Red Sox CEO John Harrington, asked about concern his star ballplayer could have been hurt, joked, "I was worried about the horse."

Mickey Vernon

Mickey Vernon and Ted Williams had parallel careers. Vernon entered the major leagues with the Washington Senators in 1939, the same year that Williams arrived in Boston, and they both retired from the game in 1960. The two great hitters were teammates on the Red Sox in 1956 and 1957. "It was a thrill for me to play with Ted," says Vernon. And much safer than playing against him, adds the former first baseman and two-time AL batting champ. "I hated playing first when Ted was at the plate because he pulled everything. You don't want to be holding someone on base when he's up—and the Red Sox always had someone on base. DiMaggio and Pesky hit ahead of him, and they were good hitters, and they'd either walk or get a hit and be on base every time. Once he crushed a sinking line drive at me and I flipped my glove down in front of my crotch, and the ball had so much topspin on it, it went right up between my legs."

∗   ∗   ∗   ∗

During the Second World War, Vernon was stationed on the tiny South Pacific island of Ulithi, which was a mile long and a quarter of a mile wide. Also stationed there were future Red Sox star Billy Goodman and the great Larry Doby, giving Ulithi more talent per square mile than any other atoll on earth. "We didn't have room to play baseball, so we played softball," says Vernon.

"Broadway" Charlie Wagner

Superstition has always been a great part of baseball. When a team is going well, no one wants to be responsible for breaking the spell. In 1938, the Red Sox were on just such a winning streak, and players went to extreme measures to keep it going. During the eight-game run, the team was served lamb chops every day. Joe Cronin chewed the same gum throughout the streak, and other players tried to maintain their regular eating routines. Perhaps it was Wagner who made the biggest sacrifice for the team. "I was on prune juice for eight straight days," he claimed. "I'm glad we lost."

*   *   *   *

You don't often hear of a player asking to be sent from the big leagues to the minors, but that's exactly what Charlie Wagner did in 1938. Starting the season with the Red Sox, he wasn't getting any playing time and felt that his skills were diminishing as a result. He went to manager Joe Cronin and demanded a demotion. "You can't watch people play," he says. "You've got to play in order to learn and not get stale." The Red Sox obliged and sent Wagner to Minneapolis, where he developed a friendship with a promising young outfielder named Theodore Williams. The next year the two were roommates with the Red Sox.

*   *   *   *

Wagner was Ted Williams' first roommate and tells many stories about the times he'd wake up to find Ted swinging an imaginary bat in the room—checking his swing in the mirror. One morning, Ted used a real bat and inadvertently smashed Wagner's bedpost, breaking the bed and waking up the man they called "Broadway" because of his natty attire. Now in his late 80s, Wagner is a Red Sox staffer at spring training every year. He even has a street named after him in the Red Sox complex at Fort Myers. Is that Broadway ... or Wagner Way? (Actually it's Charlie Wagner Way.)

*   *   *   *

Charlie Wagner was thrown out of only one game during his years in the majors and it was just for trying to get a little summer tan.

Wagner had pitched the day before and was in the visitors clubhouse in Detroit, so he missed umpire Bill Summers ordering Tom "Scoops" Carey off the top step of the dugout. In the early 1940s players were not supposed to sit on the top step of the dugouts at Briggs Stadium. Summers and Jimmie Foxx had been going at it a bit, but things had calmed down when Wagner emerged and sat down there to catch a few rays. Next thing he knew Summers was coming over, barking at him, "All right, Broadway. You're out! Get going!"

Wagner awoke as out of a trance, Roger Birtwell reported in the *Boston Globe,* and asked, "Eh-what? What's that, Bill? I didn't say anything. What did I do?"

"Never mind," roared Summers, "Get out of the park." So Wagner ended up with a Summers ban instead of a summer tan.

Tim Wakefield

Unfortunately, Tim Wakefield just kind of ran out of time. The two-time World Champion knuckleballer was going to turn 45 years old in August 2011 and was coming off the 2010 season when he was 4-10 with an ERA of 5.34. He had 179 wins for the Boston Red Sox. Two pitchers were tied for the most wins in Red Sox history: Cy Young and Roger Clemens. Both had won 192 games for the Sox. Each, like Wakefield, also had wins for other teams. But Wakefield had a chance to secure the status of the winningest pitcher in Red Sox team history. He got 23 more starts in 2011, but only won one game in his final 10 starts. His 7-8 season saw him add seven wins to his total, thus ending his career six wins short of tying Cy and the Rocket. With four wins in 2010 and seven in 2011, he might have gotten to the franchise record in 2012, but one assumes there came a point when the team and the player agreed not to spend another season devoted to chasing that record.

It's not as though Tim Wakefield was ever shooting for the mark in the first place. In fact, in the first place, he wasn't even a pitcher. When he began his career in the Pittsburgh Pirates organization, he was an infielder.

His father Steve taught him the knuckler and he rode its unpredictable flutter to a stellar career. Brought to the Red Sox by GM Dan Duquette, he experienced several stretches of brilliance, perhaps none more than in 1995 when he led in wins for the first-place Sox. There were downs, too, though, such as the season-ending home run the Yankees' Aaron Boone hit off him in

Tim Wakefield unleashes the classic knuckler.

extra innings in Game Seven of the 2003 ALCS. "I just became Bill Buckner," he told Red Sox clubhouse man Joe Cochran right after the game. To his genuine surprise Red Sox fans, the most knowledgeable fans in the game, rallied around this ultimate team player.

There was some inconsistency in the way the Red Sox used him, both as a starter and a reliever, and sometimes both in the same season. He was, he once said, "a one-pitch pitcher. Here it is. If they hit it, they hit it." He readily admitted he had no idea where the ball might go, once it left his hand. It was the most unpredictable of pitches.

Boone or not, the fans loved him. He was sort of the "everyman" type of pitcher, not some freak of nature and talent. He'd given up his start to throw garbage innings in the Game Three blowout, but was available to relieve in Game Five of the 2004 ALCS against the Yankees and he threw the 12th, 13th, and 14th. After the Sox swept the final four games, Yankees manager Joe Torre placed one call to the Boston clubhouse—to congratulate Tim Wakefield.

His total of 3,006 innings pitched for the Red Sox ranks first all-time.

Murray Wall

When folks talk about "The Wall" in Fenway, it's a safe bet that few are thinking of Murray. This Wall started with the Boston Braves in 1950, appearing in one game in early July and working four innings. He gave up six hits and had five runs scored on him, and then disappeared from major league rosters for several years.

Wall never gave up, however, and in 1957 he was back with Boston, this time with the American League's Red Sox. He went 3-0 that year, and followed up with an 8-9 record and respectable 3.62 ERA in 1958. Homers hit off him over the Green Monster were said to have been "Wall to Wall" homers.

The next year Wall was 1-4 with a 5.40 ERA when he was abruptly traded to Washington for Dick Hyde, who turned out to be something of a Dr. Jekyll. It seems that Hyde had hidden a sore arm and the trade was rescinded, but not before Wall had pitched one and one-third innings for the Senators, giving up a home run and two other hits. Hyde returned to the Senators and Wall wended his way back to Boston, having recorded the shortest and most unproductive stay in Washington since President William Henry Harrison.

Wally "The Green Monster"

When Wally made his first public appearance on April 13, 1997, he was booed lustily by some elements in the crowd—just as a few other left-field denizens at Fenway have been. Wally's initial introduction to Fenway Park was even the subject of a question in the April 14, 1997 Department of State briefing by spokesman (and Red Sox fan) Nicholas Burns. Mr. Burns was not pleased about the emergence of a mascot at Fenway Park. From the official record, Burns is quoted: "I think it's an abomination. Don't you? It's an abomination. It's an affront

Wally "The Green Monster" (The Boston Red Sox)

to our decent values and right thinking. Do you know what we're talking about? This new mascot, Wally the Green Monster at Fenway Park." Burns later was sent to Greece to serve as United States Ambassador to that faraway land.

Wally turned out to be a humanitarian of the first order, though, and his good works won over even his most vocal critics. Today Wally does a great deal of charity work in the Greater Boston area, particularly with children in need. He bears a resemblance to Oscar the Grouch although his disposition is much brighter and his hygiene impeccable. As with many celebrities, his popularity soared following a number of appearances on television, in Wally's case aided by the invaluable PR he received from cronies Jerry Remy and Sean McDonough on Red Sox telecasts.

Wally became so popular that in September 1999, he was rewarded by being taken on a road trip. It turned out to be an eventful one for the little guy. On September 5 in Seattle, early in the West Coast swing, Wally was struck by a foul ball off the bat of Nomar Garciaparra as horrified viewers back home watched the Sunday game on live TV. The blow knocked him off his perch atop the TV monitor and he had to be taken from the broadcast booth on a tiny stretcher hastily fashioned out of Popsicle sticks. A tiny ice pack (one cube in a little sack) was placed on his head. He reported that everything was a bit fuzzy until he realized that he was looking at his own nose. Nomar was as upset as anyone in the ballpark. Wally was attended to by team doctors and then taken to a nearby hospital for an MRI, which proved negative.

A few days later, Wally was fully recovered and—apparently feeling his oats a bit on this first trip away from Fenway—went out on the town with Rich Garces and Pedro Martinez and stayed out a little too late. Wally was grounded for breaking curfew; the pitchers reportedly got off easier. Jerry Remy explained, "Wally is still learning how to travel. He hasn't traveled much, you know." Wally settled down and stayed pretty low-key until he got back to Boston.

Wally did get a little boisterous at the Ryder Cup and was actually detained by security personnel at The Country Club, and arrested for heckling.

"He knows very little about golf etiquette," commented Jerry Remy afterwards, again excusing Wally's inappropriate behavior. Bewildered a bit by the intoxication of his sudden rise to fame, and perhaps a little chastened, Wally snapped to again and settled back into a baseball groove. On his first visit to New York, he visited Monument Park inside Yankee Stadium where, showing courage and pluck of the first magnitude, he stared down the Babe himself, an act that won him even more admirers back home as the Sox swept that series. His showdown with the Babe is also said to have inspired Pedro Martinez to make an even more blatant challenge to the Bambino (See Martinez entry for details).

Perhaps recalling Clinton appointee Nicholas Burns's slur on his character, it is hardly surprising that Wally decided to throw his Red Sox hat into the ring in the 2000 federal election. He announced his candidacy for the President of the United States, carrying the banner of the newly formed Mascot Party. Unfortunately his life came under the media microscope and rumors of scandal plagued his campaign. He was seen talking on his cellphone to female fans in the stands during Sox games. That was just the beginning. The name "Slick Wally" started to appear on internet sites as unsubstantiated accusations of a romantic involvement with tennis glamour girl Anna Kournikova spread. This scandal-mongering backfired however, and his "friendship" with Kournikova made him even more popular than ever.

Just as this scandal began to subside, reports circulated about a brawl with former Yankee player Bucky Dent. Again, these reports only served to increase his popularity with Boston voters, although presumably not in voter-rich New York. Wally had no shortage of potential running mates, and the media buzz suggested that the fuzzy thinkers such as the Philly Phanatic, Pat Patriot and Ross Perot were on his short list.

Wally stayed quiet throughout 2001, a generally uninspiring year for all Sox fans. Wally huddled with potential buyers for the Red Sox but wisely declined to join any particular group. As we go to press, though, there are rampant rumors about Wally's seething ambition to replace Sean McDonough as Jerry Remy's broadcast partner. Wally will be 90 in 2002, but that never held back Strom Thurmond. It's possible that he may mount a bid for a U.S. Senate seat if John Kerry runs for President. Bosox fans everywhere hope the little guy gets to see the Red Sox win another World Championship before too long. He's been waiting since 1918.

John Wasdin

Nomar Garciaparra hit his first major league homer off John "Way Back" Wasdin. "It's a funny story because I didn't know who I hit it off until John was traded to the Red Sox. I don't really know pitchers. I found out in spring training that it was Wasdin. He had just come over to our team, and I didn't know him. We were all doing our stretching exercises, and he came up to me and said: 'You know, you haven't even thanked me yet.' And I go: 'For what?' And he said: 'I got your career started.' Then we just laughed. He's a really good guy and we became very good friends. I just said: 'Alright! Thank you!' Even to this day, we'll joke around. He'll say to everyone: 'You know who got Nomar started, right?' I'll say: 'It was John Wasdin, right here. If it wasn't for him, I don't know where I'd be.'"

Earl Webb

His career may have been short—a mere 650 games—but while in the major leagues, Earl Webb tried to double his fun. He totaled 155 lifetime two-baggers, and in 1931 banged out 67 for the Red Sox, a major league record. The previous year he had 30, and in a 1932 season split between Boston and Detroit, managed another 28. The closest any player has come to Webb's mark in the last 70 years is Todd Helton's 59 in 2000.

Billy Werber

Baseball humor exists at all levels. Billy Werber was a practical joker and a Duke graduate. "He was never without a firecracker, an electric buzzer to shake hands with, a stink bomb or any other weapon of that kind on which he could lay his hands," wrote one Werber observer. Among the stunts he pulled were putting a possum in Johnny Orlando's hotel bathroom, a stink bomb in Tom Yawkey's bedroom on the train and a dead fish in Al Schacht's berth. He gave Dolf Luque a mutilated necktie into which he'd sewn bolts, screws and buttons. All that was missing from Werber's repertoire was the fake dog doo-doo.

*   *   *   *

When the reconstructed Fenway reopened in 1934 and the players showed up to see their new clubhouse in April, they found that "the floor was covered with a thick layer of wood dust, and several area alley cats, none of which had signed a Red Sox contract, were in obvious residence." One of the players gave a broom to outfielder Dusty Cooke. Bill Werber said, "A cat would jump on top of a locker and run its length with Dusty swinging wildly and overcoat flying. The dust was so thick in the air, he looked exactly like Lawrence of Arabia in a sandstorm. The cats escaped through an open transom, leaving behind cheering Red Sox, atop stools, sore from laughing and covered with dust."

*   *   *   *

Billy Werber was a swift and aggressive baserunner. On August 24, 1934, Werber was walked in a game against the Tigers. As he trotted down toward first, he noticed that neither the shortstop nor second baseman was paying attention. So he turned on speed as he hit the first base bag and made it safely to second before either infielder could get into position to take a throw. The catcher indeed threw wildly into center, and Werber wound up at third. He scored the tying run on a sac fly.

*   *   *   *

On opening day 1935, Yankees catcher Bill Dickey dropped a third strike, then fired the ball to first. An alert Werber, who had been on third base, saw his opportunity, shot home and scored the winning run in a 1-0 Red Sox victory.

*   *   *   *

Werber told us, "I remember a lot of jokes I did play. I don't mind sharing one of them that was very effective. Wesley Ferrell was a single fellow and he rented Chevrolet cars when he was in Spring training in Florida.

"The Chevrolet car sat out in front of the Sarasota Terrace Hotel. It was sitting out there one evening after dinner, and I went out behind the hotel and I got a double handful of crab guts and fish heads and stuff like that and I went to his car and I put all of that junk behind the seat. Not under the seat in the rear, but behind it. I took the seat out and I put it behind there. There it sat all the next day, in the hot sun. Roy Johnson asked Wesley if he could borrow the car that night. He had a date and Wesley wasn't going to use it and he said sure and gave him the keys.

"Well, when Roy Johnson opened the door, it like to knocked him down. That smell. There was a pair of pants and a pair of shoes lying on the floor there in the back and Roy threw those out on the grass. Wesley fished in Lake Myaka.

*   *   *   *

"Roy went on down to pick up his date and when they came back by the hotel they had all the doors open. Roy was out one side and the girl was out the other. Somebody asked him the next day how things went.

"'Not too good,' he said. 'She thought it was me and I thought it was her.'

"Now the next day, Wesley pulled the stool out of his locker and said if the no-good S.O.B. would acknowledge that, he'd whup him! And if two guys had anything to do with it, he'd whup 'em both. All the players were sitting around laughing and clapping and shouting 'Give it to him, Wesley! Give it to him, Wesley!' He never did find out who did that.

"He was so mad. He couldn't use his Chevrolet after that. He had to turn it in."

Tom Werner

One of the new Red Sox owners, Tom Werner, had an early Fenway connection. Though born in Manhattan, Werner recalls becoming entranced with Fenway early on. "I remember going to Red Sox games when I went to Harvard over 30 years ago," Werner said. "I would take off a lot of time and ditch classes, and come to Fenway Park in the afternoon."

In 1971, the Harvard senior produced a short documentary film about Fenway Park—and later went on to produce *The Cosby Show, Roseanne, 3rd Rock from the Sun* and other popular TV shows.

Sammy White

This story comes from the "true or falsie" department. Parnell claims that White had some rather unconventional catching equipment. "Sammy used to use a woman's falsie as a sponge in his glove. When you think about it, it is the ideal thing because it fits the hand perfectly and creates that air vacuum between the rubberized sponge and the glove, which would soften the impact of the ball hitting in his glove. One day, he goes over to the wall after a foul ball and hits the wall, and the glove flies off, and darned if the falsie doesn't land in a girl's lap. She was so embarrassed; she thought people would think it was hers. Her face was as red as can be. Everyone wanted to laugh but they couldn't. It took Sam to think of that."

*   *   *   *

Mickey McDermott has another true falsie story about Sammy White. "Sammy goes into a department store, and he see these falsies in a barrel. He says to the lady clerk: "What size do you have there?" She said: "You mean for your girlfriend?" He said: "No, for me." She said: "Oh, my God!" He buys two of the falsies and painted the nipples red, and they fit between his two fingers perfectly and when they were doubled up they made a great sponge for this catcher's mitt—because when you set down and catch fastballs all day long, your hand gets killed. We didn't have those big padded gloves in those days. Well, there was a close play at home plate one day where the lead runner from third was coming home and the anchor runner is coming around third and almost catches the lead runner. It should have been a sure double play—bang bang—at home plate for Sammy. As he tags one, the other runner hit him, and his glove flew off, and there were the two big shiny tits with bright red nipples lying in the middle of the field. The place went nuts. They thought he was a cross-dresser and they'd knocked his bra off or something, that he didn't have a chest protector, he had a bra on. Sammy had a locker full of those things."

*   *   *   *

"OK, catcher. I've seen enough. You just don't have it today. Hit the showers!" When Boston pitcher Bill Werle missed the strike zone with nine consecutive pitches during a game in 1954, manager Boudreau came out and pulled catcher White, not pitcher Werle.

Del Wilber

This Sox catcher pinch hit in '53 and drove a home run off the first pitch thrown to him. Next time up, same thing. Two pitches, two pinch-hit homers.

Dick Williams

Williams was the acerbic manager of the 1967 Red Sox, transforming the team that had finished in ninth place the previous year into the Impossible Dream pennant winners. Lacking any discernible diplomatic skills, he didn't make many friends in the process. He told Joe Foy that he was so fat he couldn't bend over for a ground ball. He was equally critical of George Scott's eating habits and had nothing much good to say about benevolent Red Sox owner Tom Yawkey, making Williams perhaps the only person in his employ ever to criticize the likeable owner.

Ted Williams

"Ted has conquered the air because he's been an ace pilot; he's conquered the sea because he's caught so many fabulous fish; and he's conquered baseball. I mean, what he needs is another planet."
—Maureen Cronin

He was a hit in Boston before he ever set foot in that often-cynical town—this tall, skinny, 147-pound kid from San Diego. Early newspaper copy about him had whetted the New England appetite for a latter-day Moses to lead them from their baseball wilderness, another Babe Ruth to replace the one sold into bondage with the hated Yankees. When he arrived at his first spring training, teammate Bobby Doerr took young Teddy Williams aside and in hushed, almost reverential tones said, "Wait until you see Foxx hit!" Instead of being impressed, the Kid's off-hand reply was, "Wait until Foxx sees ME hit!" Ted Williams downed milkshakes to put on weight, smiled easily and positively bristled with self-confidence. He was a wild, funloving, clean-cut kid who'd shout at the bad guys in the movies and had been known to fire his shotgun out of a speeding car on the plains of Minnesota. His sole ambition was to walk down the street and have people say: "There goes the greatest hitter who ever lived." On dusty small town roadways, bustling city sidewalks and today's information superhighway, people have been doing just that for the last half-century.

✳   ✳   ✳   ✳

Williams always had a keen eye. When he returned to Fenway for batting practice after being mustered out of the service mid-way through the 1953 season, he had been away from baseball for over a year. He stepped into the box for batting practice, took a few swings and then stepped out and asked what they'd done to the plate while he was away. No one knew what he was talking about. "It's out of line," he said. "You're nuts," was the reply. Williams insisted, measurements were taken and—sure enough—the plate was about one-quarter-inch out of alignment.

✳   ✳   ✳   ✳

Ted was always a favorite of umpires. The general consensus among them was that if Ted didn't swing at a pitch, it must not have been a strike.

✳   ✳   ✳   ✳

Boston Herald writer Tim Horgan once interviewed a blind man who'd come to a Red Sox game and asked him why he didn't just stay at home and listen to the play-by-play on the radio. "I can tell when Ted comes out of the dugout," the man said, "then when he comes to the plate—just by the crowd reaction. There's no other player like Ted."

*   *   *   *

Had Ted not lost nearly five prime seasons to military service in World War II and Korea—having been called up the second time at age 34—projections show him hitting 701 home runs. If the competitive Williams had gotten that close to Babe Ruth's record, one can bet he would have found a way to hit 14 more before retiring.

*   *   *   *

Although writers were Ted Williams' sworn enemies, he still managed to inspire many a Boston columnist to literary flights of fancy. When he committed an error in left field one fine afternoon at Fenway, he was booed enthusiastically by Boston fans. When he homered later in the same game and was cheered by these same fans, it was more hypocrisy than Ted could stomach. He showed his contempt by spitting toward left field, then right field and finally toward the press box. One scribe, carried away by the exhibition, referred to Williams' performance as his Great Expectorations.

*   *   *   *

In Game Three of the 1946 World Series, Joe Garagiola had four hits and drove in three runs to lead the St. Louis Cardinals to a 12-3 victory over the Red Sox at Fenway Park. The next morning, the proud catcher rushed down to his hotel lobby to buy the morning newspaper, anxious to see how the Boston press had heralded his heroics. Much to his chagrin, the headline read: WILLIAMS BUNTS!

*   *   *   *

Ted Williams demonstrates a perfect follow through to a perfect swing.

When Teddy Ballgame was inducted into the National Baseball Hall of Fame, he wrote out his own speech the night before. It was an impassioned plea for recognition of the great Negro ballplayers who'd been excluded from the Hall of Fame only because the color barrier had kept them out of the big leagues for so long. "A chill goes up my back when I think I might have been denied this if I had been black," Ted said five years later in a speech at Howard University.

★   ★   ★   ★

Ted Williams was a hero to fans and an idol to fellow hitters, but he was looked on with awe by big-league pitchers. Rookie pitcher Pedro Ramos once struck Ted out and then had the gall to enter the Red Sox dugout and ask the Splendid Splinter to autograph the ball used to strike him out. "Get the hell out of here!" roared Terrible Ted. "I'm not signing any ball I struck out on." Ramos, who idolized Williams, was crushed and tears welled in his eyes. Seeing this, the great Williams relented. "Give me the damn ball, and I'll sign it," he said. During the next Red Sox homestand, Ted once again faced Ramos. This time he tore into the pitcher's first offering and drove the ball deep into the right-field bleachers. As he trotted around the bases, he turned to the pitcher and shouted: "Go find that SOB, and I'll sign it for you too."

*　　*　　*　　*

On July 14, 1946, the Boston Red Sox and Cleveland Indians met for a doubleheader at Fenway Park. In the first game, Ted Williams feasted on Indian pitching, hitting three home runs as the Red Sox won the marathon contest 11-10. Between games of the double-header, Williams decided to reward himself. When the last out had been recorded, he slipped through the door in the left field score-board and then through a trap door leading to the street. Still in full uniform, he walked to a nearby restaurant and placed his order: a large dish of ice cream. After consuming the frozen delight, Ted paid his bill, trotted back to the ballpark and emerged once again in left field, refreshed and ready for the remainder of the afternoon.

Ted's devastation of the Indians in game one had been so complete that it inspired Indians player-manager Lou Boudreau to introduce the infamous "Boudreau Shift," also known as the "Williams Shift." In Ted's first at-bat in game two, he doubled home three runs. Boudreau, who had watched his own record four doubles and a homer in game one go to waste, was so disgusted that he decided drastic measures were called for. He knew that lefty Ted was a dead pull hitter to right, and therefore he positioned his fielders on the right side of the ballpark.

If Fenway had been a ship it would have capsized to starboard. The first baseman and the right fielder were hugging the right-field foul line. The center fielder moved to deep right-center. The second baseman played a shallow outfield position, closer to first than to second, while the shortstop moved into the vacated second base position. The third baseman was in foreign territory directly behind second. Only the left fielder remained more or less true to Abner Doubleday's original concept, positioning himself in shallow left center field. Ted grounded out to Boudreau in his next at-bat and walked twice. Williams was to be faced with variants of the Shift throughout his career, stubbornly refusing to compromise his hitting principles by going to left field.

*   *   *   *

The Williams Shift was sometimes carried to ridiculous extremes. During a spring exhibition in Dallas in the late fifties, the manager of the opposing team placed all three outfielders in the right-field stands when Ted Williams came to the plate.

*   *   *   *

In early spring 1946, an agent of the Mexican Baseball League made a blatant attempt to coerce, cajole and entice Ted Williams into jumping from the majors to the Mexican circuit. Through an interpreter, he promised that Williams could "name his own figure and his own terms." The agent threw out a figure of $300,000 for three years. He told Ted that the right-field fences were short in Mexico and that the wind was always blowing toward the outfield. Williams appeared to be weakening. He squinted at the agent and asked: "Have you signed Bob Feller yet?" The agent asked why he wanted to know about the American League's best pitcher. "Well, if you've got Feller," said Williams: "I think I'll stay in the American League."

*　　*　　*　　*

On June 9, 1946, Joseph A. Boucher was seated in row 33, deep in the Fenway Park bleachers, watching the second game of a double-header between the Boston Red Sox and the Detroit Tigers. It was a beautiful day for baseball, with the wind blowing out, although the bright sun made it difficult for fans in the bleachers to look toward home plate. Boucher heard the public address announcer introduce the next batter: Ted Williams. Then he heard the crack of the bat and the roar of the crowd, so he knew something significant was happening. However, not until Ted's home run drive had landed on the top of his head, denting his straw hat, did Mr. Boucher realize that he had become a footnote in Red Sox history. The drive was measured at 502', and today that seat has been painted red—standing out like a beacon in a vast sea of green. "They say it bounced a dozen rows higher, but after it hit my head, I was frankly no longer interested," admitted Mr. Boucher.

*　　*　　*　　*

Ted Williams hit 12 home runs off Detroit's Virgil Trucks—more than he managed against any other pitcher. Trucks recalls his first encounter with his nemesis: "I will never forget watching Ted take batting practice during my first trip to Fenway Park in 1942. He was hitting the ball over the fences in the deepest parts of the ballpark. Unfortunately, when the game started—with me on the mound for the Tigers—he must have thought I was still pitching batting practice. In fact, everyone on the Red Sox seemed to be under that impression that day. The first batter hit a single on the first pitch; the second batter hit the first pitch for another single. Then up comes Williams. He smoked the first pitch for a double. With that, our manager, Steve O'Neill, came to the mound and so did my catcher, Bob Swift. O'Neill said to Bob: 'Doesn't Virgil have it today?', and Swift replied: 'How the hell would I know; I haven't caught a ball yet!'"

*　　*　　*　　*

When Robert Redford played Roy Hobbs in the movie *The Natural,* he modeled his character after his hero: Ted Williams. He wore number 9 and tried to imitate Ted's swing. Redford explains: "The spirit and courage that Williams epitomizes was the guiding force behind my performance in *The Natural,* and I feel strongly that this performance was, in its way, my tribute to Ted." Why? "Any heroes I had when I was a kid were pretty much born out of reading Greek mythology. In real life, in real time, there was only one: Ted Williams. He was left-handed. I was left-handed. He was from Southern California, as was I. He was a baseball player. I wanted to be one when I grew up. Incidentally, I never achieved either objective."

*   *   *   *

In 1946, the All-Star Game was played at Fenway Park. To no one's surprise, Ted Williams stole the show. After homering early in the game, he came to bat in the eighth to face Rip Sewell, whose trademark was the so-called "eephus" pitch. Sewell threw the ball on a slow arc that reached a height of some 25 feet. No hitter had ever managed a home run against this blooper, and experts claimed that such a feat was impossible because the hitter had to supply all the power. When he stepped into the batters box, Ted shouted to Sewell: "You're not going to throw me that #$@^% pitch—not in an All-Star Game?" Sewell grinned and nodded. The first offering was indeed the dreaded eephus, and after a moment of indecision, Ted swung and drove a vicious foul into the stands behind the third base dugout. The second pitch—another blooper—was outside. The one-and-one offering was a fastball, but Ted didn't bite. The Kid then proved the experts wrong. The next pitch, a classic eephus, floated slowly toward the plate like a deflating dirigible. Taking a single stride toward the ball, Ted drove it on a high arc into the right field bleachers. From their gleeful reactions, it was hard to decide who was most pleased—Rip or Ted. Today, Ted claims that if it had been a regular-season game, he would probably have been called out—he was two and a half feet out of the batters box when he hit the ball!

*   *   *   *

Ted Williams, the man with the perfect baseball swing, was a mere mortal with a golf club in his hands. At the end of one particularly brutal round, the hitting perfectionist was so disgusted with his performance that he threw his clubs, bag and all, into a lake adjacent to the 18th hole. With a flurry of oaths disturbing the peaceful surroundings, he stalked to his vehicle only to discover that he had left his car keys in the golf bag.

Rolling up his pants legs, he waded into the pond and retrieved the bag. At this point, most people would have reconsidered their original rash act and cooled off. Not Ted. He retrieved his keys and promptly threw the clubs back in the water.

*   *   *   *

It was the Splendid Splinter vs. Slammin' Sammy—a classic dispute between two legendary athletes over the relative difficulty of their respective sports. Golfer Sam Snead, possessor of perhaps the smoothest swing in golf history, and Ted Williams, the best pure hitter in the annals of baseball, were friends and fishing buddies. When it came to arguments, however, they both came out swinging.

Snead once visited the Red Sox dugout, where he and Williams discussed the merits of their two sports. "Golf's an old man's game!" taunted Williams, the ultimate needler. "You use a club with a flat-hitting surface and hit a ball that's not moving. In fact, it's teed up so that you can hit it better. On top of that, the galleries remain dead silent so as not to distract you. Meanwhile, I'm up there trying to hit a 100 mile-an-hour fastball or a curveball that looks like it's rolling off a table top. And at least half the time, a hostile crowd is yelling for me to strike out—and that's at Fenway Park!"

"Maybe so," said Snead, "but as a golfer I'm trying to get a ball in a four-and-a-half-inch cup. You're practically hitting into the whole world out there." "Not true!" countered Williams. "If I swing a split second too early, I pull it foul into the right field stands; too late, and I foul it into the left field stands." Snead paused for a moment before delivering the coup de grace. "Yes, Ted, but you don't have to wade into the stands to play your foul balls like I do." Williams' reply was not recorded.

* * * *

"He took time off for the war to rest. I didn't have that opportunity. I had to stay and play....I got tired."—*Bob Uecker, explaining why Ted Williams hit .344 lifetime with 521 homers, and he managed only a .200 average and 14 home runs.*

* * * *

Ted quizzed everyone about hitting, even pitchers. "One day, Ted was about to bat against José Santiago," recalls southpaw ace Mel Parnell. "I was standing at the bat rack, and Ted asked me: 'What does this guy throw?' I went on to relate what I thought he threw and Ted said 'OK' and went up to the plate and hits the first pitch out of the ballpark. I said: 'Hell, you sure had a lot of confidence in a pitcher's opinion.'"

* * * *

In February of 1994, Ted Williams, then 75 years old, suffered a serious stroke. Lying in a hospital and hooked up to an assortment of tubes and wires, Ted lapsed in and out of consciousness. He later told writer Dave Anderson about one particularly vivid dream; a dream that says it all about Ted Williams. As Ted tells it, he was half asleep and imagined he was back in spring training working with the young Red Sox hitters as he once did. Suddenly, fearsome left-hander Randy Johnson appeared on the mound, and the young Red Sox hopefuls were egging him on to hit against The Big Unit.

"I tell them: 'I haven't hit in years, and I just had a stroke, and I can't see too well,' but they keep teasing me and I say: 'Yeah, I'll do it.' But as I'm walking to home plate, I'm thinking: *I'm not going to try to pull this guy because he can really throw.* The first pitch he laid one right in there. I pushed at it. Line drive through the box for a base hit." Which only goes to prove what we already suspected: Ted Williams could hit today's pitching in his sleep!

*   *   *   *

Ted was apparently the last of the red-hot hitters. In a roundtable discussion organized by *Sports Illustrated* for an April 1986 cover story, hitters Ted Williams, Wade Boggs and Don Mattingly discussed the intricacies of their craft. Williams brought the conversation to an abrupt halt when he casually asked: "Have you ever smelled smoke from the wood burning on the bat?" Boggs was flummoxed at the very notion that such bat speed could be generated. Williams explained that five or six times in his career, he had faced good fastball pitchers and had just barely fouled the ball back, presumably causing the seam on the ball to burn. "That's the damnedest thing I've ever heard!" admitted Boggs, a future Hall of Famer.

*   *   *   *

Ted Williams was a hero to fans and an idol to fellow hitters, but he was looked on with awe by big-league pitchers. Satchel Paige was one of the best pitchers in baseball history, but, due to the color barrier, only fans of the Negro Leagues knew of his greatness. He finally made it to the major leagues when he was well past his prime but still more than a match for most hitters. In a key game during the hotly contested 1949 pennant race, the Red Sox faced Paige's Cleveland Indians. As the starting pitcher struggled, the 43-year-old Paige, as well known for his laid-back philosophy as for his superb pitching, warmed up alongside rookie reliever Mike Garcia. Paige, the elder statesman, tried to calm the nervous rookie.

"Those Red Sox don't have a hitter worth a moment's worry," soothed Satch. No sooner were the words out of his mouth than

Boston's number nine hitter ripped a single to left. Leadoff hitter Dom DiMaggio then stepped to the plate. "DiMaggio is certainly not his brother. No sir, this is Dominic, not Joseph." DiMaggio promptly singled. Runners at first and second, no one out.

Johnny Pesky was next up. "He's a banjo hitter. All you have to do is pitch him around the knees," said Paige with a dismissive wave of his hand. Pesky lined a clean single to load the bases. As Ted Williams strode to the plate, the banter ceased, and Satchel grew uncharacteristically quiet. With the frenzied Fenway crowd roaring in anticipation, the Cleveland manager walked purposefully to the mound and signaled for Paige. Feeling like a man reprieved, Garcia waited for further words of wisdom from his guru, but none were forthcoming. Satch remained silent. Finally, he trudged from the bullpen with all the enthusiasm of a prisoner on death row. "One last thing, son," he drawled, rolling his eyes skyward. "When you're playin' these Red Sox, put your trust in the good Lord."

✳   ✳   ✳   ✳

Even "Temperamental Ted" smiled sometimes.

He was the Splendid Splinter, not a splendid sprinter, but Ted nonetheless set one speed record that still stands—although legitimate speedster Rickey Henderson duplicated it in the 2000 season. Ted was the only player in major league history to have stolen a base in each of four different decades. Williams had a lifetime total of just 24 stolen bases, but he spread them out efficiently: two in 1939, 14 in the 1940s, seven in the 1950s and one in 1960.

*　　*　　*　　*

Only once did Ted Williams hit under .300. In 1959, suffering several injuries that limited his number of at-bats to 272, Ted managed only .254. He decided to play one more year but stipulated that it would be on the condition that he be given a 30% pay cut. Ted felt he hadn't earned his salary. Owner Tom Yawkey reluctantly complied. There was no players' union to argue that the best-paid hitter in baseball shouldn't be allowed to dock himself for a bad year.

*　　*　　*　　*

Ted Williams was truly in another league when it came to hitting. Williams batted a cool .344 in a career that began in 1939 and ended with a dramatic homer in 1960 (with interruptions for service in WWII and Korea.) During that same period, the American League average was .260, a 0.84 differential.

*　　*　　*　　*

Fans in New York and Boston still argue about which is the more incredible baseball feat: Joe DiMaggio's 56-game hitting streak, or Ted Williams's .406 batting average. Both took place in 1941. There is no question that Ted had the better offensive numbers for that season. He hit 37 homers to Joe's 30; his on-base percentage of .551 bested Joe's .440 mark; his slugging average was .735 to Joe's

.643, and of course he out-hit DiMaggio .406 to .357. But how did the two men compare during the 56-game streak? Joe batted a stellar .409 during his streak, but that was only a mere three points higher than the average that Ted maintained over the course of a full season.

Hank Aaron: "I'd have to agree that 56, 755 and .406 are three of the most significant numbers in baseball history. When fans think about hitting streaks, they think DiMaggio; when they think about home runs, it's me or Ruth. But when you think about hitting, it's Ted Williams and .406."

$$* \quad * \quad * \quad *$$

In 1942, Ted Williams won the Triple Crown with a .356 batting average, 36 homers, and 137 RBIs. Ted also led the A.L. in runs, bases on balls, total bases, slugging percentage and on-base percentage, as well as in runs produced. The Yankees' Joe Gordon batted .322, hit 18 homers, and drove in 103 runs. What did Gordon lead in? Only two statistics—strikeouts (with 95) and grounding into double plays. He also committed 28 errors, more than any other player at his position. So who was voted American League MVP in 1942? Joe Gordon by a vote of 270-249.

$$* \quad * \quad * \quad *$$

In Korea, Ted served his second tour of duty (he'd already given up three years of his career to serve in World War II), this time as a United States Marine fighter bomber pilot. He served in the same squadron as John Glenn, and was Glenn's wingman on many missions. Twice Ted's plane was hit by enemy ground fire, and once his jet exploded in flame just seconds after he crash-landed it on a nearby base. Glenn offered an appraisal of Ted's contribution:

"I'd guess probably half the missions that Ted flew in Korea he flew as my wing man. ... He did a great job and he was a good pilot. He was out there to do a job and he did a helluva good job. Ted ONLY batted .406 for the Red Sox. He batted a thousand for the Marine Corps and the United States."

* * * *

Ted Williams never got beaned in the majors, but he did get hit in the head once in the minor leagues. "Bill Zuber got me in the back of the head," recalls Ted. Sid Hudson came closest to beaning Ted in the majors. "I went to a 3-2 count on him in Washington and he hit the bill of my cap and turned my cap right around."

* * * *

Billy Consolo recalls: "Ted Williams. 1953. I was in the clubhouse when he was coming back. I saw them put this uniform in the locker. Number 9. I said, 'Oh, my God.' My locker was right near the toilet. Of course, all the rookies get right near the toilet, you see. I was six lockers down from him. He had two lockers. Everybody else had one. He was next to the bat rack also. Johnny Orlando put out that uniform and, boy, I sat in my locker until he walked in—with about a hundred sportswriters. And cameras. Those old cameras. These were those tripod things. And they were shooting him. I mean to tell you, I get chills even talking about that day.

"Then he went out and took batting practice. With his golf gloves. Nobody used golf gloves in those days. They call them batting gloves now. He had been out of shape. They gave him about 30 days to get in shape so he wore those gloves to protect his hands. He had to start off from scratch. That was exciting. That was quite a day.

"And then to see him come out of the ballpark at night after a ballgame, and those people just a hundred deep. They wouldn't let his car out of the parking lot. They wanted to see him, touch him. He never traveled with us in the end. He and Paul Schreiber—the batting practice pitcher—they roomed together at different hotels than where we stayed. He couldn't walk through the lobby of a hotel, with people knowing the Red Sox were in that hotel. It was like playing with Babe Ruth."

* * * *

The Splendid Splinter carried on a tempestuous feud with the Boston press, giving them the finger, spitting at the press box, making remarks about the smell of manure as he'd pass a reporter in the clubhouse. His boyish Western enthusiasm was met with some cynicism by a hard-drinking press corps who seemed to resent the too-good-to-be-true youngster from the Coast. When they starting prying into his family, Ted felt they'd crossed the line in the competitive quest for headlines, using him—even prodding him—for fodder, and he withdrew. As time went on, he learned to work the press, and there are those that allege he stirred up some of the controversy himself later on as a way to energize himself, to pull himself out of slumps. He often seemed to explode out of a doldrums after one of the incidents.

"I put up with a lot of nonsense from Ted. I started covering baseball in '51 or '52. It was tough in the press box, especially when you're breaking in new. I was fresh out of college, and I ran into a buzz saw with this guy. I was kind of proud, got a job with a metropolitan newspaper, and all of a sudden this guy's telling me I'm a bum. He was tough. He was indiscriminate."—Tim Horgan, *Boston Herald*

*   *   *   *

"The fans turned on him. I think because he is a combative person that it actually fed him and he used it. Some shrinking violets would have been crushed by that sort of treatment, but he was a courageous, stand-up guy and that fed him. He likes competition, he likes rivalry, he likes an argument. He had a different personality from DiMaggio and Musial who were both quiet guys who kept to themselves and weren't flamboyant."—Paul Gleason, actor and friend of Ted Williams

"What made Ted great was that he refused to think that a pitcher could get him out. I mean he just refused to buckle, and that's what it takes to be great. Somehow you've just got to feel that you are the best. That's how he played the game and that's how he left the game, as the best"—Hank Aaron

Billy Consolo adds another memory: "When I was a kid 18 years old, I remember going north, barnstorming, with Ted Williams, and every town we went into—like Bloomfield, South Carolina, towns like that—the whole town would show up to see one man: Ted Williams. They didn't even know who the other players on the Red Sox were. It was only one guy. There were people sitting on mountains, looking over ballparks in the south. One game every day. You'd get on the train and barnstorm north. We used to go up with the Phillies a lot of times and the Braves a lot of times. But everybody came to see Ted Williams, let's face it. It was jam city when he played. That was exciting."

✳   ✳   ✳   ✳

Ted loved to fish in New Brunswick, Canada, and keeps a house there on the Miramichi, one of the world's great salmon rivers. He's also helped inspire the battle to save the endangered Atlantic salmon and he still funds the Ted Williams Conservation Award, a highly prized award for writers who have helped the cause. In 2001, Ted was inducted into the Atlantic Salmon Hall of Fame and author Jim Prime accepted on Ted's behalf.

Those who know sport fishing considered Ted one of the greatest sport fishermen of all time. He's a member of the International Game Fish Association Hall of Fame and still holds the record for one of the largest fish ever caught (off the coast of Peru.) Ted's fishing prowess has been reflected in his induction into two other halls of fame for anglers: the Atlantic Salmon Hall of Fame and the National Freshwater Fishing Hall of Fame.

In all, Ted Williams is a member of the following Halls of Fame:

> San Diego Hall of Champions
> National Baseball Hall of Fame
> Atlantic Salmon Hall of Fame
> National Freshwater Fishing Hall of Fame
> International Game Fish Association Hall of Fame
> Boston Red Sox Hall of Fame
> United States Marine Corps Sports Hall of Fame
> Florida Sports Hall of Fame
> Hispanic Heritage Baseball Museum

One Hall of Fame that has not inducted Ted is the Hitters Hall of Fame in Hernando, Florida—but that is because it is part of the Ted Williams Museum and Ted specifically asked that he not be included.

The Ted Williams Museum is the first museum ever dedicated to a living athlete. Visitors can view taped video tributes to Ted recorded by four United States Presidents—Richard Nixon, Gerald Ford, Ronald Reagan and George H.W. Bush.

Ted is closest to George Bush, a former college first baseman at Yale, and President Bush participated in the Museum's annual event in 1995. Ted has campaigned for a number of political candidates for office—so long as they're Republican.

＊   ＊   ＊   ＊

Ted's father was a friend of California's Governor Merriam. When the young Ted was first introduced to Merriam, with typical unselfconscious irreverence, he simply greeted the Governor with a spirited "Hiya, Guv!"

"I just wish I could have voted for you. But you had to be a $%#@% Democrat!"
            —Ted Williams to astronaut and former U.S. Senator John Glenn at "An Evening with #9 and Friends" in 1988.

I hardly know Ted. The only time I remember Ted was when we played him in the All-Star Game in Fenway Park, in 1946. He hit a couple of home runs and I was playing shortstop, and as he rounded second base he looked over at me and gave me a big wink, and he says, "Kid, don't you wish you could hit like that?"—Marty Marion

＊   ＊   ＊   ＊

*Finding a Ted Williams card was cause
for celebration.*

Vic Power remembers an episode from his past that is reminis-
cent of Tom Sawyer's famous whitewashing encounter. "I played
with some characters. Like Tony Oliva. . . . Well, I was living in
Minnesota. It's cold up there during the winter and I had to get
up every morning to shovel snow to take my car out of the garage
to drive my kids to school. I was tired of it.

"I was reading in a psychology book that in life man takes
advantage of other men to get ahead. Okay, I thought, let me see
if this works.

"Now I'm sitting in my house with Tony. I said, 'Tony, you
know what I just read? I was reading Ted Williams's book, and Ted
said that the secret to his success was shoveling snow.'

"Ted Williams was the greatest hitter—the most power, the
most intelligent, the last guy to hit .400. And he said his secret is
shoveling snow."

"The next day Tony was at my house with a shovel. I was inside
laughing, and he was outside shoveling snow. Then come October,

the end of the season, and Tony Oliva was the batting champion. He said, 'Vic, you were right.'

"And now look what happened: Kirby Puckett became the batting champion. I think he's been telling Puckett to shovel snow."—*They Played the Game*

The following story from *A Bittersweet Journey* explains a lot about the drive that made Ted Williams the greatest hitter of them all. Jimmy Piersall recalled,

"They were tough on him, but you know why? They sort of sensed that when they got on him, he played better. He hit better. Ted used to say to me when I got mad about something, 'I'll take care of it, kid. Don't worry.' He used to talk through his teeth when he got mad. I said, 'Ted, why are you getting so mad all the time?' And he said, 'You know why? Because I've got to be good every day. You don't.'"

$$\ast \qquad \ast \qquad \ast \qquad \ast$$

Ted, on not wanting to settle for a .3995 on the last day of the 1941 season: "I want to have more than my toenails on the line." Ted chose to hit, and went 6-for-8, boosting his average to .406.

$$\ast \qquad \ast \qquad \ast \qquad \ast$$

How often does a ballplayer demand a decrease in salary? Ted did, after he only hit .254 in 272 at-bats in 1959.

"I'd just go in and see Mr. Yawkey, and we'd talk a little fishing and we'd talk a little hunting, and he'd ask me how I felt, and I'd sit down and sign my contract. They doubled my salary every year for the first five years, and when it got to $125,000, they kept it there every year for the last ten years. But when they gave me the usual $125,000 for the 1960 season, I tore it up right in Mr. Yawkey's face. I threw it down on the table and told him to give me $90,000, because that's all I deserved."

*   *   *   *

Actor Paul Gleason, who was friendly with beat generation writer Jack Kerouac, reports that the young Kerouac admired Ted's rebel side and would often hitchhike into Boston from his native Lowell to catch games in Ted's first few years. "He let things flow and that was what Kerouac looked for in everything in life—people who didn't revise their behavior, didn't conform ... in Ted's case, he just let it fly."

*   *   *   *

"Ted the first rebel? No. A rebel to me is a guy who goes out of his way to create problems. Ted was absolutely true to himself. I don't think there was anything rebellious about it. I think the guy was just honest, the first really honest guy. And maybe the last one, too."—Bobby Knight

*   *   *   *

Ted's high school principal Floyd Johnson appreciated his attitude.

"When Williams attended Hoover High School, he habitually dropped into my office for a chat. During these chats, it never occurred to me that Ted would usually slump down into his chair and put his feet up on the principal's desk. The subject would usually be either baseball or fishing, subjects I was just as interested in as Ted. And I'd be enjoying the conversation so much I'd be completely oblivious to his posture and unconventional way of talking to the school principal. This was never impudence on Ted's part. To him all folks on the school campus were the same—faculty, principal, or kids."—*Ted Williams* by Arthur Sampson.

*   *   *   *

Sparky Anderson wrote:

"In spring training a while back, we played the Red Sox in Winter Haven.

"In batting practice before the game, a man walked up to shake my hand.

"'Hi, Sparky. I'm Ted Williams,' he said.

"I almost fell over. I started to laugh.

"'Ted, that's the funniest thing I ever heard,' I said.

"'What do you mean?' he said.

"'You telling me that you're Ted Williams,' I answered. 'Everybody knows you. You don't have to say who you are.'

"'No, Sparky, it can't be that way,' he explained. 'I would never want you to be embarrassed if you happened to forget who I was.'

"Now just imagine. This was Ted Williams. This was one of the greatest players in the history of our game making sure that I wasn't embarrassed.

"That's not only success. That's class.

"After that, I never meet anyone to whom I don't introduce myself before the other guy gets a chance. I always walk up with my hand out. 'Hi, I'm Sparky Anderson.'"

—*Sparky!* by Sparky Anderson

*   *   *   *

Talk to players from the 1950s. Every one of them will tell you: when Ted stepped into the box to take batting practice, everyone else stopped and watched. Then silence was punctuated only by the hard shots of balls hit deep. "It was a picture swing," says former roommate Broadway Charlie Wagner. "You don't have to be prejudiced about it. He stopped everything in the ballpark, just with his swing. When he went to bat in batting practice, the whole park got silent as a church. Beautiful swing. A classic swing. Nobody's had it since."

When Ted took over right field for the Red Sox in 1939, he displaced Ben Chapman, who had hit .340 the year before. It wasn't all bad news for Chapman. Forever afterward, harking back to an earlier job change, he bragged that he lost his job twice to two good men—to Joe DiMaggio of the Yankees and Ted Williams of the Red Sox.

*   *   *   *

In his book *Oddballs,* author Bruce Shalin talks about becoming a navel explorer courtesy of Ted Williams.

"Both leagues had just made an adjustment in the strike zone for the '88 season, so I asked Williams what he thought about it. 'Where's my belly button?' he growled. I pointed at his midsection, and he said, 'Where is it? Show me where it is!' I pointed my finger at his waistband. 'No, that's not it!' He pulled down the waistband of his baseball pants, grabbed my finger and stuck it in his belly-button. So there I was, with my finger in the navel of the greatest hitter who ever lived. 'Here it is,' he said. 'Now this ball at the bellybutton has got to be a strike.' "

*   *   *   *

Ted invited Tony Gwynn to receive an award at the Ted Williams Museum's annual event in 1995. Tony doesn't like dinners and awards, but this was, of course, Ted Williams making the invitation. Tony told his agent John Boggs, "There'll probably be a million people there and I'm going to get some award and probably see Ted Williams for about two seconds."

That was basically what happened the first evening. The next day, it looked like a reprise of the evening before when Bob Costas asked Tony to sit down for a one-on-one discussion between him and Ted. "We went back there," Boggs recalls, "and it was Costas and his producer, the cameraman, technician, President Bush, Ted Williams and Tony. And I'm sitting there thinking, 'Man, this is unbelievable.' President Bush left and Tony took the President's seat, and they started talking. And I am telling you, it was like the student and the pupil. You could tell that Tony wanted to relate his batting theories when Ted was asking the questions, but always had this hesitancy he was going to say the wrong thing. You got this sense of relief every time Ted would say, 'Absolutely!' "

Tony himself adds, "I was like a kid in a candy store. When he was talking, I was like a little kid. But I hung in there and made a few of my points, talked about how I do it. That was clutch."

*   *   *   *

A Red Sox utility player had just returned from a public appearance for which he was paid the grand sum of $35. He met Ted Williams who was on his way to another appearance—this one for $1,000. "How can they justify the difference in money?" whined the long-forgotten player. "Just think of it as the difference between .238 and .388," explained Ted.

*   *   *   *

Having tried unsuccessfully to get Ted out any other way, former teammate Jimmy Piersall came up with a unique new strategy to foil the Splendid Splinter. With Ted at the plate in the late innings of a close game, Piersall, now playing outfield for the Cleveland Indians, sprinted back and forth repeatedly from his position in center field to left field. Instead of distracting Ted, the bizarre maneuver got Piersall ejected from the game.

Ted Williams was asked if the inside-the-park homer he hit to win the pennant-clinching game in 1946 was the easiest he ever hit. "Hell no, it was the hardest. I had to run."

*   *   *   *

What about the Holy Ghost? Ted Williams hit a HR off Thornton Lee in his first year, 1939 (the 28th of his career) and off Thornton's son Don Lee (the 517th) in September, 1960, the final month of his final year.

*   *   *   *

In 1999, Ted Williams was back in Fenway Park for the third, and possibly last All-Star Game ever to be played there. Once again, he was the center of attention as current stars and Hall of Famers gathered around him, like starryeyed kids. True to form, Ted could be heard giving hitting instruction to Mark McGwire and Sammy Sosa, who had only combined for 136 homers the previous year.

* * * *

Ted claims that he can remember in detail each of his first 300 major league home runs—who the pitcher was, what the count was, the kind of pitch and where the ball landed. He also remembers the strikeouts. Billy Crystal, a great Yankee fan, once cornered Ted Williams at a cardsigning show and informed him that he had home movies of Ted striking out. The actor-comedian related a specific time more than three decades previous, when Ted had struck out in a key situation against a Yankee pitcher. Ted nodded knowingly. "Curveball," he said. "Low and away."

Ted managed the Washington Senators in 1969. The team performed well above expectations, as did several individual players. Ted was voted Manager of the Year, but he was on safari in Africa when the award was announced. Told he'd been honored as Manager of the Year, Williams expressed pleasure but then added, "I'll tell you something. It was just another case of the writers being wrong again. Weaver and Martin deserved it more."

* * * *

Umpire Joe Paparella told Larry Gerlach about Ted's uncommon courtesy. "I worked with so many outstanding players. ... Ted Williams stood ceiling-high. He very rarely looked back at an umpire at the plate. And he would help you even to the point of getting players off your back. If you finished the season with

Boston, he'd come to the dressing room, shake your hand, wish you and your family a happy winter, and thank you for being associated with the game. He was the only one to ever do that."

*   *   *   *

Ted leaves baseball to fight bigger battles.

Had Ted not missed the 1943, 1944 and 1945 seasons while serving in the Navy during World War II, he almost certainly would have had another 100 home runs—to which he might have added yet another 50 had he not spent most of 1952 and 1953 serving in the Korean War. Ted actually did hit one home run at Fenway Park during a 1943 game, but you won't find it in any record books. To support the war effort, the Boston Braves played a special team of allstars drawn from the armed services. Ted played on the allstar team and hit a home run. His manager? Babe Ruth.

*　　*　　*　　*

In his book *Cobb,* A.L. Stump asserts that Ted and Ty Cobb had a bitter falling out over an incident in which they were comparing their all-time line-ups. Williams argued for the inclusion of Rogers Hornsby on his all-star squad. Cobb objected, presumably due to his intense personal dislike for Hornsby. Ted, probably unaware of this and arguing his point, added recklessly that Hornsby's .424 season had even outdone the Georgia Peach. Cobb, the story goes, became enraged, shouting "Get away from me! And don't come back!" And he never spoke to Ted again. Ted refutes this version, telling Jim Prime, "Ty Cobb was a close friend of mine and we remained friends up until the time he died."

*　　*　　*　　*

When Ted tried his hand on the pitching mound in an August game in 1940, his catcher was Joe Glenn, the same man who had caught the final pitch thrown by another pretty good hitter named Babe Ruth. Glenn was a catcher for the Yankees in 1933, the last year Ruth appeared on the mound in a major league game.

*　　*　　*　　*

In 1954 Ted Williams reported to spring training and on the first day of workouts, fell in the outfield and broke his collarbone. He was sent back to Boston where doctors inserted a steel pin in his shoulder, and as a result Williams missed all of spring training. After a period of recuperation, he took batting practice for a few days and rejoined the Red Sox in Baltimore, where he was put in to pinch-hit. He flied out to center field.

The Red Sox then moved on to Detroit for a double header against the Tigers. It was during this twin bill that the Red Sox left-fielder single-handedly set spring training back 50 years. Ted went

8 for 9 in what announcer Curt Gowdy calls, "The most amazing batting show I think I've ever seen.

"Before the game," recalls Gowdy, "I asked him how he felt and he was moaning. 'Oh, I'm not swinging the bat well. I shouldn't even be playing.' And then he goes out and hits every pitch they throw to him. The New York Yankees were playing the Indians in Cleveland, and the next morning Casey Stengel was reading about Ted's feat in the morning paper. The old perfessor said, 'I'm gonna get them steel pins put in all my players' shoulders.'"

*　*　*　*

Even superstars took a backseat to Ted Williams. American League MVP Jackie Jensen once confided to roommate Dick Gernert: "You crouch in the on-deck circle and watch them throw four wide pitches past the big guy, and you think of your kid days, when the other pitchers were afraid of you. With Williams on your side, they're never afraid of you up there. They'd rather pitch to anyone but him. Then if you don't get on base yourself, you're the goat."— from *The Jackie Jensen Story*

*　*　*　*

Ted was famous for his great eye at the plate. He seldom swung at any pitch that wasn't in the strike zone and pitchers knew this all too well. So did umpires, who respected his patience and his infallible knowledge of the strike zone. The Yankees were about to play the Red Sox and during a clubhouse meeting they were going over the various hitters. Catcher Bill Dickey advised pitcher Spud Chandler to pitch Ted either "high and tight" or "low and away. Chandler, one of the Yankees' best hurlers, was not impressed with this advice. "Ok, Bill," he said sarcastically. "I throw one high and tight, and the next one low and away. Now it's two balls and no strikes. Then what do I do?"

*   *   *   *

Hall of Famer Jim Palmer recalls: "The first time I met Ted was when he was managing the "Washington Senators. He was giving a hitting clinic and I remember telling him our second baseman, Davey Johnson, that you need to have a six-degree upswing. Davey worked hard on that. He had about 148 different batting stances for the year trying to get that six-degree upswing. He'd swing and then he'd ask me, 'You think that's six degrees?' and I'd say, 'No. It's only about five and a half.'"

*   *   *   *

Even the best hitter in history had his off days. The only player in ML history to face a pitcher three times in the same inning? Ted Williams. He set the major league record in the seventh inning of an Independence Day game between Boston and Washington. Ted walked twice and grounded out once. The Red Sox scored 14 times that inning, but Ted didn't have a hit in the entire game—the only Red Sox player who didn't.

*   *   *   *

"I am building up strength to do a lot of slamming as we head down the stretch," Ted said in late July 1946. "Thursday night down at Pawtucket," Mel Webb wrote in the *Boston Globe*, "he did as well in the banquet league as he has been doing all along at the dish. And here's the damage Teddy did:

 3 shrimp cocktails
 3 cups of fish chowder
 1 1½ inch thick steak
 10 rolls
 1 pound of butter
 2 orders of string beans

2 2½ pound broiled lobsters
1 chef's salad
3 ice creams with chocolate sauce
plus an undetermined amount of iced tea

Legendary Sox announcer and longtime friend of Ted Williams, Curt Gowdy recalls a phone call he received a few years ago from the erstwhile "Kid." "Seven a.m.," he says. "I was sound asleep. I heard this gruff voice, 'Gowdy! It's Teddy Ballgame. Wake up! I want to ask you something. Where in the hell are those golden years?' And then he hung up.

Ted's Philadelphia Story

Ted Williams was a great hitter for many reasons: great eyesight, hard work, a will to succeed, and last but not least, his listening abilities. From his time in the minor leagues, right up through his entire major-league career, Ted sought out the Svengalis of swing and the high priests of hitting. He learned at the feet of Rogers Hornsby, Ty Cobb and Eddie Collins. He conferred with Bill Terry. He interrogated Collins about Shoeless Joe Jackson, Babe Ruth, Lou Gehrig and Cobb. Some of the advice he dismissed as incompatible with his own approach to hitting. Cobb's theories, for example, were completely foreign to Ted. Others he embraced, enhanced and added to his repertoire.

September 27, 1941 was a drizzly late summer evening in Philadelphia. It had rained hard earlier in the day, canceling the ballgame, and passersby rushed heads down along the tree-lined streets, scarcely noticing the tall athletic man and the shorter, stockier man walking along in animated conversation. Few of the onlookers were aware that the taller man was on the verge of a feat so rare that it has not been repeated in any baseball season since.

They walked through business areas and neighborhoods with immaculately manicured lawns. Occasionally, the shorter man would duck into a bar for a quick refresher, while the athlete went for ice cream. The taller man, Red Sox phenom Ted Williams, and his less imposing friend, clubhouse boy Johnny Orlando, were talking hitting—specifically the next day's season-ending doubleheader between the Red Sox and the hometown Athletics. Ted reckons they walked about ten miles that night. Exactly what was said is long forgotten, but knowing Williams, he was analyzing the pitchers he would see the next day—what they might throw in particular situations and on specific counts.

The last time anyone had batted .400 was 1930, more than a decade earlier, when Bill Terry batted .401 for the National League's New York Giants. Terry had been the closest thing Ted had to a boyhood idol. The last American Leaguer to reach the mark was Harry Heilmann, way back in 1923. As he walked, Ted remembered the encouraging words he had heard from Heilmann a few weeks earlier: "Just hit the way you can hit, and you'll be all right."

Going into the twin bill, Williams was batting precisely .39955—which for math majors everywhere, and certainly by major league baseball standards, would make him a .400 hitter. But Ted's personal standards were even higher. He did not want to leave his fate up to the discretion of a statistician in some airless league office. Earlier that same evening, Sox manager Joe Cronin had suggested that maybe Ted would like to sit out the last two meaningless games to preserve the coveted mark. Ted's reply was as blunt as it was powerful. "If I can't hit .400 all the way, I don't deserve it," he said. There was no argument.

Just before this crucial two-game finale, Al "Bucketfoot" Simmons, then a coach for the Athletics, swaggered into the Red Sox dugout, intent on planting doubts in the young hitter's mind. Four times in his career, Simmons, a lifetime .334 hitter, had averaged over .380, leading the American League in 1930 and '31. He and Cobb had always criticized Williams for being too selective at the plate. Approaching Ted, he taunted: "How much you wanna bet you don't hit .400?" Lesser men would have found the challenge from a bona fide Hall of Famer disconcerting, if not devastating. Not so Williams. If anything, it had the opposite effect, galvanizing Ted to the task at hand.

September 28 broke cold, damp and dreary at Shibe Park—the sort of day that signaled the imminent move from the diamond to the gridiron. The crowd of 10,000 who braved the unpleasant conditions was rooting for the kid from Boston. In fact, they were pulling for him all the way. As he entered the batter's box, he heard home plate umpire Bill McGowan mutter: "To hit .400 a player has got to be loose." Ted had always enjoyed a great relationship with umpires; he respected them and never showed them up, and they, in return, marveled at his uncanny knowledge of the strike zone.

Ted was undeniably loose. He singled sharply in his first at-bat, then homered to straightaway center field, and finished the game with two more singles and a walk. After game one, there was no way he could fail to hit .400, and many felt he would sit out the second game with a clear conscience. To the surprise and delight of the Philadelphia fans, however, Ted trotted out to his position in left field. In game two, he confirmed his legend by doubling off the loudspeaker in right field and adding another hit. At the end of the day, he had accumulated six hits in eight at-bats, raising his average to .406.

Heilmann had been right; Simmons dead wrong! Ironically, perhaps appropriately, in 1927, Heilmann had also battled down to the wire before capturing the American League batting title. Like Ted, he had refused to sit out the second game of a doubleheader to preserve his title. He picked up three hits to raise his average to .398 and win handily over the runner up—one Al "Bucketfoot" Simmons.

Jimy Williams

During Jimy Williams's tenure as Red Sox manager, he compiled an enviable 414-352 win-loss record (.541 winning percentage) and although his on-field strategies sometimes baffled Sox fans, his baseball know-how won admirers throughout baseball. He was voted manager of the year in the A.L. in 1999 and at the time of his abrupt dismissal in the midst of the 2001 pennant race, he had the injury-ravaged Red Sox 12 games over .500 with a 65-53 record, just two games out in the wild-card race and not far behind the league-leading Yankees. The team collapsed after his departure, playing sub .500 ball the rest of the way.

*   *   *   *

Bill Lee; "Jimy Williams did a great job of pissing everybody off and getting them to do things they never would have. Jim Palmer was like that with Earl Weaver.

"Dick Williams was like that in 1967 when we won the pennant."

*   *   *   *

Williams was criticized for being less than open with the media and fans. He often refused to discuss strategic moves, cutting off reporters' questions with the blunt explanation "manager's decision." Some of his homegrown expressions rivaled Yogi Berra for their obscurity.

Some examples of what the *Boston Globe* termed "Jimywocky":

During his first press conference as Red Sox manager in 1996, Williams stunned the Boston media with the following observation: "If a frog had wings, he wouldn't bump his booty."

Williams was once asked about a home run by Manny Ramirez that appeared to start out foul and then turn fair: "I'm not the ball. I think the ball is the only one who knows."

Asked to assess Japanese reliever Tomo Ohka's fastball, he said: "He had some giddy-up. How do you say giddy-up in Japanese? 'Hi-ho, Silver?'"

When asked if reporters could see him earlier in the morning, he replied: "As long as I've got my cup on."

When he was asked under what conditions his base runners should steal, he offered the following thoughts: "The runner dictates it. The pitcher dictates it. The catcher dictates it. The score dictates it. The situation dictates it. But I'm not a dictator, whatever that means."

His reaction to Seattle's Kingdome being torn down: "One less racquetball court."

Asked to pinpoint his hometown of Arroyo Grande, California: "It's about three miles past 'Resume Speed.'"

Fall 2001, with Sox pitching in shambles, everyone wondered who'd be starting when the team returned from Cleveland.

Williams was asked about the state of his rotation. His response? "It's in Ohio, and Friday it will be in Boston."

When asked if the '99 Sox were a surprise, Williams answered, "I don't know about that, surprise, or all those other adjectives, or what do you use, adverbs? Prepositions? I like gerunds. I went to high school with a guy named Gerand Thornquist. His dad drove a bus for Greyhound. He was almost the valedictorian. You'd have to be with a name like that."

No one can remember the question, and it became irrelevant when Williams responded, "I guess, you know, when I was a little kid, I liked to play marbles. You know, everybody has different games they like to play. I liked to play marbles. A lot of you people think I've lost mine, I don't know. I still got them at home in a big brandy snifter. I really do."

✳   ✳   ✳   ✳

Williams is highly regarded in baseball and was quickly snapped by the Houston Astros practically the minute the season was over. One assumes he will adapt to his new environment. Jimy was once asked to offer his evaluation of Enron Field (which happened to be the home of the Astros before they bought back the naming rights in the wake of the Enron scandal): "What position does he play?

Jim Willoughby

"They never should have taken out Willoughby."

Along with "They should have taken out Buckner!", "They should never have sold Babe Ruth!", and "They should never have started Galehouse," this statement ranks right up there as a hot-stove league perennial when discussing the great mysteries of Red Sox history. In Game Seven of the 1975 World Series, the Red Sox and Cincinnati Reds were tied 3-3 going into the ninth inning. Jim Willoughby, a willowy sinker-ball artist, had been brought on in the seventh and silenced the Reds' big bats, retiring Johnny Bench with the bases loaded. He then mowed down the Reds 1-2-3 in the eighth. But in the bottom of the eighth, with a runner on first and two out, manager Darrell Johnson pinch-hit for Willoughby, thereby removing Boston's best reliever from his arsenal. As every Red Sox fan knows, the Reds scored against his replacement, Jim Burton, in the top of the ninth and clinched the World Series.

Rick Wise

Rick Wise was a talented right-handed pitcher who won 188 games during his 18-year major league career. From 1974-77, he pitched for the Red Sox, winning 19 games for the pennant winners of 1975.

While with the Red Sox, Wise was a member of the infamous group known as the "Buffalo Heads" who succeeded in making manager Don Zimmer's life less than pleasant during his time in Boston. Other members were Bill Lee and Ferguson Jenkins. The group was supposedly named after Zimmer because, as Jenkins so kindly put it, "a buffalo is the dumbest animal on earth."

Perhaps Wise should have thought back to his own baseball past before joining such a group. While pitching in the National League against San Francisco he was once hit in the head by a line drive and was immediately rushed to the hospital where x-rays were taken. Fortunately the results were negative, but when Wise opened the newspaper the next day, he was confronted with the following sports page headline: "X-rays of Wise's Head Reveal Nothing."

Smoky Joe Wood

"Can I throw harder than Joe Wood? There's no man alive that can throw harder than Joe Wood," —Walter "Big Train" Johnson

Smoky Joe Wood's 1912 pitching record was an amazing 34-5—the best of the century with the possible exception of Walter Johnson's 36-7 slate in 1913. Wood recorded 258 strikeouts, a

Smoky Joe Wood (Brace Photography)

1.91 ERA and 10 shutouts. He pitched 35 complete games and a total of 344 innings! On September 6, 1912, Wood and Johnson met in the most anticipated and hyped sporting event of the young century. To add to the drama, Wood was looking for his 14th consecutive win in front of the hometown crowd at Fenway Park. Johnson, known because of his blazing speed as the Big Train, had set the record earlier that same season when he won 16 straight. It was a promoter's dream; a match made in Cooperstown. It would be difficult to imagine a modern equivalent, but picture Roger Clemens in his prime taking the mound against Pedro Martinez, and you get some idea.

To say that the game was a pitching duel is like saying that Ali vs. Frazier was a mild disagreement. The two moundsmen did not disappoint the capacity crowd, throwing fastball after fastball past overmatched batters. Not until the bottom of the sixth inning did the Red Sox finally spoil the two neat rows of zeros on the scoreboard. With two men retired, Tris Speaker, Wood's best friend and roommate, doubled. Duffy Lewis followed with another double to score Speaker. Appropriately, the final score was 1-0, with Wood emerging victorious and winning his 14th in a row. He would go on to win his next two as well to tie Johnson's new American League standard.

✴   ✴   ✴   ✴

"Smoky Joe could throw harder than anyone." —Satchel Paige

"I threw so hard I thought my arm would fly right off my body." —Joe Wood

✴   ✴   ✴   ✴

Wood shared one thing with Babe Ruth—they were both excellent pitchers *and* excellent hitters. Ruth is more known for his hitting career, obviously, but—largely in his years with Boston—he did win 94 games to just 46 losses and posted a 2.28 career ERA! Smoky Joe Wood, on the other hand, is remembered only as a pitcher; he had precisely the same win-percentage ratio as Ruth (.671) with a 116-57 record and a career 2.03 ERA. He's best remembered for his spectacular 34-5 season for the Red Sox in 1912, with 344 innings pitched.

Nevertheless, Wood was also a good hitter. Back in those days, the pitcher always hit anyhow, but after the Red Sox sold his contract to Cleveland before the 1917 season, Wood played the outfield and hit a respectable .297 over six seasons. His lifetime average was .283.

Smoky Joe Wood and Babe Ruth both appeared for the Red Sox in one World Series as pitchers and in another World Series as outfielders.

Tris and Smoky

Surely the most productive roommates in Red Sox history were Tris Speaker and Smoky Joe Wood. In 1912, the two friends led the Red Sox to the American League pennant and a World Series championship. Wood won 34 regular-season games and notched three World Series victories. He pitched 35 complete games during the season, and boasted a microscopic 1.91 ERA. Speaker batted .383 and, in the middle of the dead ball era, led the A.L. in doubles with 53, and homers with 10.

Joseph Frank Wood, the son of Red Sox fireballer Smoky Joe Wood, pitched three games for the Red Sox in 1944. This Wood was hardly a chip off the old block. He went 0-1 with a 6.52 ERA.

John Wyatt

Caught in a rundown between third and home, pitcher John Wyatt dropped several items from his Sox pitching jacket. The excess baggage included a tube of Vaseline, a pack of cigarettes and his car keys. We're not sure what Sherlock Holmes would deduce from those clues, but possibly, just possibly, Wyatt was up to no good.

Carl Yastrzemski

"I loved the game. I loved the competition. But I never had any fun. I never enjoyed it. All hard work; all the time." —Yaz

W hat's in a name? Carl Yastrzemski was so popular in Boston that Sherm Feller used to introduce him only by his number: "Number 8!" Only Yaz and Ted (# 9) have reached that numerical level of fame with the Red Sox.

*   *   *   *

Bill Lee suggests that Yaz's longevity had much to do with the number he wore: "When he lies in bed at night, it forms the algebraic symbol for infinity."

*   *   *   *

Like Ted Williams, his predecessor in left field, Carl Yastrzemski was often the target of abuse from the fans down the left field line at Fenway. He once turned the jeers into cheers by trotting to his position, and with great show, removed large wads of cotton from his ears.

*   *   *   *

In 1967, Carl Yastrzemski hit 44 homers, had 121 RBIs and a .326 batting average to win the Triple Crown—a feat that hasn't been achieved in either league since. He was named the American League MVP. More significantly, Yastrzemski led the Red Sox out of the baseball wilderness to their first American League pennant in 21 years. Ninth-place finishers the previous year, they had entered the campaign as 100-1 long shots, and even those odds seemed overly optimistic at the time. The Sox had languished in the doldrums for several years since Ted Williams retired, and interest in the team had faded. But in 1967, they caught fire, led by this Polish son of a Long Island potato farmer. Yaz did it all for the Red Sox that year. He hit for average, and he hit with power. He ran the bases with calculated abandon. He played left field like no one before or since. The Green Monster was his personal domain, and he used it to his advantage. There may have been better statistical years on paper—but Yaz came through in the clutch so many times, it was almost supernatural. His name was gold and suddenly everyone, even those who could spell little else, could spell it perfectly.

*   *   *   *

As the pressure-packed pennant race moved toward its climax, Yaz just got better and better, batting an astounding .523 in the last two weeks of the season. In the last two games of the season against Minnesota, he hit safely in seven of his eight trips to the plate, sealing two victories for the Sox and making the Impossible Dream a reality. In the '67 World Series, Yaz batted .400 in a losing cause, winning respect from both leagues and fans across America.

*   *   *   *

Ted Williams once observed: "I never played with Yaz, but Bobby Doerr told me that in 1967 he had the best single year he ever saw, and Bobby played with *me* for 10 years! For that one year, he was Babe Ruth, Ty Cobb and Honus Wagner all rolled into one."

*   *   *   *

In the midst of the red-hot 1967 pennant race, Chicago White Sox manager Eddie Stanky questioned Boston's Carl Yastrzemski's baseball smarts, calling him "an all-star from the neck down." This psychological warfare gambit backfired. During the next series against the White Sox at Fenway, Yaz made several unbelievable plays in left field and went 6 for 9 at the plate. He put a giant exclamation point on the performance by homering and then tipping his hat to Stanky as he rounded third base. When he crossed home plate, Red Sox fans held a sign aloft that read: STANKY: A GREAT MANAGER FROM THE ANKLES DOWN.

Carl Yastrzemski (Brace Photography)

*   *   *   *

Following his MVP performance in 1967, and a valiant effort in a losing cause in that year's World Series, Carl Yastrzemski was on top of the world. After being told how wonderful he was by everyone in Boston, even the usually humble Yaz was beginning to believe his press clippings. Until he went on a postseason Florida excursion with some friends, that is. Checking into the hotel, one of Yaz's friends asked if Mr. Carl Yastrzemski's room was ready. The clerk, obviously not a baseball fan, asked if he had a reservation.

After considerable ribbing from his companions, the group made its way to the room where a vase of flowers and a bowl of fruit awaited them on the dresser. At last, Yaz was getting the sort of respect he deserved, and he crowed to the others: "See, they do know me around here." Picking up the attached card, he read, to the vast amusement of all present: "Welcome, Charles Yastrzemski." Yaz says that even today, those friends call him Charles.

*   *   *   *

Yastrzemski holds the distinction of having played longer for one team than any other ballplayer. During his 23-year career with the Red Sox, he batted over .300 six times while playing under six U.S. Presidents. The *Boston Globe* pointed out that he reached that batting standard once during the presidency of John F. Kennedy, twice each while Lyndon Johnson and Richard Nixon occupied the White House, and once under Gerald Ford. Jimmy Carter and Ronald Reagan failed to inspire him to this level during their time in the office.

On September 12, 1979, Carl Yastrzemski made Red Sox and American League history by becoming the first player in the junior circuit to reach 400 homers and 3000 hits. He had achieved the 400 round-tripper milestone in July of '79. Hit number 3000 came off Yankee Jim Beattie, who as a boy growing up in the state of Maine had idolized Yaz.

✷   ✷   ✷   ✷

In 1975, after striking out on a called third strike, Carl Yastrzemski showed his dissatisfaction with what he thought were repeated bad calls by umpire Lou DiMuro by scooping dirt into a large pile on home plate. He was quickly ejected from the game. "Yaz never thought an umpire had a right to call him out on strikes," recalls Bill Lee. "So he made a sand castle on home plate."

✷   ✷   ✷   ✷

You've heard of giving a player a hotfoot? Renowned practical joker Carl Yastrzemski once carried the joke a bit farther north. He used newspapers to start a fire under unsuspecting teammate Doug Griffin's chair. While the rest of the team watched the conflagration grow, Griffin continued to read his newspaper, totally unaware of the flames lapping around him. Finally, the plastic chair got so hot that he shot out of it like a cannonball. Yaz was literally a pain in the ass.

✷   ✷   ✷   ✷

"He was the worst dresser in baseball," claims Bill Lee.

"We called him Columbo, although he wasn't as sartorially attired. We tried to get rid of that damn raincoat. He must have had more than one. I remember once, he went into a slump in Minneapolis and at the hotel, he took all his clothes and set them on fire and called the fire department." On another occasion, Doug Griffin and Yaz were walking to the team bus, looking like two actors about to audition for the starring roles in *Dumb and Dumber*—Yaz had the entire back of his raincoat cut out, and Griffin was sporting trousers cut off at the knees.

✷   ✷   ✷   ✷

Carl Yastrzemski

Don Zimmer once sent Yaz a special delivery COD package. It cost Yaz $148 to find the box contained dead fish, dirt and rocks.

＊　　＊　　＊　　＊

"He arrived in Boston to fill a void. He departed leaving one."

—Friend & Zminda

Newspapers regularly misspelled his name, but in box scores he was usually Y'str'mski. When Carl Yastrzemski retired at the end of the 1983 baseball season, people throughout baseball paid tribute to his 23-year career. Perhaps it was Tony La Russa, then White Sox manager and one of the most astute baseball minds of our time, who paid him the most fitting compliment. "I have a little quirk when filling out my lineup cards for the opposing team. I never use vowels except for Yastrzemski. I just feel it would be disrespectful to him not to spell his name out. As a Red Sox fan back in 1967, I remember vividly every hit he got that year. All through his career he's been a game-breaker."

＊　　＊　　＊　　＊

On the eve of his retirement, Yaz recalled some of his best catches and most important hits for the *Boston Herald*.

Defensive Plays:

#1 "The best was the play I made off Reggie Jackson in the third game of the '75 playoffs. "This was the game in which he cut off a ball that looked like a sure two-run triple and held Jackson to a single. After the game, Jackson allowed that "only two people could have made that play: Carl Yastrzemski and God."

#2 The diving catch in Yankee Stadium off Tom Tresh in the opening game of the 1967 "Impossible Dream" season. The catch temporarily preserved a no-hitter by Red Sox rookie pitcher Billy Rohr. Rohr lost the no-hitter on a hit by Elston Howard with two out in the ninth inning, but many people point to this game and this play as the inspiration for the rest of this miracle "cardiac kids" campaign.

Biggest Hits:

"Just about every hit I had in 1967 could be the biggest," Yaz rightly says. "But I'd say the top five were the three-run homer off Jim Merritt on the second-to-last day of the 1967 season; the bases-loaded single which tied the game the next day; the two-out, ninth-inning homer off Fred Lasher that tied a game in Detroit earlier that year (Dalton Jones won it with a homer in the 11th); my home run off Vida Blue in the 1975 playoffs when we were losing 3-0; and my 400th homer off Oakland's Mike Morgan not only because it was the 400th but because it won a game in a pennant race." *Boston Herald* Oct. 2, 1983

* * * *

Now playing third base: Carl Yastrzemski. "When Rico was hurt in 1973, Yaz filled in for 11 games. He logged ten errors.

* * * *

Carl owned a car dealership in Massachusetts named Yaz Ford. Every time the team would be on the bus and pass an auto junkyard, Luis Tiant would shout out, "Hey, there's Yaz Ford. Nah, that can't be it. Those cars look better than the ones you've got."

* * * *

In *Tales From the Red Sox Dugout,* we told about an incident involving Yaz and slicing up clothing, which related to Doug Griffin. Another time after several players had sliced up each others' clothes, Yaz walked through the hotel lobby with his shirt and

Williams, Foxx, Garciaparra, Yastrzemski

sweater all torn. Luis Aparicio was with him. By coincidence, the Miss Minnesota pageant had just spilled out and a few of the losing contestants were in the lobby sobbing. Gary Peters said hello to them, then added, "Don't feel bad. Look at these guys. I just dragged them off the street to have a meal."

Another time in Minneapolis, Yaz had cut up all of Peters' clothing and stuffed them in his suitcase. Out for dinner the next night, Peters (who'd never said a word about it) excused himself, grabbed a cab and shot over to the team's hotel. He cut up Yaz's clothes, and then set fire to them in the middle of the room but found himself unable to extinguish the flames. Just then Yaz, who'd followed his instinct, burst into the room and found the mess.

The next morning, Yaz checked out very early. When he got to the park, the police and a fire chief were waiting. Yaz said the mess was due to a can of Sterno they'd knocked over warming some fish.

*   *   *   *

"Carl Yastrzemski is the only guy in baseball who can not only read an eye chart but understand it. He's retiring from baseball because they won't let him grow potatoes in left field. Anyone who spends 20 years running into a wall has to be lonely." —Don Rickles

*   *   *   *

Carl is the last player in baseball to win the coveted Triple Crown. He accomplished the feat in 1967, hitting 44 homers (tied for first with Minnesota's Harmon Killebrew), 121 RBIs and a .326 batting average.

The 1968 season was a pitcher's dream and a hitter's nightmare. Carl Yastrzemski batted .301 and led the American League in batting! No other player, not even a part-timer reached the .300 standard that season. Yaz's teammate Ken Harrelson led the circuit in RBIs with a modest total of 109 and actually finished seventh in the batting race with a .275 average!

* * * *

Yaz, sadly, made the final out in the 1967 World Series, the 1975 World Series and the 1978 one-day playoff against the Yankees to determine the pennant winner.

* * * *

In 1978 Buddy LeRoux, then vice-president and part owner of the Red Sox was telling a Polish joke in the locker room at Fenway Park. LeRoux is speaking loud enough to ensure that the most famous Pole in the room hears every word. When the joke is completed, Carl Yastrzemski turns to his tormentor and says "I got something for you, Buddy. I'll leave it in your office. I'm on the way there now." With that Yastrzemski gets up from his chair and walks past LeRoux into the washroom.—*Sport,* October 1978

* * * *

The two best-remembered exits by Red Sox stars couldn't have been more different. In 1960, Ted Williams hit a home run in this last at-bat and refused to tip his hat to adoring fans. When Yaz left in 1983, he did it with less fanfare but more *savoir faire,* circling the field and shaking hands with fans.

Yaz Jazz:

"YAZ, SIR, THAT'S MY BABY."—sign seen at Fenway during '67 season.

"Ed (Runge), you're the second best umpire in the league. The other 23 are tied for first."

"I knew when the ball was going out [over the Green Monster]. It was something I worked into the decoy, but it used to tick the pitchers off.

"Bill Monbouquette used to say, 'Can't you at least make it look like you can catch it?' Meanwhile, the ball would be on its way over the fence to a spot three-quarters of the way out to the railroad tracks."

"I'm very pleased and very proud of my accomplishments, but I'm most proud of that [hitting 400 home runs and 3,000 hits]. Not [Ted] Williams, not [Lou] Gehrig, not [Joe] DiMaggio did that. They were Cadillacs and I'm a Chevrolet."

"I think about baseball when I wake up in the morning. I think about it all day and I dream about it at night. The only time I don't think about it is when I'm playing it."

"The 3,000 hit thing was the first time I let individual pressure get to me. I was uptight about it. When I saw the hit going through, I had a sigh of relief more than anything."

"They can talk about Babe Ruth and Ty Cobb and Rogers Hornsby and Lou Gehrig and Joe DiMaggio and Stan Musial and all the rest, but I'm sure not one of them could hold cards and spades to Williams in his shear knowledge of hitting. He studied hitting the way a broker studies the stock market, and could spot at a glance mistakes that others couldn't see in a week."

"And if I have my choice between a pennant and a triple crown, I'll take the pennant every time."

Tom Yawkey

Red Sox owner Tom Yawkey was often accused of running his team like a country club and spoiling his players. The truth is that Yawkey was the biggest Red Sox fan in town and wanted a winner more than anyone. He was a wealthy man with a down-to-earth approach to life. His generosity to his players went beyond money and was rewarded with a fierce loyalty seldom seen in today's game. When Mel Parnell pitched his no-hitter in 1956 at the age of 34, Yawkey was like a little kid. "When I got to the clubhouse, he was the first man to greet me," Parnell recalls. "He had a new contract and a pen in his hand and he said: 'Sign this!' I said: 'Mr Yawkey, you already pay me to do this kind of thing.' He said:' Sign this already.' How many owners would do that? Not many."

Tom Yawkey (Brace Photography)

His generous spirit was not confined to his ballplayers. Parnell remembers his love of kids and his love of the game. "Whenever we went away on a road trip, he'd work out at Fenway with Vince Orlando and take batting practice, and the kids around the neighborhood would go out and shag flies for him. When he was finished, he'd give them all a $20 bill. The kids loved that. He sent a lot of our batboys to college and one of them, John Donavan, came back to be our team lawyer."

*   *   *   *

Yawkey's highest paid ballplayer was Ted Williams, and while he was the most generous owner in baseball, his generosity did have limits. He could tolerate Williams offering hitting tips to players on second-division teams who were struggling, but when he saw him counselling the Yankees' young superstar Mickey Mantle, it was too much for even this kind man to bear. He asked Ted what the hell he was doing helping a hitter from the Red Sox' biggest rival.

Ted's reply says a lot about his love of the game. "T.A., just remember this: if you don't have any hitting in baseball, you don't have any excitement. When you're two or three blocks from a major league ballpark and you hear the crowd roar, somebody hit the ball! We've got to get more hitting in the game. Better backgrounds. So what if I help them a bit? It adds excitement to the game." Yawkey, who also loved the game above all else, agreed with his star.

*   *   *   *

Yawkey was beloved by his players because of his unassuming manner—a manner that included dressing very casually, certainly nothing like the sometimes-ostentatious owners of today. Sitting in front of his locker after a game one day, Bernie Carbo spotted his benefactor approaching. "Go get me a couple of cheeseburgers, would ya?" said Carbo. When Yawkey explained that he was the Red Sox owner, Carbo apologized. "I thought you were the club-house man," he explained sheepishly.

*   *   *   *

When Tom Yawkey ran the ball club, it was a different era, with the reserve rule in place and no sports agents mediating between the players and the ball club. Yawkey was very wealthy, though he remained a down-to-earth guy who didn't put on airs and could readily be mistaken for one of the clubhouse attendants. He was also very generous with players and as a result, a strong loyalty was returned. At the end of Johnny Pesky's first year with the Red Sox, he was changing in the clubhouse and was sent a message to come upstairs. Ballplayers weren't allowed upstairs without being summoned, so Johnny was understandably apprehensive. Eddie Collins gave him an envelope from Mr. Yawkey. Inside, the rookie found a bonus check, enough to buy his parents a house to live in back in Portland, Oregon.

Even Sparky Anderson, after his Cincinnati Reds had just defeated the Boston Red Sox in the 1975 World Series paused to praise Yawkey. "Tom Yawkey was the greatest gentleman I've ever met in baseball," said Sparky.

Tom Yawkey was owner of the Boston Red Sox but he was also a baseball fan who loved to hang out with ballplayers. This created numerous problems for manager Joe Cronin, according to Cronin's daughter Maureen:

"Tom Yawkey was a bit of a rascal so it was tough on dad. He'd be trying to get the players to come in at a certain time and the players would be out drinking with Tom Yawkey. A couple of times it was funny because dad would be waiting up in the hotel lobby and in would come Tom with a player and dad couldn't really say much about that. Guys like Mickey McDermott and Walt Dropo would probably admit that they drove dad a bit crazy. Yawkey loved the ballplayers. He used to like to go down into the clubhouse and wrestle with them."

Bill Lee on Tom Yawkey:

"It was weird the day that Tom Yawkey died. There wasn't a cloud in the sky, and then he died, and right before the game a cloud passed over and delayed the game. It was kind of a homage to him. I was driving to the ballpark that day, and a pigeon stopped me going into the parking lot. I tried to pull to the left, and he walked to the left; I'd cut my wheels back to the right, and he'd move over that way. And he refused to let me go in there. I knew then that Tom Yawkey had come back as a bird because of all the DDT he had sprayed to kill spruce bud worms in his pine forests in South Carolina. In the process, he killed all the birds there. We'd talked about that, and I told him that he would have to do penance and come back as a bird. He was undergoing chemotherapy at the time. We got along great. Someone said that at the end of that ball game there was a pigeon that went up into the air and dove headfirst and committed suicide into the bleachers at Fenway Park. Even today, I'm always seeing Tom Yawkey out in the field. He's matriculated up. Now he's a crow."

Rudy York

Teammate Mel Parnell recalls Rudy York: "The big Indian led the league in burning up hotels. I think he set three hotels on fire. In my first year, 1947, I was rooming with Bob Klinger, and we could hear fire engines running around Kenmore Square like crazy, so we look out, and they're all going to the Myles Standish Hotel—a block away. When the fire was extinguished, the police brought Rudy over to our room at the Kenmore Hotel. We said: 'Rudy, what happened?' and The Chief says: 'I don't know. Some guy upstairs must have been smoking a cigarette, and he threw it out the window, and it blew in my window and set it on fire.' Actually, he had fallen asleep with a cigarette, and the next day the pictures of the ruined hotel room ran in the newspaper with bottles in sight on the dresser. So Mickey Harris cut the pictures out and put them by his locker. Rudy had a few choice words for him."

*   *   *   *

Rudy York was one of the few teammates to criticize the great Ted Williams. And he was man enough to do it to his face. In 1946, when the Red Sox were in hot pursuit of the American League pennant, York and some other Sox players felt that Ted hadn't hustled on a ball hit to left field. York confronted him in the clubhouse after the game. "We're about to win the pennant," York told him angrily. "Everybody's in this together. Anyone who loafs has got to answer to me." Williams took the criticism in the spirit it was intended, and the two teammates remained close friends. The Red Sox went on to win the '46 pennant.

*   *   *   *

Rudy York once drove in an astounding 10 runs in a single 1946 game against the St. Louis Browns. But the amazing part is that he had done that by the fifth inning and still had two more plate appearances coming. York started his incredible day with a grand slam in the second inning. He followed that with another grand salami in the fifth frame. Both round-trippers came at the expense of Browns reliever Tex Shirley. Rudy struck out in the seventh with one man on, and hit into a double play with two on in the ninth.

Of the 11 major league players who have hit two grand slams in a single game, two others were Red Sox: Jim Tabor in 1939 and Nomar Garciaparra in 1999.

Cy Young

Y is for Young,
The Magnificent Cy;
People batted against him,
But I never knew why.
—Ogden Nash

Cy Young is a name known to every fan of major league baseball. The award named for him is one of the most prestigious in sport and is synonymous with pitching excellence. Had the coveted award existed at the turn of the century, Young would have been a perennial candidate to capture it. Four times he won 30 games, and 15 times he won 20 or more. His final totals were 511 wins and 316 losses, with a lifetime ERA of 2.63. On May 5, 1904, the big right-hander spun a perfect game against the Philadelphia Athletics—the first one since 1880. He struck out eight batters in a quick-paced contest that consumed only one hour and 20 minutes.

* * * *

Born just a few years after the end of the Civil War, Cy Young pitched in the major leagues for 22 years with five different clubs and averaged more than eight innings a game during that stretch! Young once pitched a record 24 consecutive innings without yielding a hit.

On June 13, 1903 when his 361st career win eclipsed Pud Galvin's 360th, Cy Young became the pitcher with the most wins in baseball history; nearly 100 years later, no one has challenged him for that distinction. Meanwhile, Cobb's record for the most career hits, Ruth's for the most home runs, even Lou Gehrig's for the most consecutive games played—all of these cumulative triumphs have all been surpassed.

* * * *

Cy Young

Young also holds the distinction of having pitched the first inning of the first official World Series game, in 1903. What could be more appropriate than having the man whose name is synonymous with pitching throw the very first pitch ever thrown in World Series competition? Although he gave up an uncharacteristic four runs, he did win two games and lose one in the 1903 Series. He held a 1.85 ERA in 34 postseason innings that year.

In 1904, the Red Sox pitching staff threw a phenomenal 148 complete games (this was when there were only 154 games each year.) The entire *team* had an earned run average of 2.12 and only surrendered 233 walks in 1406 innings of play. The Sox posted 21 shutouts. Forty one—yes, 41—of the complete games were authored by Cy Young! Young's biographer Reed Browning states that he retired 76 consecutive hitters without a hit over 24 innings as part of a stretch in which he threw 45 consecutive scoreless innings. This is the *equivalent of five consecutive complete game shutouts!* For good measure he also tossed a perfect game during this stretch.

Obviously, the man whose name now symbolizes excellence in the art of pitching was a great pitcher himself. In June of 1908 at the ripe old baseball age of 41, Young threw his third no-hitter, this one against the New York Highlanders in New York. Young began the game by walking the first batter, Harry Niles. Niles was quickly erased trying to steal second base. Young then confounded the remainder of the Highlanders' line-up en route to an 8-0 gem.

✳   ✳   ✳   ✳

Cy Young's 511 wins—his 192 wins for Boston puts him in a direct tie with Roger Clemens for top spot in that category—is such a staggering total that a pitcher would have to be a 20-game winner for 25 straight years and then win another 12 games the year after that to top him. Pitchers can have long careers—Nolan Ryan pitched for 27 years, but he "only" won 324 games. Young threw 749 complete games; Ryan only appeared in 807 total (but an impressive 222 of those were complete games.)

In fact, Young pitched in so many games that he also holds the records for the most losses of any pitcher: 315. Not surprisingly, Ryan is close behind with 292. Nevertheless, Cy's .619 winning percentage was outstanding by anyone's standards.

*   *   *   *

Young hinted that he was not above using any method available to get batters out. "I admit that some of my cutplug tobacco would get on the ball."

*   *   *   *

In 1908, a "Cy Young Day" was held for Young at the old Huntington Avenue Grounds in Boston. Over 20,000 fans turned out to honor the man who had gone 22-15 the previous season, and had finished with a 21-11 record in '08—with a no-hitter thrown in. Not bad for a 41-year-old man! In fact the old Young was almost as good as the young Young: at age 41, in 1908, he pitched 30 complete games and posted a yearlong ERA of just 1.26. *Sporting Life*, poking fun at Young's longevity, commented after his 1911 season, "The old boy is said to look better than any previous season since 1663, considered by many to be his best year since the Summer of 1169." Young received various gifts on that day, including about $7,500 in cash. The most telling gift however was presented by the American League umpires association—a traveling bag. Cy was sold that fall to Cleveland for $12,500.

Matt Young

Matt Young proved to be a pretty disappointing pitcher for the Red Sox, averaging about five walks every game, and possessed a horrible psychological condition whereby he often could not throw the ball to first base, either on a bunt or a pick-off. He did have one moment, however, when the sun shone briefly through the clouds before becoming obscured once again. In a game against the Cleveland Indians in Municipal Stadium, Young pitched a complete game without allowing a hit. It wasn't ruled a no-hitter because the home team never batted in the bottom of the ninth—the Indians were ahead and won the game 2-1 in large part due to all the walks Young granted that day.

Norm Zauchin

What do you do with a caged bear? Norm Zauchin was up with the Red Sox for just five games in 1951, but then he had to go in the service. He made it back in 1955 and had his best year, contributing 27 home runs to the Red Sox cause. On State of Maine Day that season, three prizes were offered: Maine hens for whoever hit the first double in the game, Maine lobster for the first triple and a bear named "Homer" for the first home run. Zauchin had himself quite a day and won all three.

They didn't actually bring the bear to the park because they didn't know if anyone would actually win it. They shipped Homer from Maine to the zoo in Birmingham, Alabama. It grew old and eventually died there. The hens and the lobster were dispatched more quickly. There was just so much food that Zauchin brought them to the chef at the Somerset Hotel and hosted an elaborate party.

Don Zimmer

"If you can't play for Don Zimmer, you can't play for anybody."
—Ted Williams

Though described as a "gerbil" by Bill Lee—who insists he did not mean it in an uncomplimentary fashion—Zimmer has had a remarkable baseball career as coach and manager and is well respected by many veterans. He had the misfortune to manage the Sox just at the time that many of them—the "Buffalo Heads"—were the most unmanageable.

With his old-fashioned attitudes, ample girth, bald head and the common knowledge that this head housed a steel plate from a past beaning, Zimmer was an easy target for ridicule. It was often said that he set off airport metal detectors. Zim soldiered on, but once or twice embarrassed himself and created additional fodder for Boston media long-hairs and young Turks. In 1976, he rushed out from the Sox dugout to argue a call, but tripped over first base and fell flat on the ground.

*   *   *   *

Don Zimmer sometimes treated his players with utter (or is that udder) disrespect. Speaking of his right fielder Dwight Evans, Zimmer once offered the following insights: "Next to Jim Rice, he's the strongest guy on the team—maybe in all of baseball— but he's got the balls of a female cow." And that's no bull.

*   *   *   *

Sadly, Zimmer was the Sox manager in 1978 when the team had built up a 14-game lead by the All-Star Game, only to see it completely erode and then had to struggle to force a one-game playoff. It was the so-called "Bucky Dent" game, in which the light-hitting Yankee hit a home run and broke countless hearts across the length and breadth of New England. In the spring of 1979 Don Zimmer and his wife were driving to Florida for spring training. It is reported that during the long drive, Zimmer would disturb extended periods of silence with the mumbled incantation: "Bucky Dent! Bucky ****ing Dent!"

*   *   *   *

Bill Lee and Don Zimmer were like oil and water; they just didn't mix. Zimmer is the prototypical old school manager who respects the unwritten rules and traditions of the game; Lee was as close as baseball gets to a wild-eyed radical. Lee once labeled Zimmer "the gerbil" and was generally a very large thorn in his side throughout his tenure in Beantown.

In Zimmer's recent book *Zim,* the former Red Sox manager and current Yankee bench coach exacts a measure of verbal revenge on his tormentor, referring to Lee as the "only man I've ever known in baseball who I wouldn't let in my house." Asked if he'd read the book, Lee replied: "No, I didn't. I don't read fiction." He had heard about it, though, and offered the following review. "I've sold a hundred thousand copies of that book for him just by that one line. Hey, I love it. You've gotta check the source. He had a lot of Richard Nixon in him. Hell, to be praised by a Yankee is damnable." He added: "Zimmer wouldn't know a good pitcher if he came up and bit him in the ass."

Is there any chance of reconciliation between the Spaceman and Zim? According to Lee, the answer is no. "I've tried. The veins in his neck just get real big. I can see him on life support and some Red Sox fan runs in and says, 'The Spaceman is here to see you.' Instant straight line!"

✱   ✱   ✱   ✱

At the beginning of the 1977 season, Zimmer had to make the agonizing decision to release longtime Red Sox third baseman Rico Petrocelli in favor of young and offensively more potent Butch Hobson. The decision was not well received throughout New England and Zimmer received death threats. One was very specific, claiming that Zimmer would be shot while getting off the plane in Boston after spring training. When the plane arrived, Zimmer confronted Jim Rice, the Boston strongman and one of Zimmer's favorites, asking him to get off the plane in front of him. "My ass!" replied Rice. "I'm not taking no bullet for you!"

Bill Zuber/Bob Zupcic

When he joined the big league club at the very end of the 1991 campaign, Bob Zupcic erased a distinction pitcher Bill Zuber had held for nearly 50 years: since 1947 Zuber had always been the final entry in any comprehensive listing of Red Sox players. "Goober" Zuber came over from the Yankees in time to go 5-1 on the 1946 pennant-winning Red Sox team. He was born and raised in Middle Amana, Iowa, one of the few communal societies in the United States. Zuber's, a restaurant he founded, still flourishes in the area. Zupcic tied a major league mark for freshmen ballplayers in 1992, his official rookie season, when he hit two grand slams.

Sox Populi

"The hardest thing to do in baseball is to hit a round baseball with a round bat, squarely."

—Ted Williams

"I gave $250 to some mission in Alaska. I wouldn't send the fine to Bowie Kuhn because it might end up in a Nixon re-election campaign."

—Bill Lee

"When I was young, I'd spend summer weekends shagging flies and pretending I was Carl Yastrzemski. Now I spend them mowing the lawn and pretending I'm Joe Mooney.

—Dan Seidman

"Pope dead, Sox Alive, details at 11."

—Charles Laquidara, WBCN announcer, after the slumping Red Sox rallied to beat Toronto in a crucial series during their ill-fated drive for the 1978 pennant.

"When he (Nomar) called to say he was coming to Georgia Tech, I turned to my wife, Gina, and said, 'Nobody knows this yet, but we just got our best player ever.'"

—Rick Jones, former Georgia Tech Baseball Coach

"We are the best team in baseball."
> —Cincinnati Reds manager
> Sparky Anderson on the eve of the 1975 World Series.

"We are the best team in baseball. But not by much."
> —Sparky Anderson after his
> team captured the 1975 World Series
> in seven hard-fought games.

"After my career, I didn't walk down streets. I walked down alleys."
> —Bob Uecker, when asked if he shared Ted
> Williams' dream of walking down the street after his career was
> over and having people say, "There goes the greatest hitter who
> ever lived."

"Defensively, the Red Sox are a lot like Stonehenge. They are old, they don't move, and no one is certain why they are positioned the way they are.
> —*Boston Globe* writer Dan Shaughnessy describes an
> unlamented Red Sox team of the of the early nineties

"If I could play shortstop like him (Nomar Garciaparra), that's what I would like to do."
> —Pedro Martinez

"Yaz, you're my idol. I want my son to be just like you—rich!"
> —Red Sox outfielder Joe Foy,
> to all-star Carl Yastrzemski

"The Red Sox stranded more men than Zsa Zsa Gabor."
> —Yankee owner George Steinbrenner on the Red Sox
> performance in Game Six of the 1986 World Series.

"They killed our fathers and now the sons of bitches are coming after us."
> —a New Haven bar owner reflecting the trauma and paranoia
> inherent in being a Red Sox fan. (as quoted by Peter Gammons
> after the '78 playoff with the Yankees.)

"Baseball is the only field of endeavor where a man can succeed three times out of ten and be considered a good performer."

—Ted Williams

"Fear Strikes Out is the worst movie ever made about baseball."

—Jimmy Piersall

Popeye's Chicken

There is little doubt that the collapsing 2011 Red Sox could have used some spinach down the stretch. They sure needed something, as they dropped 20 of their last 27 games. Unfortunately, certain Sox starters were apparently more interested in Popeye's fried chicken than the green stuff that enabled the Sailor Man to defeat Bluto.

News that Josh Beckett, John Lackey, and Jon Lester (among other Sox players) sent out for vittles from the fast-food establishment on Brookline Avenue during games was met with disbelief and anger by Red Sox fans and management alike—though owner John Henry said a couple of days after the controversy broke big that he'd not even heard about it. Probably the only person who was pleased with the famous clientele seemed to be franchise owner Jon Stilianos.

"If they were winning, it wouldn't be a problem, know what I'm sayin'?" 20-year-old Jamal Mason, told the *Boston Globe.* "If you think about it, how did Big Papi become Big Papi? It was because of the chicken, man." Not that Big Papi was alleged to be among the offenders.

Just the Facts

The Red Sox scored 23 runs in a single postseason game in '99. According to *Baseball America,* there have been nine postseason series in which the two teams combined failed to score 23 runs in the entire series.

The following Red Sox players have had their numbers retired: Joe Cronin (#4) 1935-1945, Ted Williams (#9) 1939-1960, Bobby Doerr (#1) 1937-1951, Carl Yastrzemski (#8) 1961-1983. Carlton Fisk (#27) 1969-1980 with the Red Sox.

"As long as I'm playing ball, it doesn't matter where I am, as long as it's not in a Yankees uniform."

—Carl Everett

"Whenever I fee 1 my ego getting away with me, I call my mom and ask if I can take out the trash."

—Nomar Garciaparra

"I like it when the pitcher thinks he has given up a hit and, the next thing you know, I'm throwing the guy out. The pitcher gets so excited. You can see it in his face."

—Nomar Garciaparra

"I'm just tired of seeing New York always win."

—Manny Ramirez

Jokes

There was a Texan, a New Yorker and a Bostonian in a sports bar drinking. The Texan throws back a shot of tequila, throws the half full bottle up in the air, takes out a gun and shoots the bottle to bits. The New Yorker and the Bostonian look at him in amazement when he says, "Where I come from we have plenty of tequila."

Not to be outdone, the New Yorker took off his Yankees cap, tossed back the rest of his glass of Merlot, then tosses the half full bottle of wine in the air, takes out his gun and blows it to bits. He says, "Where I come from we have plenty of fine wine."

The Bostonian slowly finishes his beer, tugs his Sox cap down snugly, takes the rest of the six pack, throws it in the air, takes out his gun and shoots the New Yorker between the eyes, then catches the six pack. He turns to the stunned Texan and says, "Where I come from we don't waste good beer, but we have too many Yankees fans."

*   *   *   *

Three baseball fans were on their way to a game when one noticed a foot sticking out of the bushes by the side of the road. They stopped and discovered a nude female dead. Out of respect and propriety, the Cubs fan took off his cap and placed it over her right breast. The Red Sox fan took off his cap and placed it over her left breast. Following their lead, the Yankees fan took off his cap and placed it over her crotch.

The police were called and when the officer arrived, he conducted his inspection. First, he lifted up the Cubs cap, replaced it, and wrote down some notes. Next, he lifted the Sox cap, replaced it, and wrote down some more notes.

The officer then lifted the Yankees cap, replaced it, then lifted it again, replaced it, lifted it a third time, and replaced it one last time. The Yankee fan was getting upset and finally asked, "What are you, a pervert or something? Why do you keep lifting and looking, lifting and looking?" "Well," said the officer, "I am simply surprised. Normally when I look under a Yankees hat, I find an a—hole."

*   *   *   *

A first-grade teacher in New York City explains to her class that she and her husband are excited about the year 2000 World Series because she is a Mets fan and her husband is a Yankees fan. She asks her students to raise their hands if they, too, are either Mets or Yankees fans.

Everyone in the class raises their hands except one little girl. The teacher looks at the girl with surprise and asks, "Janie, why didn't you raise your hand?"

"Because I'm not a Mets or Yankees fan," she replies.

The teacher, still shocked, asks, "Well, if you are not a Mets or Yankees fan, then who are you a fan of?"

"I am a Red Sox fan, and proud of it," Janie replied.

The teacher cannot believe her ears. "Janie, why are you a Red Sox fan?"

"Because my mom is a Red Sox fan, and my dad is a Red Sox fan, so I'm a Red Sox fan, too!"

"Well," says the teacher in an obviously annoyed tone, "that is no reason for you to be a Red Sox fan. You don't have to be just like your parents all of the time. What if your mom were a moron and your dad were a moron—what would you be then?"

"Then," Janie smiled, 'We'd be Mets and Yankees fans."

Two young boys are playing baseball on a vacant lot in a Boston suburb. Suddenly one of the boys is attacked by a rabid Rottweiler. As the vicious dog is about to finish off his helpless victim, the other boy takes his bat, wedges it into the dog's collar and gives it a mighty twist, breaking the dog's neck.

A reporter who witnessed the dramatic event dashes across the street to interview the young hero. He starts writing in his notepad: "Young Red Sox Fan Saves Friend From Vicious Animal".

Looking over the reporter's shoulder, the young boy protested: "But I'm not a Red Sox fan." "Sorry," replies the reporter. "I assumed that everyone in Boston was a Red Sox fan." "Not me," replied the boy proudly, "I cheer for the world champion New York Yankees!"

Without hesitation, the resourceful reporter crossed out the headline and wrote: "Little New York Bastard Kills Beloved Family Pet".

✳   ✳   ✳   ✳

A man from Boston dies and goes to Hell. The devil ushers him into a room and says: "I hope you're prepared for some pretty hot temperatures." The man replies: "No problem, I'm from Boston."

The devil leaves the room and turns the thermostat up to 100 and the humidity to 80. He returns 15 minutes later and asks the Bostonian how he's doing.

"No problem. Boston gets this warm in June." A bit surprised, the devil goes out and turns the thermostat up to 150 and the humidity to 90. Again the devil asks the man from Boston how he's doing. "Just like Beantown in July," the man replies. "Makes me feel right at home." Frustrated, the devil cranks the heat up to

200 degrees and the humidity to 100. When he looks in the room, he sees that the guy from Boston has removed his shirt and there is some sweat on his brow, but he still seems to be enjoying the weather. "Just like Boston in August," he says dreamily. By now the devil is at the end of his rope. He goes back to the thermostat and turns it to minus 150 degrees. All of Hell immediately freezes solid, and even the devil himself is shivering. To his complete amazement, he opens the door and sees the Bostonian jumping up and down in ecstasy. "What could you possibly be so happy about?" demands the devil. The man replies: "THE RED SOX WON THE WORLD SERIES! THE RED SOX WON THE WORLD SERIES!"

*   *   *   *

One day four baseball fans were climbing a mountain. Each was a fan of a different team in the A.L. East and each proclaimed to be the most loyal of all fans of their baseball team.

As they climbed higher, they argued as to which one of them was the most loyal of all. They continued to argue all the way up the mountain, and finally as they reached the top, the Toronto fan hurled himself off the mountain, shouting, "This is for the Jays!" as he fell to his doom. Not wanting to be outdone, the Baltimore fan threw himself off the mountain, proclaiming, "This is for the O's!"

Seeing this, the Boston fan walked over and shouted, "This is for THE SOX!" . . . and pushed the Yankee fan off the side of the mountain.

*   *   *   *

The Boston Symphony Orchestra was performing Beethoven's Ninth. In the piece, there's a passage about 20 minutes long during which the bass violinists have nothing to do. Rather than sit around the whole time looking stupid, some bassists decided to sneak offstage and go to the tavern next door, grab a quick beer and catch an inning of the Sox on TV. After slamming several ales in quick succession, one of them looked at his watch. "Hey! We need to get back!"

"No need to panic," said his fellow bassist, "I thought we might need some extra time, so I tied the last few pages of Seiji's score together (Sox fan Seiji Ozawa) with string. It'll take him a few minutes to get it untangled." A few minutes later they staggered back to the concert hall and took their places in the orchestra. About the same time, a member of the audience noticed the conductor seemed a bit edgy, fussing with things, and said as much to her companion. "Well of course," said her companion. "Don't you see? It's the bottom of the Ninth, the score is tied, and the bassists are loaded!

Stealing Home

T he Pawtucket Red Sox, the top minor-league affiliate of the parent Boston Red Sox, hosted the longest game in baseball history: a record 33-inning marathon against the Rochester Red Wings. The game began on April 18, 1981, and continued for eight hours, well into the morning of April 19, when it was finally called with the score tied 2-2. When one of the Pawsox players returned home in the wee hours of the morning of April 19, his wife was justifiably suspicious and demanded an explanation. The exhausted and bedraggled player pleaded innocence, explaining that he had been playing baseball until a few minutes previous. His wife remained skeptical until he showed her the morning newspaper featuring front-page accounts of the game. The grueling contest was eventually concluded on June 23.

✱   ✱   ✱   ✱

The game finally ended when Marty Barrett scored on a Dave Koza hit to give the Red Sox a 3-2 victory. Koza went 4-for-13 in the contest. Future Boston Red Sox star and 3000-hit third baseman Wade Boggs managed 4 hits in 12 trips to the plate, while future Orioles iron-man Cal Ripken Jr., playing third for Rochester, went 2-for-13.

✱   ✱   ✱   ✱

This game established more records—and created more trivia questions—than many entire seasons. Here are some of the 14 records set in this marathon: Most innings: 33; most putouts, one team: 99 (Pawtucket); most putouts, both teams: 195; time: 8:25; most strikeouts, one team: 34 (Rochester); most strikeouts, both teams: 60; most pitches thrown: 882 (423 by Rochester; 459 by Pawtucket); most at-bats: 14 (Dave Koza, Lee Graham, Chico Walker).

EPILOGUE

Halley's Comet appears only every seventy-five years or so, but it's practically a frequent flyer when compared with the eighty-six year span between Red Sox World Series championships. Twice in a lifetime is about all you can expect to see the reclusive comet, and millions of people were born and died between the Red Sox titles in 1918 and 2004.

Agonizingly close calls came in 1946, 1948, 1949, 1967, 1972, 1975, 1978, and 1986—every one of them ending in defeat on the very final day. In 2003, the Red Sox once again came close to ending the drought that had begun in 1918. Manager Grady Little inexplicably left Pedro Martinez in the game one inning past his expiration date and soon Grady was the ex-manager of the Boston Red Sox. Enter Terry Francona, the newest in a long line of Moses wannabes vowing to lead the Red Sox from the World Series wilderness to the promised land.

In 2004 the Red Sox finally did it, toppling the Yankees in "the greatest comeback in baseball history," and then besting the National League champion St. Louis Cardinals in four games. It was their first World Series since Ted Williams was born. Red Sox Nation went berserk, and rightly so.

"Not since the visiting Redcoats lost to the hometown Colonials in 1776 has Boston celebrated like this," reported TIME magazine in a cover story that pushed other world events to the back pages.

Doug Mientkiewicz did not catch Halley's Comet but the orb that he did snare was just as rare. It was the ball that ended an odious eighty-six year odyssey. The journeyman first baseman caught the ball for the final out of the 2004 World Series, the first Red Sox World Series championship in eighty-six years.

The ball had been pitched by reliever Keith Foulke, hit by batter Edgar Renteria, stabbed by Foulke, and thrown to Mientkiewicz. After the ball settled into his mitt on that historic moment on October 27, 2004, it became the most revered piece of horsehide in New England since Paul Revere's mount took him on his famous ride.

Mientkiewicz decided he was going to keep the ball, joking that it was his "retirement fund." The public was outraged and the first baseman received death threats, hate mail, and even became the subject of a lawsuit. "I don't want to be remembered as "the guy who stole the ball," he told ESPN.com's Wayne Drehs. "You would have thought that I took the Green Monster and said I was never giving it back." He had no plans to sell the ball. "Its baseball history," he acknowledged. In actual fact his plan was to put it in a case along with the glove that caught it.

The Red Sox finally asked for the ball's return but, stung by Larry Lucchino's description of him as a "rent-a-player," Mientkiewicz resisted. He agreed to loan the relic to the Red Sox, allowing them to take it on tour across New England with the Series trophy. Ultimately the parties agreed that the ball belonged in the Baseball Hall of Fame which is where it resides today.

There was a funny side to the unpleasant episode. During a regular season game in 2005, Mientkiewicz suffered a concussion after colliding with Mike Lowell and had to be taken off the field in a stretcher. As he was being ministered to, a Fenway fan yelled "Quick, while he's unconscious somebody get the ball."

The incident taught the player a lesson. He gave the following advice to future players in his position: "Catch the ball, look at the umpire, make sure he calls the final out, then take the ball out of your glove, drop it on the ground and run to the pile to celebrate with your teammates."

If you like your heroes bloodied and wounded, then meet Curt Schilling, the Braveheart of the 2004 Red Sox. Schilling was the ace of the pitching staff and a courageous leader. In the ALCS, he was driven to pitch under extreme duress, with his ankle tendon stitched in place so that it wouldn't escape from its sheath.

Reassuringly, his doctor had first tried the procedure on a cadaver. In Game Six of the ALCS at Yankee Stadium blood could plainly be seen soaking through his white sanitary sock. Schilling went on to win that game, 4-2—and for an encore pitched and won (6-2) Game Two of the World Series.

If you prefer that your idols come out of nowhere, the hero of Game One of the 2004 World Series was quiet, humble Mark Bellhorn. With the score 9-9 and Jason Varitek on base in the bottom of the eighth, he drove a Julian Tavarez pitch off the Pesky Pole in right field for what proved to be the winning runs. It was the second straight game in which the scrappy second baseman homered off the right-field pole. The previous one came at Yankee Stadium in the ALCS clincher.

It's not often that a World Series is anti-climactic, especially when the winning team hadn't won since Woodrow Wilson was in the White House, but the 2004 version certainly had that feel to it. The ALCS against the Yankees was so unprecedented, so unbelievable, that even the Fall Classic paled in comparison. It was, after all, a win over the hated Yankees. And what a win it was. The Red Sox were down three games to none, the third Yankees win being a 19-8 evisceration of the Boston team in front of a home crowd. It was a deficit that only Federal Reserve Chairman Ben Bernanke, and possibly the government of Greece could relate to.

Principal Red Sox owner John Henry, another man who knows something about numbers, put the odds of the Red Sox emerging from the 0-3 hole at 6.25 in 100. After the series, TIME magazine pointed out that "If you want to bury a ghost, you have to dig a very big hole." The hole the Red Sox had dug seemed to be for their own interment – with the Yankees as willing pallbearers. That the Sox came back to win four games in a row and a trip to the World Series was miraculous. But the Red Sox won Game Four, then Game Five, then Six and all of a sudden they had defeated the pinstripes and were in the World Series. It was the most unlikely appearance by a team since Jerry Lewis was reunited with Dean Martin at the MD telethon.

"I can't wait till next year when we go back to Yankee Stadium and don't have to hear that 19-18 chant anymore," said Derek Lowe.

Johnny Damon was the best leadoff man in baseball in 2004. He called himself and his teammates "idiots" and added, "If we use our brains we're only hurting the team." Idiot, he may have been. But was he a deity? He had disciples, not fans and during his miraculous period in Boston, he did sport a beard that was not unlike the graven images of the Son of God. T-shirts at Fenway asked WWJDD? (What Would Johnny Damon Do?). His arm however threw lobs not lightning bolts, inspiring the popular line "Looks like Jesus, throws like Mary" (when he went to the Yankees after the 2005 season, the words "acts like Judas" were added by embittered Bosox fans). Asked after the World Series about the comparisons to God and His son, Johnny modestly replied, "Those guys are awesome." At that joyous moment, Boston fans might have added "too."

Damon liked to roam the Red Sox clubhouse naked, although he was so hairy in 2004 that some people might not have noticed.. He played cards naked, did exercises naked, and ate the pre-game meal naked. "The guy is always naked," said manager Terry Francona. "Then, 15 minutes later, I'll see him standing on second base." Fully clothed, one would assume. "We don't have rules here," said Damon. "And if we do, we can't read them."

Further gratuitous nudity was threatened by Mr. Red Sox himself, Johnny Pesky. Pesky, then eighty-five years of age, had never won a World Series while playing or coaching with the Red Sox. On the eve of the Series he said, "I want to see us win one time. I can die happy then. If they win, I'm going to take all my clothes off and run through the ballpark." Fortunately, the Red Sox clinched in St. Louis where such things are frowned upon.

Much of the spark for the 2004 Red Sox run came from Kevin Millar, a free spirit who kept the team loose. After the World Series, Millar admitted on Fox Sports' *Best Damn Sports Show Period* that some of that free spirit came in a bottle. "Before starting Game Six (of the ALCS against the Yankees), it was thirty-five degrees out there at Yankee Stadium. I got a thing of Jack Daniels and we all did shots about ten minutes before the game. And we won Game Six. So Game Seven, of course we had to do shots of Jack Daniels. And we won Game Seven, so guess what? I'm glad we won (the World Series) in Game Four because those Crown Royal shots and Jack Daniels shots started to kill me."

Writer Thomas Boswell was struck by the fact that the final World Series game was played during a lunar eclipse. Said Boswell, "The victory that arrived on this evening for the Red Sox and their true believers was far too rare and precious, too long overdue and spectacular in its consummation, to be upstaged by something so commonplace as the earth, moon and stars."

After years of disappointment and frustration Boston fans could be forgiven if they couldn't quite believe they were world champions. Too many times they had seen victory snatched from them at the very last minute. A few days after the World Series was over, long-suffering Red Sox fan Frank Solensky, was still paranoid. "There's no way the Sox can be the first team to lose the World Series after winning the first four games, right?" he asked.

Bill "Spaceman" Lee, the philosopher king of baseball, former Red Sox southpaw, and self-confessed Yankee hater, watched the 2004 ALCS at a bar in Hawaii. The place was split evenly between Red Sox and Yankee fans. As the Red Sox fought back and began to beat their foes, Lee said that the Yankee supporters seemed to shrivel up "like testicles on a frosty Vermont morning."

$$*\quad*\quad*\quad*$$

After an eighty-six year famine, four years is little more than the time between the entree and the dessert. In 2007 the Red Sox captured their second World Series of the new millennium. *Boston Globe* columnist Bob Ryan pointed out that the wait this time was only 3 percent as long as the last. "We didn't have to raid nursing homes to find people who actually saw the Red Sox win their last World Series," he wrote, adding, "You're probably one yourself."

The 2007 Red Sox swept the Los Angeles Angels three straight in the ALDS, earning the right to face the Cleveland Indians in the ALCS. Unlikely heroes emerged for the Red Sox, none more-so than the often-vilified J. D. Drew who hit a first-inning grand slam off Fausto Carmona in Game Six.

Promising new stars like outfielder Jacoby Ellsbury emerged and contributed like veterans. Ellsbury batted .438 in the World Series and knocked out four hits in Game Three. Talk about fast starts—he was still eligible for Rookie-of-the-Year honors in 2008 and finished third in the voting.

Teammate Dustin Pedroia, a second-round pick in the 2004 draft, also showcased his undoubted potential in the postseason. On the strength of a three-run double and a two-run homer, the rookie second sacker drove in five runs in Game Seven of the ALCS against the Indians. The Red Sox had a new ace in Josh Beckett, who headed up a staff that also included Jon Lester and Daisuke Matsuzaka. Meanwhile one-time starter Jonathan Papelbon had blossomed into the best reliever in the American League. One could probably fill a whole book of tales from Papelbon's locker in the clubhouse; at least once "Cinco Ocho" was spotted sighting a crossbow in the clubhouse.

✳   ✳   ✳   ✳

After Game Three of the 2007 World Series, with the Red Sox on the verge of a sweep, usually carefree Manny Ramirez was left to sound a note of caution. "You don't want to eat the cake before your birthday," he said.

Jon Lester, who a year earlier was receiving chemotherapy for lymphoma, pitched and won the final game. Lester kept the Rockies off the scoreboard for 5 2/3 innings before leaving the mound. And Mike Lowell, a testicular cancer survivor, homered, plated two runs and was declared Series MVP.

Kevin Youkilis is one of the most popular players on the Red Sox. Even before he came to Boston, he had a nickname, "the Greek God of walks," bestowed by Billy Beane and made famous in Michael's book *Moneyball*. Turns out there are at least two things wrong with the appellation. The first is that he's not Greek, and Terry Francona explained the other. "I've seen him in the shower," said Francona. "I wouldn't call him the Greek god of anything." Maybe not, but in 2007, he played like one.

This time it was closer Jonathan Papelbon who ended up with the ball from the final out of the World Series. He struck out pinch hitter Seth Smith on a 95-mile-per-hour fastball to seal the deal at five minutes past midnight Boston time. Papelbon recorded 10 2/3 scoreless innings in the postseason. Pursued relentlessly by media and fans about the whereabouts of the final game ball, he replied that a dog had eaten it.

The same Red Sox franchise that had gone seven games only to lose the World Series of '46, '67, '75, and '86 had now won two in four years, both in four-game sweeps.

The 2007 World Series champion Boston Red Sox were invited by President George W. Bush to the White House. The President was presented with a Red Sox jersey with his name on the back along with the number "07." Absent from the event was—guess who?—Manny Ramiriez, prompting the best line of the day from President Bush. "Sorry ... Manny Ramirez isn't here, I guess his grandmother died again," he deadpanned.

✴   ✴   ✴   ✴

In 2012, the Red Sox "celebrated" the 100th anniversary of Fenway Park by recording their worst season since 1965 (69-93) and finishing dead last. Manager Bobby Valentine was replaced by John Farrell and in 2013 took the Sox from worst to first, capping off the dream year with a World Series victory over the St. Louis Cardinals.

In 2014, the wonky American League East elevator once again let the Red Sox off in the basement as they managed only 71 wins against 91 losses. The 2015 season was no better as they continued to plumb the depths with a 78-84 futility mark.

In 2016, the Red Sox rebounded behind the inspirational leadership of the retiring David Ortiz, putting together one of the best final seasons a player ever had, with the team winning the division before being swept by the Cleveland Indians in the ALDS. The Indians then bowed to the Cubs, who overcame a 108-year-long curse to become World Champions. There were more than a few former Red Sox personnel, on the field and in the front office, who helped that all come about.

And the 2017 season gets underway with many ranking the Red Sox a solid contender to reach the postseason once again. Time will tell.

BIBLIOGRAPHY

Berry, Henry. *Boston Red Sox* (Collier Books, 1975)

Blake, Mike. *Baseball Chronicles* (Cincinnati: Bitterway, 1994)

Boyd, C. Brendan and Fred Harris. *The Great American Baseball Card Flipping, Trading and Bubble Gum Book* (Warner Books, 1975)

Broeg, Bob. *Memories of a Hall of Fame Sportswriter* (Champaign, IL: Sagamore, 1995)

Cataneo, David. *Tony C* (Nashville: Rutledge Hill Press, 1997)

Clark, Ellery. *Boston Red Sox* (Hicksville, LI: Exposition, 1975)

Clemens, Roger with Peter Gammons. *Rocket Man* (The Stephen Greene Press, 1987)

DiMaggio, Dom with Bill Gilbert. *Real Grass, Real Heroes* (NY: Zebra, 1990)

Gammons, Peter. *Beyond the Sixth Game* (Houghton-Mifflin Co., 1985)

Golenbock, Peter, *Fenway* (NY: Putnam, 1992)

Harrelson, Ken and Al Hirshberg. *Hawk* (NY: Viking, 1969)

Hirshberg, Al. *The Red Sox, the Bean, and the Cod* (Boston: Waverly House, 1947)

Honig, Donald. *The Boston Red Sox: An Illustrated History* (Prentice-Hall, 1990)

Lautier, Jack. *Fenway Voices* (Camden, Maine: Yankee Books, 1990)

Lyons, Steve. *Psychoanalysis* (Champaign, IL: Sagamore, 1995)

Nowlin, Bill and Mike Ross with Jim Prime, *Fenway Saved* (Champaign, IL: Sports Publishing Inc., 1999)

Piersall, Jimmy & Al Hirshberg. *Fear Strikes Out* (Lincoln, NE: University of Nebraska Press, 1999)

Prime, Jim and Bill Nowlin. *Ted Williams: A Tribute* (Indianapolis: Masters Press, 1997)

Prime, Jim & Ted Williams. *Ted Williams' Hit List* (Indianapolis: Masters Press, 1996)

Reynolds, Bill. *Lost Summer* (Warner Books, 1992)

Sullivan, George. *Picture History of the Boston Red Sox* (Bobbs-Merrill, 1980)

Tiant, Luis and Joe Fitzgerald. *El Tiante* (NY: Doubleday, 1976)

Walton, Ed. *Red Sox Triumphs and Tragedies* (NY: Scarborough, 1980)

Walton, Ed. *This Date in Red Sox History* (NY: Scarborough, 1978)

Williams, Dick and Bill Plaschke. *No More Mr. Nice Guy* (San Diego, NY and London: Harcourt Brace Jovanovich, 1990)

Yastrzemski, Carl and Gerald Eskenazi. *Baseball, the Wall and Me* (NY: Doubleday, 1990)

Zingg, Paul J. *Harry Hooper* (Urbana: University of Illinois Press, 1995)

Our definitive statistical source was *Total Baseball,* edited by John Thorn and Pete Palmer

6/17